BEYOND THE GREAT WAR

Beyond the Great War

Making Peace in a Disordered World

EDITED BY NORMAN INGRAM AND
CARL BOUCHARD

UNIVERSITY OF TORONTO PRESS
Toronto Buffalo London

Toronto Buffalo London
utorontopress.com

ISBN 978-1-4875-4274-0 (cloth)
ISBN 978-1-4875-4275-7 (EPUB)
ISBN 978-1-4875-4276-4 (PDF)

Library and Archives Canada Cataloguing in Publication

Title: Beyond the Great War : making peace in a disordered world / edited by Norman Ingram and Carl Bouchard.
Names: Ingram, Norman, 1959 – editor. | Bouchard, Carl, 1971– editor.
Description: Includes bibliographical references and index.
Identifiers: Canadiana (print) 20210236612 | Canadiana (ebook) 20210236949 | ISBN 9781487542740 (cloth) | ISBN 9781487542757 (EPUB) | ISBN 9781487542764 (PDF)
Subjects: LCSH: World War, 1914–1918 – France – Peace. | LCSH: World War, 1914–1918 – Europe, Western – Peace. | LCSH: International relations – History – 20th century. | LCSH: France – Politics and government – 1914–1940. | LCSH: Treaty of Versailles (1919 June 28)
Classification: LCC DC389 .B49 2022 | DDC 944.081/5—dc23

We wish to acknowledge the land on which the University of Toronto Press operates. This land is the traditional territory of the Wendat, the Anishnaabeg, the Haudenosaunee, the Métis, and the Mississaugas of the Credit First Nation.

This book has been published with the help of a grant from the Federation for the Humanities and Social Sciences, through the Awards to Scholarly Publications Program, using funds provided by the Social Sciences and Humanities Research Council of Canada.

University of Toronto Press acknowledges the financial support of the Government of Canada, the Canada Council for the Arts, and the Ontario Arts Council, an agency of the Government of Ontario, for its publishing activities.

Funded by the Government of Canada | Financé par le gouvernement du Canada | Canada

Contents

Acknowledgments

This book had its origin in a two-day workshop we organized at Concordia University and the Université de Montréal in October 2018 around the theme "1919: World (Dis-)Order," at which fourteen historians from Great Britain, France, Canada, and the United States presented papers dealing with the various ways in which the end of the Great War triggered a number of reflections on order and disorder within political, diplomatic, social, and scientific communities. Not all the historians present at the workshop have been included in this book, while others who were not at the conference have been added.

We are greatly in the debt of the Social Sciences and Humanities Research Council of Canada for provision of a Connections Grant, which enormously facilitated the hosting of this conference. At Concordia University, we extend our thanks to the Department of History and the Webster Library. At the Université de Montréal, we record our thanks to the Faculty of Arts and Science, the Department of History, the McConnell Chair in American Studies, and the Rare Books and Special Collections Library. The Deans of Arts and Science at both our institutions, André Roy for Concordia and Frédéric Bouchard for UdeM, were highly supportive and gave stimulating opening remarks. We are grateful to Harvard University, the Royal Military College of Canada, Utah State University, California State University at Sacramento, and the Chair in Global History at the University of Glasgow for their financial support. Half the papers included in this book were written in French; we are thankful to our translator, Rhonda Mullins, for a job well done. We also thank the three anonymous readers for the University of Toronto Press for their insightful comments; we hope they will not be disappointed with the final product. Finally, we thank our editor at the University of Toronto Press, Dr. Stephen Shapiro, who has expertly guided us through the publication process.

Norman Ingram
Carl Bouchard

BEYOND THE GREAT WAR

1 1914 or 1919? The Aetiology of a Disordered World

NORMAN INGRAM AND CARL BOUCHARD

Robert Gerwarth has written that "it is difficult to suggest that post-imperial Europe was a better, safer place than it had been in 1914."[1] Yet that is precisely the historical argument that is usually made about the birth of a new world in 1919. It is acknowledged that mistakes were made in 1919, but the Paris Peace Conference is usually seen as the midwife at the birth of a world that was safer, more predictable, and generally better than the pre-war European civilization that went before it. That birth might have been difficult, it might even have been a forceps delivery in some respects, but the resulting world order was, all things considered, better than what had gone before. In some respects, however, it all depended on where one lived. Eastern Europe was a cauldron of ethnic animosities, which led rapidly to the creation of the "bloodlands," as Timothy Snyder calls them.[2] To cite Gerwarth again, "post-war Europe between the official end of the Great War in 1918 and the Treaty of Lausanne in July 1923 was the most violent place on the planet."[3] He does not distinguish between Eastern and Western Europe in this statement, even though most of his book deals with the defeated empires of Central and Eastern Europe and the successor states that emerged out of them. Spatially and temporally, the "ending" of the war meant different things across the breadth of the European continent. In Ian Kershaw's view, it is 1924 and the Dawes Plan that really represent its final end.[4] Much also depends on whether one is speaking of the victors or the vanquished. As Norman Ingram has argued, the war "was never really over for the French – either in 1923 or even during the Second World War."[5] Recently, French historians – notably Bruno Cabanes – have engaged in a thorough examination of the "sortie de guerre," which marks the more or less long transition from the norms of war to those of peace.[6] The passage of time also had other casualties. John Horne and Alan Kramer have written insightfully about a kind of selective amnesia with regard to German atrocities in the Great War.[7] What was remembered (or repressed and forgotten) when, by whom, and to what ends is thus very important. Historical time is a submerged theme in this book, a sub-stratum, but it is subtly interwoven with geopolitical situation and political culture.[8] The result is that it becomes difficult to assign endpoints to what 1919 meant across the European landscape or, rather, that these varied enormously.

In Western Europe, the illusion that all was well lasted a little longer. But even here, there were problems that simply could not be ignored. As Victor Basch, a philosophy professor at the Sorbonne and the then vice-president of the French Ligue des droits de l'homme (LDH), insisted in 1922, while not all of the clauses of the Versailles Treaty were good, nevertheless it had been only natural that the Allies should have succumbed to "quite understandable ill feelings" of vengeance in 1919.[9] This was a song he was still singing ten years later, albeit in more nuanced tones and this time as the Ligue's president at the LDH's congress in December 1932 just before the Nazi seizure of power. At that congress, the Ligue finally debated the question of "the controversy over the treaties." It had taken almost fourteen years, but Basch had finally come out in favour of "adjustment" but not outright treaty "revision." Adjustment meant merely eradicating the injustices contained in the treaties, of which there were apparently many, but not calling into question the entire structure of the new post-1919 (European) world. In some respects, it was too little too late. By December 1932, the Nazi seizure of power was less than six weeks away. The result was that Europe was in a bind, according to Basch: "if one laid a brutal and clumsy hand on the unfortunate diplomatic instruments created in 1919, one would run the risk of creating a catastrophe that would make 1914 look like child's play."[10]

The Second World War was certainly going to prove the truth of that. Violence on all levels – between states, within states, and genocidal violence directed against entire peoples – rose to unheard of, unimagined levels in the 1939 war. Was this the unintended result of the way the Great War ended, with an armistice instead of a surrender, was it the fault of the 1919 peace treaties, or was it because of the way the war had begun, with a doubtful aetiology which one hundred years on is still the subject of historical debate? Or perhaps it was a combination of all of these elements? In short, was the global instability of the interwar period that led to the Second World War the heritage of 1919 or of 1914?

These are important questions which find parallels in recent political history. One-fifth of the way through the twenty-first century, we are still trying to keep together a fragile world order that is the result of the way the second war ended. That post-1945 world order has – until very recently perhaps – succeeded in maintaining a fragile peace. At times, it has been a frayed peace, but in general terms it has lasted, at least as far as the first world is concerned; beyond that, its success has been more doubtful, but surrogate wars and wars of decolonization notwithstanding, there has been nothing like the Second World War for over seventy-five years now. If Europe is indeed the "dark continent," to use Mark Mazower's title, at least it has plumbed the depths of its soul and pulled itself back from the brink of nuclear annihilation.[11] Thanatos has, for the most part, been stared down since 1945.

The fact that the Second World War occurred is testament to the malignant effect of the First. It is thus important to distinguish between the effects of the Great War itself – both its origins and its prosecution – and the peace which ultimately ended it. In this sense, all the essays presented in this volume argue that despite the good intentions of the peace makers at Paris, the result was ultimately an unhappy one. Part of the reason for this was the heritage of four and a half years of war which inflicted wounds on the European body politic so deep and so grievous that it is difficult to imagine how any peace – Carthaginian or not – could have rectified the situation.

For a very long time, the historical consensus was that the treaties that ended the Great War were a disaster. This was gradually supplanted by a revisionist view which held that there was much good in the 1919 treaties. Historical consensus today underlines the extreme difficulty of creating a stable international order and seeks to understand how the system established in 1919, however awkwardly, was equally an innovative one (with regard to the relationship between internationalism and nationalism, on the question of sovereignty, the rights of minorities, and civic participation through plebiscites, among others).[12] The treaties, which were the result of an arrangement representing the interests of the victorious powers, were also a compromise between great innovative principles and the reality of international relations, all of which was conducted in the context of negotiations the likes of which had never been seen before. Even more fundamentally, the treaties illustrate the imperfect and incomplete transition between two systems: the first from before 1914, based on force and the dominance of the "great powers," and the other of the post-war period, which sought to establish an international community of powers in the service of order in which violence would cease to be a way of resolving the differences between states. It is the contention of the authors of this volume that the catalyst of this transition was a world war which, through a snowball effect, spun out of control into instability. Put another way, the disorder which followed on from 1918 was in many respects a nascent order, an order in the state of "becoming."

This belief also assumed that 1919 was the zero hour. The period after the end of the Great War and the Paris Peace Conference brings to mind Wordsworth's verse on the French Revolution: "bliss was it in that dawn to be alive ... When Reason seemed the most to assert her rights." Paradoxical and counter-intuitive though it might seem, the only way in 1919 to deal with the 1914 problem was in a selective forgetting – forgetting or misremembering the complex origins of the war, forgetting the various and vain attempts to forge peace during the war itself as blood flowed like a river in both eastern and western Europe, and denying, in a very real sense, the recent past. In short, the only way to live with the trauma of the war was to make of it a crusade, moreover a crusade that had ultimately been successful. The heritage of the war was rescued by turning it into, in William Mulligan's apt phrasing, the "Great War for Peace."[13] This happened right from the outset in 1914. For the Entente side, the war was almost immediately a crusade to defeat Prussian militarism and defend the rights of small nations (Serbia and Belgium), while for the Central Powers, it was a crusade to protect the rights of empires and more crucially to defeat the attack on western civilization of eastern, i.e. Russian, barbarism. On both sides of the conflict, war aims would henceforth not be limited to the simple acquisition of territory or the creation of a new regime of force under the thumb of the victor but instead would express the noble and universalist character of sacrifice. The perverse effect of such a conception of the war took form at the very moment it became a war of attrition: at what point would idealistic expectations be satisfied? The inflationary character of these universalist war aims, increasingly unattainable as the body count increased into the millions, imprinted as a consequence a new and paradoxical dynamic onto the conflict: the "Great War for peace" did not allow for a rapid end to the conflict.

After 1918, for a time, some parts of Europe were indeed able to "forget" the war – more in the West than in the East – while at the same time paradoxically remembering it. In particular, the Entente Powers, especially Great Britain and France, were able to deal with the trauma of the war by a huge collective will which believed that the war had been fought for the noblest of motives and that the world which emerged from it was, almost by definition, going to be better. Both of those assumptions were dubious, and their dubiety began to become evident for all to see by the early 1930s.

The problem with this is that both of these positions occluded what happened before 1919, that is to say, in 1914. If we assume that 1919 was a fresh start – the zero hour – then this analysis might have something to commend it. But 1919 was not a fresh start. It was not the zero hour. To extend what Sebastian Döderlein writes with regard to the historiography on Alsace-Lorraine, arguing that history reads only forward from 1919 is to assume that there is no pre-history, no anteriority to 1919 in general. But there was. And that pre-history was the debate over the explosion of the war in 1914. It is that which underpins the critical analyses of all of the historians in this volume. That is why the 1920s were the "decade of things that might have been,"[14] rather than the beginning of a genuinely new world. Positivist ideas of progress and idealism had both been killed in the trenches. There remained only the husk of these notions when the victorious Allies met in Paris in January 1919. That is what makes the Paris Peace Conference so tragic: it became an epic struggle between a largely American vision of a new sort of international relations and a European view which was still mired in the Great Power politics of the nineteenth century, even if important parts of French and British public opinion supported precisely the kind of new world order that Wilson seemed to represent. For a time, the illusion could be maintained. It was certainly worth the hope and the effort. Not to have tried to realize it would have been an even more grievous tragedy. But tragedy it still was: Elvis had already left the building.

The difficulty was that history – recent history – could not easily be transcended, and despite the existence of ideas and plans to make the brave new world safer and better, these plans and ideas were at least partially vitiated by the very historical fact of the war itself. There was too much unfinished business in 1919. Disorder trumped order, perhaps not immediately but ultimately and incrementally. Even if one were to discount the difficult heritage of 1914 – essentially by looking forward only – it is clear that the 1914 problem was the *toile de fond* for the Paris Peace Conference and that its resolution, posited by the peace treaties of 1919, was pregnant with consequences for the future.

In a sense, the problem with 1919 is the same as with the Great War itself. The war, in the West at least, had become bogged down in a trench warfare which could seemingly never be transcended or broken free of. Great advances in technology were insufficient to end the war of stasis after the first battle of the Marne, and so the war ground on relentlessly, neither side capable of the knockout blow which would have led to a war of movement (*Nach Paris! À Berlin!*) and in turn to victory. Technologically induced sclerosis begat an infernal machine that was capable of killing millions of men but not of producing a decisive breakthrough for either side. On the diplomatic level, the response was a kind of "atony of the conscience," among both the Entente and Central Powers, with regard to the appalling human cost of the war.[15] The result was the carnage of the Western Front. An analogous problem faced the peacemakers of 1919 when they tried to rebuild and reorder the world. Excellent ideas inspired by an internationalism reacting to the human catastrophe of the war there were aplenty, but, like the problem of technology during the war itself, the distance between theory and practice, *Dichtung* and *Wahrheit*, between *Idealpolitik* and *Realpolitik* was too great. So, while the half-illusion of progress was tenable during the 1920s, it began to unravel in the 1930s, only to end with the still more calamitous Second World War.

None of this was obvious at the time. The men and women who worked tirelessly for the success of internationalist ideals did so in all good faith. For a time, it seemed that Europe would be able to transcend the experience of the hecatomb, that all the good ideas regarding the re-ordering of national and international society would take root and that the future could be saved. It was possible to take this position during the 1920s by resolutely looking forward; by denying parts of the past; by refusing to confront the historical problems posed by 1914; by, in a sense, paradoxical though it might seem, negating recent history. But the past was still there. It did not go away and what the treaties of 1919 unwittingly did was merely to occlude, or hide, the issues raised by the war itself and store up the rancour of 1914 for a later day.

Much recent discussion of the Great War has underlined the extent to which it was a *world* war, a war of empires, a war of peoples, which ended with an enormous impact on the colonial world.[16] We certainly do not discount that. By the time the war ended in November 1918, it was undoubtedly all those things. But recognising that does not mean one may ignore the fact that it began in Europe with a settling of European accounts and that it ended with a peace conference in Europe. Moreover, the next war, which began in 1939 was also, at its outset, very much a European war, too – a settling of European accounts from the last war. This book, then, makes the case that the relationship between order and disorder begotten of the Peace Treaties of 1919 needs to be understood in a European–American context.

As the next ten chapters show, we approach the problem of the 1919 treaties and the heritage of the Great War from several complementary angles. The answers to the questions posed above are multilayered and complex. As will become evident, some look backwards more than forwards for answers. Both approaches, however, take a critical stance vis-à-vis the Peace Treaties of 1919.

Internationalism and Political Disorder

There is no doubt that high hopes were held for the post-war world. Peter Jackson and William Mulligan argue that paradoxically a major war seems necessary for the emergence and development of internationalist ideas. They structure their argument around the idea that since the wars of the French Revolution "the longer and more destructive the war, the greater the appetite for internationalist projects for peaceful cooperation."[17] Their analysis provides a cautionary reflection of present-day political concerns. They write that the rules-based international order that was the result of the Great War and perhaps even more of the Second World War "is now under threat as we enter the third decade of the twenty-first century." What catalysed the internationalist reaction was not merely the destruction of the "credibility of the political practices that produced the conflict in the first place" – the utilitarian or humanitarian reaction to so much suffering[18] – but paradoxically also the "practice of justifying unlimited war as necessary for permanent peace opened up possibilities for new approaches to world politics based on cooperation and the creation of institutions beyond the state to promote peace and the rule of law."[19] There is a rather pessimistic paradox here. War, the bloodier the better, becomes necessary for the creation and elaboration of new internationalist ideas which will henceforth prevent war. This is the quintessence of what Martin Ceadel calls the "crusading" ideal type in international relations[20] or, as Romain Rolland put it in quite a different ideological context, "*par la révolution, la paix.*"[21] Viewed from this angle, it is certainly possible to see 1919 in a positive light, as the beginning of a new era in internationalist thinking, but this, we would argue, is only possible by looking forward from 1919 alone and by ignoring the human cost required to get to that point. To cast even the briefest of glances backwards to 1914 is to encounter "the world we have lost."[22]

Andrew Barros provides some immediate historical context to the internationalist ethos in 1919 through the lens of the work of the Carnegie Endowment for International Peace (CEIP) and its work from 1910 to 1920. He demonstrates the immense dissatisfaction with the final product of the many members of the CEIP who were delegates to the peace conference. The organization was handicapped, however, by the rising tide of American isolationism and by Wilson's failure to secure passage of the peace treaties through the American Senate or American entry into the new-born League of Nations. Barros's analysis supports Jackson and Mulligan's thesis; he writes that "For the CEIP the First World War marked above all a weapon for peace," but ultimately he sees the disorder created by the war and indeed by the peace which followed it as "stronger than [the legacy] of those who … attempted to harness it in the construction of a liberal internationalist order."[23]

European socialists were obliged to repair to Switzerland for their first post-war international conference; convening in Paris had been banned by the Allied governments. Talbot Imlay's essay makes a cogent case for examining socialist internationalism in the wake of the Great War. He argues that this has been ignored by scholars in favour of a bipolar analysis of internationalism as either of the liberal/Wilsonian variety or else of the Bolshevik/Leninist sort. Taking inspiration from Geoff Eley's felicitous phrase, "enabling indeterminacies,"[24] which itself is consonant with the analyses of all the authors in this volume, Imlay seeks to understand the non-communist socialist position on peace and war in 1919. He describes the politics of the Vienna Union, a revolutionary but democratic answer to both the "national-reformist" socialism of the pre-war years and at the same time to the anti-democratic Bolshevik revolutionary socialism of the Russian Revolution. He argues that this "vibrant" socialist internationalism was more "coherent" in its critique of the post-1919 political order than liberal internationalism could ever hope to be.

Between Order and Disorder: The Case of France

Some of the essays in this volume examine the impact of the treaties moving forwards from 1919 and posit that far from creating order they ultimately contributed to the disordering of European society. Others, however, look more explicitly back to 1914. From whatever angle they analyse the legacy of the treaties of 1919, the question of France and its role in the post-war world is central. While much excellent scholarship has underlined the extent to which the Great War was a global phenomenon or that, following Christopher Clark's compelling analysis, it was a war which began (at least) as a third Balkan war, we believe an argument can be made that it was also in its essence a Franco–German war.[25] This is not meant to be a zero-sum argument: the importance of one perspective does not negate the validity of the others.

Norman Ingram argues that "French political society had just as much trouble dealing with the victory of Versailles as the vanquished nations had in dealing with defeat."[26] He does this by underlining the importance of looking backwards from 1919 to the beginning of the war and suggests that provisions of the treaties, which in a forensic way attempted to look back to 1914 in the laying of war guilt on Germany, vitiated from the outset any hope that the post-1919 world would ultimately be a better, safer place. The chickens of 1919 came home to roost in 1939 in a cataclysm far greater than that of 1914. In the French context, the debate on 1914 eventually came close to destroying the quintessentially republican Ligue des droits de l'homme in France. This debate had two ancillary effects, equally portentous for the future of France: first, the war guilt debate became the historical catalyst for the emergence of a new style of pacifism in France, and secondly, this very development itself led to the creation of a particular type of pro-Vichy political position during the Second World War. The two world wars are thus intimately linked in French history, and the *trait d'union* between them is the knotty problem of war guilt from 1914.

Sebastian Döderlein offers a highly original look at the reintegration of the "lost provinces" of Alsace-Lorraine into the French body politic in 1919. For Döderlein, the end of the war was not a triumphal return of these contested lands to the motherland but rather a decidedly ambiguous end to the Great War. His examination of the end of the war as a "pivot," a fulcrum, in history is insightful. For Germany, Alsace-Lorraine enters History as the Reichsland in 1871 and then exits from it with the end of the war in 1918. For France, on the other hand, Alsace-Lorraine became a much-regretted memory in 1871 and only re-entered History with the Armistice of November 1918. Alsace-Lorraine is thus caught in an historical neverland – for German historiography it ceases to exist in 1918, and for French historiography its history really only begins at that point. The reality on the ground in 1918–19 was quite different from the triumphant version of history usually articulated by French historians. There was little of the unanimous joy at the arrival of the French troops that is often spoken of. The social reality of the end of the war was ambiguous, largely for material reasons: the inhabitants of Alsace-Lorraine wanted the war to end because it would bring an end to economic privation. Lofty ideals of nationalism played a surprisingly small role. And when the French authorities proceeded to effect an ethnic cleansing of Alsace-Lorraine by removing many German-born residents from the territory, the results were negative.

Bruno Cabanes raises the problem of reparations for wounded and disabled veterans in France. His analysis reveals the gendered nature of French notions of reparations along with the extent to which reparation payments were as much a civilian issue as a military one. What is important in Cabanes's approach is the fact that the initiative to enshrine the right to reparations did not come from the State – despite the State's role in the drafting of the reparations section of the Paris peace treaties – but rather from within civil society. The initiative came from veterans, wounded ex-soldiers, and war widows.

They demanded not assistance from the State, but on the contrary recognition of their right to reparation as a function of the social contract of civil society. And, at the same time, under the leadership of René Cassin and other French social and legal experts, this social contract was expanded to a humanitarian right of international dimensions. As Cabanes writes, this humanitarian campaign existed at the "margins of traditional diplomacy" and itself became a "humanitarian diplomacy" which posited alternative visions of what nations must do in the aftermath of war.[27]

Carl Bouchard takes the original approach of questioning the way in which Woodrow Wilson and his ideas were received in France, not by looking at diplomatic documents or newspaper articles and editorials, and certainly not by examining the person of Wilson. Rather, he examines the letters sent to Wilson by French people from November 1918 to June 1919 and the anonymous writings of Fernand Pila, director of the department of the economy and trade in the French Foreign Affairs Ministry and a staunch disciple of Wilsonian ideas. The result is an excellent examination of raw public opinion that is not filtered through any of the normal channels mentioned above. Bouchard's analysis makes clear how people in 1919 – and more particularly those who qualified as "Wilsonians," that is to say, the men and women who subscribed until the end to the Wilsonian promises of a new world – genuinely believed they had a role in shaping world events, no matter how much these hopes were to be dashed by what eventually transpired at the peace conference. For Wilsonians, 1919 was indeed a zero hour, the birth of a new world. Bouchard argues that "Wilson was the only leader who arrived in Paris in December 1918 with a new idea"; he certainly was the only leader who arrived with a fully fleshed-out design for a new world order.[28] Unfortunately, it was all for naught and, in Bouchard's words, "despite the creation of the League of Nations, the 1919 order was essentially the same that had led to global disorder in 1914–1918. Who could dare believe that it would not lead to further disorder?"[29]

Science, Gender, and Race in a Disordered Post-war World

Science, gender, and race relations were all profoundly disrupted by the Great War, themes which the final section of this book examines. One American scientist, William Noyes, struggled, ultimately unsuccessfully, to return the international scientific community to its ante-bellum principles. The final two chapters in this book underline the extent to which 1919 ought not to be seen as a grand liberating moment in terms of gender and race relations. All three chapters in this final section demonstrate how, at the level of mental structures, many of the ideas of 1914 were still dominant at the end of the war.

Marie-Eve Chagnon analyses the reconciliation efforts of the American chemist, William Noyes, in the period immediately following the end of the war. Central to Noyes's concerns was the establishment of the International Research Council (IRC) in 1919, which was specifically designed to exclude German and Austrian scientists. The year 1919 thus represents the introduction of still more disorder into the international scientific community rather than the lancing of the boil caused by the war. Despite the efforts of Noyes and other Americans, it proved impossible to return to the *status quo ante* in international science, to go back to "a science with integrity that recognized no borders and that operated above politics."[30] As Chagnon richly demonstrates, the internationalist desires of some were negated in 1919 by the heritage of the war, of 1914 itself. Disorder, whether it stemmed from 1914 or from its attempted, yet stillborn, resolution in 1919, could not be transcended by the international scientific community.

Both Marie-Michèle Doucet and Mona Siegel offer analyses of 1919 that look forwards to greater gender and racial equality. The Great War and the peace conference appeared to open up the possibility for greater participation by women in the political sphere. On one level this happened: women received the vote in some form or other in the United States, Great Britain, Canada, Germany, and elsewhere. They did not, however, in France, despite the active role of French women in both the councils of international feminism, the peace movement, and politics generally. Doucet analyses the conundrum faced by French women in 1919. Some were drawn to the ideas of pacifism and internationalism, while for others, the siren call of nationalism and revenge against the Germans proved too strong. Siegel complicates the story of American women's participation in the 1919 Zürich congress of the Women's International League for Peace and Freedom (WILPF) by introducing the question of race into the equation. Doucet demonstrates how much ideas of revenge continued to dominate French feminist politics, lending credence to James McMillan and Susan Grayzel's arguments that the Great War ultimately changed little for French women.[31] Both Doucet and Siegel go beyond this rather reductive argument, however, and examine on their own terms the feminist response to the 1919 peace treaties. Here, their analyses add much to our understanding. The fact that Doucet's "unknown mother of the unknown soldier" was able to make her voice heard at all against the claims of a masculine-inspired French nationalism is significant. Siegel's description of Mary Church Terrell's campaign for racial and gender equality is instructive. The Women's International League for Peace and Freedom (WILPF) was not allowed to hold its 1919 congress in Paris at the time of the peace conference, which is why it met in Zürich instead. As for racial equality, the peace conference showed clearly how little the great powers, especially the United States, cared for the issues involved. Woodrow Wilson does not come off well in this telling of the story. But what is noteworthy are the truly progressive positions of the WILPF on issues of race and gender – positions which continue to find resonance all the way down to the present day.

Where does this leave the historian who wishes to understand what happened just over one hundred years ago at the Paris Peace Conference? Several points need to be made. First, the authors in this volume do not discount in the slightest the positive effects of the Paris Peace Treaties of 1919, most notably in the creation of the League of Nations. The world was arguably a better place, in the 1920s at least, because of the existence of the Genevan institution. The fact that the League, as well as the Paris treaties themselves, ultimately failed is due to the unresolved issues embedded both in the League Covenant and in the discussions in Paris. The diplomacy of Paris failed to galvanize world opinion behind it: Bouchard's analysis of French public opinion and Siegel's examination of the race question both strikingly demonstrate that. Secondly, however, part of the problem with weighing the success or failure of the 1919 Paris peace treaties is that 1919 is represented as a caesura, a starting point, a new beginning devoid of historical antecedents and contextualization. It could never be that. The weight of historical experience caused by four and a half years of the bloodiest war in human history would not, indeed could not, permit it.

The analyses presented here portray 1919 as a social, gendered, political event, but not primarily as a diplomatic one. Our purpose is not to write another history of the "high politics" of 1919 but rather of the deep currents roiling Western society as a result of 1919 and the war that preceded it. Even Jackson and Mulligan, despite a point of departure that is anchored in diplomatic history, agree that internationalism, or rather its success, is rooted in calamitous wartime experiences. John Maynard Keynes argued that the Versailles Treaty in particular was a "Carthaginian peace."[32] Even that is perhaps to give too much credit to the Paris peace process. What made the disorder, disillusion, and disappointment with the peace of 1919 possible was the truly Carthaginian war which preceded it. That war and the peace which followed it are two sides of the same coin. Much of the failure of 1919 was the result of the failure to drain the abscess of 1914.

NOTES

1 Robert Gerwarth, *The Vanquished: Why the First World War Failed to End, 1917–1923* (London: Allen Lane, 2016), p. 7.
2 Timothy Snyder, *The Bloodlands: Europe between Hitler and Stalin* (New York: Perseus Books, 2010).
3 Gerwarth, *Vanquished*, p. 7.
4 Ian Kershaw, *To Hell and Back: Europe, 1914–1949* (New York: Penguin, 2016).
5 Norman Ingram, *The War Guilt Problem and the Ligue des droits de l'homme, 1914–1944* (Oxford: Oxford University Press, 2019), p. 266. Gerd Krumeich rightly pointed out in an intervention at the conference on "30 ans d'histoire des relations internationales," sponsored by the Ministère des Affaires Étrangères de France and the Université de Paris 1 Panthéon-Sorbonne, on 14 December 2012, that for many Germans the First World War really ended when German troops marched up the Champs-Elysées in 1940.
6 Bruno Cabanes, *La victoire endeuillée: La sortie de guerre des soldats français, 1918–1920* (Paris: Seuil, 2004); Stéphane Audoin-Rouzeau and Christophe Prochasson, *Sortir de la Grande Guerre. Le monde et l'après 1918* (Paris: Tallandier, 2008); Bruno Cabanes and Guillaume Piketty, "Sortir de la guerre : jalons pour une histoire en chantier," *Histoire@Politique*, no. 3, 2007; Stéphane Tison, *Comment sortir de la guerre? Deuil, mémoire et traumatisme (1870–1940)* (Rennes: Presses universitaires de Rennes, 2011).
7 John Horne and Alan Kramer, *German Atrocities, 1914: A History of Denial* (New Haven: Yale University Press, 2001).
8 On the importance of the geopolitical situation and political culture in an understanding of the peace and war question, see Chapter 8 ("The Determinants of the Debate") in Martin Ceadel, *Thinking about Peace and War* (Oxford: Oxford University Press, 1987), pp. 166–89.
9 Victor Basch, "Notre voyage en Allemagne: les impressions de M. Victor Basch," *Cahiers des droits de l'homme* 22, no. 17 (25 August 1922), p. 399.
10 Victor Basch, "La Controverse sur les traités: I. Les Principes. Discours de M. Victor Basch" in *Le Congrès national de 1932. Compte-rendu sténographique. Paris, 26–28 Décembre 1932* (Paris: Ligue des droits de l'homme, 1933), pp. 202–3.
11 Mark Mazower, *Dark Continent: Europe's Twentieth Century* (London: Allen Lane, 1998).
12 Marcus M. Payk and Roberta Pergher, eds., *Beyond Versailles: Sovereignty, Legitimacy, and the Formation of New Polities After the Great War* (Bloomington, IN: Indiana University Press, 2018).
13 See William Mulligan, *The Great War for Peace* (New Haven: Yale University Press, 2014).

14 Norman Ingram, *The War Guilt Problem and the Ligue des droits de l'homme, 1914–1944* (Oxford: Oxford University Press, 2019), p. 264.

15 Much later, the French pacifist Georges Pioch used the phrase "atony of the conscience" to criticize the position of non-engagement of the French Ligue des droits de l'homme on the Moscow Purge Trials. See "Discours de M. Georges Pioch," in "Les Procès de Moscou" in the debate on the Rapport moral in *Congrès national de 1937. Compte-rendu sténographique. Tours, 17–19 juillet 1937* (Paris: Ligue des droits de l'homme, 1937), pp. 147–9.

16 See, for example, Erez Manela, *The Wilsonian Moment: Self-Determination and the International Origins of Anticolonial Nationalism* (New York: Oxford University Press, 2007); Michael S. Neiberg, *Fighting the Great War: A Global History* (Harvard: Harvard University Press, 2009). Recent German scholarship has also laid emphasis on the global nature of the conflict and the peace treaties. See Jörn Leonhard, *Der überforderte Frieden: Versailles und die Welt, 1918–1923* (Munich: C.H. Beck, 2018) and Eckart Conze, *Die Grosse Illusion: Versailles 1919 und die Neuordnung der Welt* (Munich: Siedler, 2018). See also Richard S. Fogarty and Andrew Tait Jarboe, eds., *Empires in World War I: Shifting Frontiers and Imperial Dynamics in a Global Conflict* (London: Bloomsbury, 2020); Lawrence Sondhaus, *World War One: The Global Revolution* (Cambridge: Cambridge University Press, 2011); Daniel Marc Segesser, *Der Erste Weltkrieg in Globaler Perspektive* (Wiesbaden: Marixverlag, 2014). See also the special number of *Geschichte und Gesellschaft* 40/2 (2014), "Der Erste Weltkrieg in globaler Perspektive," edited by Oliver Janz. The Oxford project, "Globalising and Localising the Great War," is also of signal importance. See http://greatwar.history.ox.ac.uk/. Another important resource is the online encyclopaedia at https://encyclopedia.1914-1918-online.net/home/.

17 Jackson and Mulligan, chapter 2 of this volume, p. 22.

18 Martin Ceadel has written that the "utilitarian inspiration" for pacifism was the single most important intellectual advance of interwar British pacifism. See Martin Ceadel, *Pacifism in Britain: The Defining of a Faith, 1914–1945* (Oxford: Clarendon Press, 1980), p. 13.

19 Jackson and Mulligan, chapter 2 of this volume, pp. 39–40.

20 See Martin Ceadel, *Thinking about Peace and War*, pp. 43–71.

21 See Romain Rolland, *Par la Révolution, la paix* (Paris: Éditions sociales internationales, 1935).

22 With apologies to Peter Laslett for the mis-appropriation of his evocative title. See Peter Laslett, *The World We Have Lost* (New York: Scribner, 1965).

23 Barros, chapter 3 of this volume, pp. 60–61.

24 Geoff Eley, "Europe After 1945," *History Workshop Journal* 65 (2008), 207–8, cited in Imlay, chapter 4 of this volume, p. 72.

25 See Christopher Clark, *The Sleepwalkers: How Europe Went to War in 1914* (London: Allen Lane, 2012).
26 Ingram, chapter 5 of this volume, p. 93.
27 Cabanes, chapter 7 of this volume, p. 142.
28 Bouchard, chapter 8 of this volume, p. 149.
29 Bouchard, chapter 8 of this volume, p. 161.
30 Chagnon, chapter 9 of this volume, p. 176.
31 For an early iteration of this idea, see James McMillan, *From Housewife to Harlot: The Place of Women in French Society, 1870–1940* (Brighton: The Harvester Press, 1981). McMillan provides a more theoretically nuanced version of his argument in McMillan, "The Great War and Gender Relations: The Case of French Women and the First World War Revisited," in Gail Braybon, ed. *Evidence, History and the Great War: Historians and the Impact of 1914–1918* (New York: Berghahn, 2003), pp. 135–53. For a similar argument, see Susan Grayzel, *Women's Identities at War: Gender, Motherhood, and Politics in Britain and France during the First World War* (Chapel Hill, N.C.: University of North Caroline Press, 1999). See also Susan Grayzel, "Liberating Women? Examining Gender, Morality and Sexuality in First World War Britain and France," in Braybon, *Evidence*, pp. 113–34. For a counterargument to McMillan and Grayzel, see Mary Louise Roberts, *Civilization without Sexes: Reconstructing Gender in Postwar France, 1917–1927* (Chicago: University of Chicago Press, 1994).
32 John Maynard Keynes, *The Economic Consequences of the Peace* (New York: Harcourt, Brace and Howe, 1920).

Internationalism and Political Disorder

2 The Great War and the Political Conditions of Internationalism

PETER JACKSON AND WILLIAM MULLIGAN

Internationalism appears to be in retreat today even as debate over the character and significance of the Paris peace settlements one hundred years ago gathers new momentum. Wherever one looks, the international institutions, regimes, and practices developed at great cost during the twentieth century are under threat. Climate change agreements and nuclear non-proliferation accords as well as core institutions such as the European Union, the North Atlantic Treaty Organization, and even the United Nations face serious challenges to their continued viability. This is of course not the first time internationalism has faltered. The decade of the 1930s witnessed the precipitous collapse of the international institutions that emerged out of the unprecedented destruction of the First World War.

This last observation begs the question: What role has war played in the evolution of internationalism? The argument advanced in this essay is that war has played a fundamental role in creating the conditions for internationalism to thrive. The First World War is an excellent illustration of the way large-scale conflicts that demand massive sacrifices of belligerent societies create fertile ground for internationalist alternatives to peace and security. The Great War was represented by all sides as a crusade for peace and justice. These representations, in turn, created the political space for internationalist discourses to flourish by transforming the normative context in which the war was waged. This transformation forced policy elites to confront different political choices when they began to plan for a new international order in 1918–19. The transnational discourse of a "Great War for peace" placed powerful constraints on political, diplomatic and even military leaders that could not be ignored. Our larger argument is therefore that *words matter in international politics.* This is especially true when it comes to political discourses of peace and international justice during wars of unparalleled destructiveness.

This assertion may seem paradoxical. Wars, and in particular long destructive wars, nearly always undermine structures and practices that facilitate cooperation between states. The First World War is often used as the paradigmatic example of a major war that wrecked the internationalist institutions. In the words of George Kennan, repeated so often they have assumed the character of dogma, the war was the "seminal catastrophe" of the twentieth century. It destroyed the allegedly restrained political and social mores of the nineteenth century, giving way to a politics characterized by dystopian visions and totalitarian practices. According to this reading, fascism, communism, and Nazism were the inevitable result of a cycle of violence that began in 1914 and reached its apogee in the Holocaust.[1] Efforts to refashion the world order after 1918 have therefore been criticized as inadequate at best. At worst, they are considered responsible for the violent political instability of the 1920s and 1930s and the coming of war in 1939. The Treaty of Versailles stands as the prime example of how failed peacemaking at the end of one war led to a subsequent war.[2]

There is a wealth of historical writing that supports this understanding of the impact of the Great War on the post-war peace settlement. The problem with this literature is that it frames the conflict in a teleological straitjacket intended to explain totalitarianism, genocide, and the Second World War. It closes off alternative readings of the First World War and its legacies, notably the new ways in which peace was imagined, constructed, and maintained. Indeed, the evidence since 1792 suggests that the longer and more destructive the war, the greater the appetite for internationalist projects for peaceful cooperation. This has been true not only within the public sphere, as many historians have shown, but also among political and diplomatic elites.

Most internationalist campaigners were aware of the opportunity afforded to them by the political context of the First World War. But the relationship between the experience of war and the influence of internationalist ideas on the policies of the great powers have been largely ignored. This is in part because influential accounts of the evolution of internationalism have tended to marginalize statecraft and diplomacy. The *Palgrave Dictionary of Transnational History*, for example, has an excellent entry on "language diplomacy." But it lacks an entry on diplomacy.[3] There exists an untenable divorce between studies of political, diplomatic, and military policymaking, on the one hand, and recent work on the history of internationalism and transnational civil society, on the other. This divide reflects not only different research concerns but also different sources and different methodological assumptions about the nature of international politics.[4]

The unparalleled violence from 1914 created political space for internationalist ideas to exercise new influence on the calculations of political and diplomatic elites. Political space for the purposes of this essay refers to the range of positions that actors can adopt on given issues. These positions are both enabled and constrained by public discourse, which provides the normative language that is used to justify high political decisions. Such an approach illuminates the way high-level decision-making is connected to, and even shaped by, the broader public sphere.

A dynamic relationship thus exists between public debate and official policy-making.[5] During the Great War, political and policy elites justified the extraordinary sacrifices governments demanded of their respective societies by making claims concerning the transformative character of the conflict. The relationship between public discourse and policy decisions was especially powerful because the objective promised by political elites was enduring and even perpetual peace. It was this claim that the war was being waged to bring about a more peaceful world that established the conditions for internationalist ideas to enter mainstream political discourse.

I

The terms "internationalism" and "internationalist" require definition. For our purposes, internationalism is a belief system that attaches vital importance to the economic, social and cultural benefits of cooperation between political communities in general and between states in particular. The form of internationalism under consideration here looked to the establishment of institutions and practices *beyond* the state aimed at facilitating political and economic relations as well as knowledge exchange and other forms of cooperation *between* states. This strain of internationalism questioned the assumption that the sovereign state was the only significant actor capable of protecting individual rights and providing security in the international system.[6]

The Great War was not the first general conflict to generate internationalist initiatives. Enlightenment notions of human progress through stages provided the ideological framework for claims regarding the transformative character of the French Revolutionary Wars. These conflicts, like the First World War, were represented as necessary for the permanent eradication of war through the introduction of shared political freedom as the basis for international society. The radicalization of revolutionary politics following the successful repulsion of the Prussian and Austrian invasion in 1792 soon led to a war of surpassing ferocity with the aim of exporting freedom and democracy to France's neighbours. Leading revolutionary Georges Danton invoked "the exterminating angel of liberty" as the necessary condition for eradicating war.[7] The First World War was justified in very similar terms. Pundits and politicians on both sides of the Atlantic characterized that conflict as the "war that will end war" and, in quasi-religious terms, as a "sacred crusade for the final triumph of peace, justice and liberty." As the conflict dragged on and exacted human and economic costs on a hitherto unimaginable scale, the public discourse on both sides became suffused with "pervasive talk of peace."[8]

It is ironic that the most acute insights into the effects of waging war for peace are offered by Carl Schmitt, one of the great enemies of twentieth-century liberal internationalism. In a 1932 work inspired by reflections on the nature of the First World War (and dedicated to the memory of a friend killed in the fighting of 1917), Schmitt argued that waging war with the aim of abolishing war was in essence an attempt to create a world without politics. Such a conflict must therefore be "considered to constitute the absolute last war of humanity." Consequently, "[s]uch a war is necessarily unusually intense and inhuman because, by transcending the limits of the political framework, it simultaneously degrades the enemy into moral and other categories and is forced to make of him a monster that must not only be defeated but also utterly destroyed. In other words, he is an enemy who no longer must be compelled to retreat into his borders only."[9]

David Bell has used this insight to argue that enlightenment-inspired projects to wage war in order to eradicate war have culminated in apocalyptic conflicts that have been far more destructive in their effects than traditional wars waged for circumscribed political aims. Bell's fundamental position, like that of Schmitt, is that war must be accepted as "an inextricable part of being human" and that the belief that it is exceptional and eradicable is "a romantic delusion."[10]

This is not our argument. We contend instead that the public justification of the Great War as a struggle for peace and freedom opened up new political space for internationalism and had important effects on international relations. The dynamic relationship between public expectations and elite decision-making was recognized before the outbreak of the war. In 1913, Kurt Riezler, adviser to the German Chancellor Bethmann Hollweg, acknowledged that the public statements of national leaders constrained decision-making. Repeated avowals of peace, Riezler observed, raised the bar for going to war. For a war to occur, it was a requirement that it be justifiable to the public. This public, moreover, was not bound by national borders. It was a transnational public. "There is no doubt," Riezler explained, "that this idealist atmosphere, even if it is only show and soap bubbles, is in itself a real power … [it] makes it difficult for most to breach these rules and practices with little cause, and it compels all to cover these breaches and to mitigate their form."[11] Some historians have argued that the facility with which the leaders in the Central Powers crafted a justification for war in July 1914 shows how easily statesmen could ignore their solemn declarations.[12] But Riezler was not naïve. The author of the "policy of risk" (Risikopolitik), Riezler was schooled in late nineteenth-century European power politics. The successful resolution of numerous diplomatic crises before 1914 had convinced him that the European public would only countenance war as a last resort in defence of a vital interest. Such a war must meet the public demand for justification and legitimation. Crucially, however, the justificatory language deployed by all belligerents to legitimize their war policies set unforeseen parameters for post-war foreign policy choices.[13]

It was not necessary that political leaders believed their own rhetoric. But it is significant that they felt compelled to justify their actions using a specific normative vocabulary. For Quentin Skinner, the founding figure of the Cambridge School of the history of ideas, words are an enabling condition for any political decision. Skinner wrote in his seminal text on modern political thought that "the problem facing an agent who wishes to legitimate what he is doing at the same time as gaining what he wants cannot simply be the instrumental problem of tailoring his normative language in order to fit his proposals. It must in part be the problem of tailoring his projects in order to fit the available normative language."[14] Absent a justificatory language, certain courses of political action are impossible – or come at such high political costs that they are self-defeating. Prominent discourses in the transnational public sphere can play an important role in shaping the conceptual parameters within which foreign policy is made.

Public justifications occupied a particularly significant place in the context of the First World War. This reflected the pressures of mass mobilization and the importance of social cohesion to national war efforts. Although all states repressed dissent and coerced both military and labour service, the war efforts of the belligerents relied mainly on consent. The degree of consent varied across time and place. It rested ultimately on broad popular acceptance of the legitimacy of the war and the need for sacrifice.[15] Efforts to legitimate the war, crucially, required a vision of the post-war international order. A variety of post-war visions were articulated on both sides in countless newspaper articles, pamphlets, and speeches by political leaders, academics, journalists, and other voices in the public sphere. The legitimacy claimed in these interventions was grounded in international structures as well as domestic society. Politicians appealed to neutrals and sought to undermine enemy claims. Our focus here is on public justifications for the war and their interaction with foreign policy decision-making, particularly the production of war aims and peace initiatives. But first let us turn to the growth of internationalism before 1914, without which the demands for a new peace order during the First World War would have been unthinkable.

II

Professions of universal values in 1914 drew on a prior history of internationalist thought and practice. The second half of the nineteenth century witnessed an explosion of internationalism. Technological revolutions in communications, transportation, industry, and commerce brought about profound structural changes in international society. The movement of people and ideas intensified considerably as part of the "expansion of international society."[16] From the late 1850s the number and variety of international institutions increased dramatically. Among the most important were those created to manage international trade and communications: the International Telegraphic Union (1865), the Universal Postal Union (1874), the International Union for Weights and Measurements (1875), the International Union of Customs and Tariffs (1890), and the International Office for Public Hygiene (1907).[17]

A growing number of transnational associations promoted intellectual cooperation. Before 1850, the number of international bodies of this kind could be counted on one hand. By the 1890s, however, ten such organizations were being established each year. One result of these trends was the emergence of what Glenda Sluga has termed "new forms of international sociability" that reflected "a world shrinking under the influence of commercial and cultural interdependence."[18] In turn, the concept of the international created a new domain for a range of social relationships that transcended state boundaries and traditional diplomatic practices. This development also had implications for interstate relations. The notion of growing interdependence was central to internationalist doctrines predicting increasingly peaceful cooperation among nation-states. This theory of interdependence provided a stimulus to older national and transnational movements to eradicate war that had emerged in the aftermath of the Napoleonic Wars. From Giuseppe Mazzini's ideal of a Europe of cooperative nation-states to Norman Angell's argument that ever-increasing commercial and financial ties had made war irrational in economic terms, internationalist thought spawned visions of a more peaceful future.

Over the course of the late nineteenth century, transnational networks proliferated and thickened. Labour, missionaries, academics, businesses, and sporting associations forged new institutions, initiated regular conferences, and published international newsletters to advance their particular interests. In many cases, they also recognized that transnational cooperation required peace. In some cases, these new actors pursued peace as an end in itself. The result of this thickening of transnational networks was the evolution of what one scholar has described as a "robust global civil society" of peace activism.[19] By 1900, there were at least 425 peace associations worldwide, many of which collaborated in the organization of large annual Universal Peace Congresses.[20] Some national political parties also organized and lobbied for peace. European socialists, for example, organized popular protests against war into late 1912.[21]

These developments in the scale and scope of internationalism coincided with the rise of international law as both a profession and an academic discipline. There was considerable ideological and sociological overlap between international law and peace activism. Both movements were drawn almost exclusively from the ranks of the well-educated bourgeoisie. The normative assumptions of both reflected the prevailing intellectual climate and in particular positivist convictions concerning the inevitability of progress and the perfectibility of mankind.[22] The interest in international law also reflected the influence of rational positivism on both sides of the Atlantic. Movements for peace and international cooperation in Europe and North America were motivated by a shared conviction that legal codes and the rational settlement of disputes without violence was a hallmark of the march of civilization. A recognition that war was retrograde supposedly distinguished "European" societies from the "semi-barbarous" and "primitive" peoples they colonized.[23]

The movement to establish international legal institutions in general, and arbitration regimes in particular, assumed that the codification of international law would impose reciprocal duties and obligations on states which would, in turn, act as constraints on the use of violence as a tool of policy. The objective of "peace through law" was understood as a gradual process requiring the perfection of existing arrangements and the creation of new institutions. Binding international arbitration agreements and the creation of a world court would provide a framework for the peaceful settlement of political disputes among "civilized peoples." By the turn of the century, a host of private associations had been created in the United States, Britain, and France to promote the cause of international arbitration. One of the most significant initiatives to emerge out of the first Universal Peace Congress in Paris in 1889 was the creation of the Inter-Parliamentary Union for Arbitration. This organization linked elected officials from both sides of the Atlantic, all of whom were committed to the cause of arbitration treaties and a permanent international court.[24]

The most important civil society organization for peace was the *Association de la Paix par le Droit.* The *Association* had been founded in 1887. By the 1890s it had its own journal, *La Paix par le Droit,* and boasted a membership of 1200 in 1902 and nearly 4000 by 1912.[25] It was at the centre of what one historian has described as "a new religion of peace through law" that would eventually constitute the backbone of the continental movement for a "society" or "league" of nations before, during and after the First World War.[26]

There were important differences in civil society conceptions of international order in Europe and North America before 1914. The varieties of British and American internationalism ranged from an emphasis on the pacifying effects of economic inter-dependence to advocacy for a new legal and moral basis to international politics.[27] Legalist approaches were strongest in France and the United States.[28] The French approach was more formalistic. The first calls for a "society of nations" to preserve peace through the imposition of the rule of international law originated in France. They were advanced by a cluster of juridically inspired internationalists around Léon Bourgeois.[29]

This flowering of internationalism culminated in the Hague Peace Conferences in 1899 and 1907. As Maartje Abbenhuis has shown, public pressure across the world compelled often reluctant governments first to attend the conference and then to respond to specific proposals, such as arbitration and the codification of the laws of war.[30] The Hague conferences were global events. Delegates from twenty-six countries attended the first conference, and forty-four countries were represented at the second. Although internationalist advocates had profound disagreements about specific issues, they agreed in general on the value of rules and institutions to order international politics. Scholars have criticized the failure of the Hague conventions to establish the bases of lasting peace. The violation of the laws of war during the First World War underlined their apparent ineffectiveness. Immediate military or naval necessity trampled over the legal restraints. And yet, as Isabel Hull and Marcus Payk have demonstrated, belligerents on both sides during the war used the Hague conventions to condemn the transgressions of their opponents. Even as the conventions were being violated, they served as a touchstone for the legal and moral standards at stake in the conflict.[31]

That said, the late nineteenth and early twentieth centuries remained an arbitrary, often violent, era. The wars that took place from 1870 through

1914 did not bring internationalist projects into the realm of peacemaking, as had been the case in 1814–15. They did not demand the intensive mobilization of European and American societies, and they were not justified with recourse to abstract aims of permanent peace.

III

From the outset, the Great War was represented to populations in all the belligerent states as a necessary struggle to defend the rule of law and achieve conditions for a perpetual peace. Almost as soon as fighting broke out, political leaders began to draw on a wide-ranging vocabulary of peace and law to frame the conflict as a crusade to end war and bring about international justice. This discourse embraced cognate concerns about nationality, constitutional rights, and international organization. Even as German leaders acknowledged that the invasion of Belgium constituted a violation of international treaty law, they resorted to arguments framed in international legal terms to justify their actions. These arguments were inevitably weak. What is striking is that they made any attempt at all to occupy the discursive terrain of international justice.[32]

It was not at first self-evident that these prescriptions would predominate over more traditional rhetorical strategies invoking the national interest and the balance of power. After taking over as Italian prime minister in October 1914, Antonio Salandra spoke of "sacro egoismo" in a speech to diplomats at the Foreign Ministry. He returned to this notorious phrase after the war, arguing in 1922 that men would never have fought for the abstractions of democracy and justice, but only for the nation.[33] Fighting for the national interest undoubtedly fell within the realm of the "available normative vocabulary" to justify the war in the public sphere. But there were other political and ethical positions within that sphere that acquired greater prominence as the war grew in scope and ferocity. On 6 July 1916, days after the beginning of the battle of the Somme, Riezler went so to far as to conjure up federal ideals of a tolerant European community, with its historical roots in the medieval Holy Roman Empire. He argued that Germany's fate was tied up with that of Europe. Germany existed "at the heart of Europe" and its chief characteristics were "federative and attractive" rather than "repellent and aggressive." What was needed, Riezler argued, was "a new synthesis" of traditional with modern political virtues. Such a synthesis would ensure "the salvation of Germany, which is also the salvation of Europe."[34]

The invocation of "vital interest," crucially, posed the broader question of what was at stake and what "the nation" stood for – or, at least, what its political leaders claimed it stood for in their public proclamations.

The nation and its "interests" often derived their significance from their relationship with other concepts, such as civilization, law, justice, Europe, and, ultimately, peace. Perhaps the best-known illustration of this is H.G. Wells' famous and influential characterization of the conflict as a "war that will end war." Surveying the "unprecedented slaughter" and "hideous butchery" of the opening phase of the war, Wells deployed very similar language to that used by French deputies in the early 1790s. Such horrific violence could only be justified if war aims expanded to embrace a "war of the mind," the purpose of which was to eradicate international conflict. This aim, paradoxically, led Wells to urge an intensification of the war effort. "This is not a war of nations," he argued, "but of mankind. It is a war to exorcise a world-madness and end an age ... this is now a war for peace."[35]

Wells' formulation entered the popular lexicon. It played an important role in structuring discourse on the meaning and purpose of the war for the next four years. It was taken up by US President Woodrow Wilson as early as May 1916 and deployed as part of a discursive strategy to depict the conflict as a crusade to usher in a new and better age. Central to Wilson's vision was a revolution in the practice of international politics. Discredited practices of exclusive alliances, secret diplomacy, and the balance of power would be replaced by a world organization animated by democratic principles.[36] The American president's call for the transformation of international relations and an end to traditional power politics generated enormous enthusiasm among the trans-Atlantic civil society of peace activists. Over the course of the war, Wilson became convinced that it was America's special mission to intervene in the conflict to establish a new moral and political basis for international relations. The creation of a League of Nations was a prominent theme in Wilson's public declarations from May 1916 onwards.[37] In January 1917, the president called publicly for "peace without victory" and argued that the traditional balance of power must be replaced by a new "community of power" based on democracy and a post-war "League for Peace."[38] These ideas remained central to his thinking and his speeches after America's entry into the war in April 1917.

Internationalist themes of permanent peace, human rights, and the rule of law structured official discourse and were part of the war culture that ascribed meaning to the conflict and provided a justification for the sacrifices made at the front and behind the lines.[39] The French variant of this "culture de guerre" has been defined as "a body of representations of the conflict crystallized into a veritable system, giving the war its fundamental meaning."[40] Within this system, crucially, the conflict was depicted as a crusade for "civilization" aimed at establishing peace through the rule of law. In French representations, France was depicted as the cradle of civilization and the defender of international justice. A German victory, conversely, would mean the triumph of brute force.[41]

The discourse of the rule of law was omnipresent in French public sphere constructions of the war's meaning. Albert Sarraut, the Radical minister of education, provided the following vision of the war's purpose for dissemination to French schoolchildren: "France's genius, unchanged through the ages and despite the diversity of its history, is eternally in the service of the same inspirations of generosity that have led it to bring to the oppressed multitudes the language of the Declaration of the Rights of Man ... France must always be the magnificent evangelist of a new rule of law."[42] The relationship between these discursive constructions and internationalist ideas was not unique to France. In Britain, the leading conservative politician Arthur Balfour similarly stressed the "sacredness of international law and the rights of international freedom" as essential reasons for British participation in the conflict.[43] The theme of future redemption through transformative peace was ever more prominent in official discourse as the war dragged on and losses mounted. David Lloyd George, about to become British prime minister, argued in 1916 that the war's "inhumanity and pitilessness" were necessary to secure a lasting peace through the destruction of German militarism. He quoted a French woman who had lost four of her five sons but nonetheless declared that "The fight will never have gone on long enough until it should have made a repetition of this horror impossible."[44] By 1917 the notion of a return to the *status quo ante-bellum* was virtually absent from public sphere constructions of the war's purpose.

References to perpetual peace, liberty, and the rule of law were less common in official pronouncements by the Central Powers. While internal government discussions stressed the need for "security for all time" in Western Europe, claims that the war must result in permanent and transformative peace were rare. When this language was deployed at all, it was usually in response to Allied rhetoric. Official pronouncements of German and Austro-Hungarian governments tended to stress the defence of European civilization against Russian barbarism, often depicted as an Asiatic threat. The idea of defending Europe went beyond a standard resort to Realpolitik invocations of the national interest. Interestingly, Allied rhetoric left its mark on German and Austro-Hungarian public debate. Themes of national self-determination, commercial liberty, and the League of Nations were prominent, particularly in Germany, where leaders such as Bethmann Hollweg judged that German security could be reconciled with a future international order based on some of these precepts. The Reichstag Peace Resolution of July 1917 asserted that territorial expansion could not be imposed by force and demanded economic peace through the freedom of the seas and open trading arrangements. It also supported the creation of an international legal organization. The resolution passed by 212 votes to 126 and thus commanded substantial support among German lawmakers. The three parties that supported it would win 75 per cent of the vote in the post-war January 1919 elections.[45]

That German politicians took up these ideas was important because it created a dynamic in which both sides had to go beyond narrow state interests in justifying the war. Just as Georges-Henri Soutou has shown that the dynamic interaction of commercial war aims of the different powers led to new economic projects, so too did the exchange of public declarations between the opposing sides (and the United States) create a dynamic that pushed the ideological stakes of the war towards internationalist ideals.[46] Public declarations about future peace placed pressure on both sides to articulate their visions of a future international order and to take account of language and concepts that transcended borders and existed within a trans-Atlantic public sphere.

The official discourse of the belligerent governments was crafted in response to an explosion in public sphere support for internationalist projects for peace that emerged over the course of the war. Internationalists in all belligerent countries were initially reluctant to argue their case publicly within the context of a sharp spike in nationalist fervour that was characteristic of 1914. Yet, as the war widened and continued to take its ghastly toll in dead, wounded, and missing, the political context was gradually transformed. Opportunities opened up for the internationalist cause to offer alternative visions of world politics. This cause had flourished in the United States throughout the war, where pre-war internationalist stalwarts such as the World Federation League and the American Association for International Conciliation were joined by the American Women's Peace Party, the Central Organization for a Permanent Peace, and the League to Enforce Peace (which by 1918 counted more than a quarter of a million supporters).[47] A collection of similar associations in support of an international organization for peace emerged in Britain from 1915 onwards. These included the League of Nations Society founded by Lowes Dickinson and the League of Free Nations Society, which amalgamated in 1918 to form the League of Nations Union.[48] In Germany, from late 1917, Matthias Erzberger led the campaign for a League of Nations. In July 1917, Erzberger had been instrumental in building a coalition of German socialists, liberals, and progressives to pass the Reichstag's Peace Resolution. He had come to repent of the stance he had taken in 1915, when he had called for unrestricted submarine warfare in response to the Royal Navy's blockade. This change owed much to the military circumstances of the war, but it was also informed by his liberal Catholic outlook.[49] Others, notably Aristide Briand and Gustav Stresemann, would undergo a similar transformation from proponents of expansive war aims to advocates of reconciliation.[50]

There was a strong transnational dimension to wartime advocacy of international organization. The Inter-Parliamentary Union for Arbitration held several meetings (without its German membership) during the war. Various French and British intellectuals toured the United States to promote the Allied case but also to encourage trans-Atlantic cultural and scientific cooperation.[51] An International Congress of Women was held at the Hague in April 1915. It was here that US and European female peace campaigners constituted the Women's International League for Peace and Freedom. This new association became a stalwart campaigner for a new international organization chaired by the Danish-German-English feminist Helena Swanwick. Glenda Sluga has observed that "[as] the war raged on, English- and French-language public spheres were bursting with the urgency of plans for a world federation."[52]

French internationalism tended to be more muscular than "Anglo-Saxon" approaches. This is borne out in an important comparative study by Carl Bouchard, who examined French, British, and American conceptions of international organization during the war. In his analysis of the vast outpouring of articles, pamphlets, and books on international cooperation produced in Europe and North America, Bouchard shows that French internationalists were almost twice as likely to favour the use of military sanctions to uphold the global order as were their counterparts in Britain. They were also more willing to accept encroachments on national sovereignty in exchange for international security. Nearly 70 per cent of French proposals for international order envisaged surrendering a measure of sovereignty as compared to only 36 per cent of those from Britain and 53 per cent of those from the United States.[53] The same dynamic existed before and after the war.[54] While the differences were of degree rather than an absolute contrast, where American, British, and German peace activists focused on shaping public opinion, their French counterparts called for formal and substantive international institutions to impose peace on an anarchical international system.[55]

Trade unions also continued to hold international meetings during the war. Labour leaders were primarily interested in the relationship between economic and political structures that gave rise to war as well as the effects of the war on labour. Allied trade unions gathered in Leeds in 1916, where they discussed how to incorporate international regulation of labour conditions into a future peace treaty. The following year, the trade unions of the Central Powers organized a conference in Bern. They drew on the published proposals of the Leeds conference and passed resolutions that were remarkably similar. Many of the proposals had featured in pre-1914 trade union demands.[56] Crucially, during the war, these demands moved from the narrow realm of labour relations to a broad conception of how a future peace would be constructed. Indeed, Carl Legien, the German trade union leader and SPD deputy, went so far as to tell the Reichstag in November 1917 that the resolutions of the Leeds and Bern conferences represented the united will of the international working class.[57]

IV

Seasoned practitioners of great power politics tended to resist pressure to re-examine their basic assumptions about the nature of international relations. And yet, from mid-1916 onwards, it became increasingly difficult for policy elites on either side of the conflict to ignore calls to make some sort of international institution for the maintenance of peace part of their publicly stated war aims. Elite foreign policy debate and decision-making was sensitive to the changing normative environment, created by the mass mobilization for war and the terms in which the war was justified. In July 1916, two senior Foreign Office officials drafted an expression of British war aims. Though their views did not represent the unified voice of the Foreign Office, let alone the cabinet, they articulated positions and ideas which would recur in subsequent debates. The document was suffused with ideas about the principle of nationality, international law and institutions, arms limitations, and the crushing of militarism. These ideas exercised growing influence within the British (and Allied) public spheres. They had been given official expression in the public declarations of successive British ministers that "all the States of Europe, great and small, shall in the future be in a position to achieve their national development in freedom and security."[58] Publicly stated aims, vague as they were on details, mattered. These ideas governed the possibilities of the territorial dispensation and the reordering of the international system.

The interplay between public declarations and foreign policy decision-making was particularly evident in the exchanges surrounding Bethmann Hollweg's peace initiative and Woodrow Wilson's Peace Note in December 1916. The German chancellor's initiative has been the subject of considerable controversy, interpreted by some historians as a charade and a trap, interpreted by others as a genuine attempt to open peace negotiations.[59] Bethmann Hollweg had multiple aims. Troubled by the escalation of the war and increasingly isolated in German domestic politics, his conservative instincts were attracted by the possibility of a compromise peace. But if the Allies rejected the proposal, then the German leadership could prepare to re-mobilize society for war and discredit the Allies in American eyes. Whatever Bethmann Hollweg's aim, the crucial point is that his initiative showed the effects of public justifications on diplomacy.

Before launching his initiative, Bethmann Hollweg had prepared the ground, notably through the Poland Proclamation, issued on 5 November 1916. He and Riezler had concluded that the principle of self-determination worked in favour of Germany. It did so on two levels. First, smaller nation-states in Eastern Europe would become dependent on Germany for their economic prosperity and military security. Anticipating the arguments of Richard Kühlmann against occupation and annexation in 1918, they understood that German power could control neighbouring states without necessarily occupying them. Secondly, it allowed Germany to pose as a champion of self-determination. As Max Weber, the liberal academic, put it: "Any policy, which is Realpolitik on the eastern side of our border is inevitably West Slavic policy, not German nationalist policy." Germany, he concluded, should present itself as the "liberator of small nations, even if we do not wish to be."[60] On 12 December, Bethmann Hollweg issued his note, accompanied by a speech to the Reichstag, in which he appealed for a compromise peace but added the jarring modification that Germany was prepared to fight to the end if the Allies did not offer a reasonable deal. Bethmann Hollweg was relying on the Poland proclamation to signal to enemies and to the neutral United States what kind of peace he foresaw.

Several days later, on 18 December, President Wilson issued his Peace Note, which called for all belligerent powers to outline their war aims. He noted that the main powers had all "stated in general terms to their own people and the world" that "each is ready to consider the formation of a League of Nations to ensure peace and justice throughout the world." Wilson's claim that the Allies' and Central Powers' declared aims were "virtually the same" – the rights of small nations, the security of the great powers, and the construction of a League of Nations – outraged the Allies, but the American president had identified principles shared by both sides.[61]

These public calls for peace negotiations and statements of aims, particularly Wilson's, put the Allies under pressure to issue a public response. Allied leaders recognized this, but they also understood that the public profession of their war aims would constitute a standard against which future decisions would be measured. The proclamations of Allied leaders since 1914, the need to maintain good relations with the United States, on which they were increasingly dependent economically, and the pressures of public opinion in their own countries required they formulate a response. In late December, Allied diplomats crafted a carefully worded public statement which restated their case that the German government and army had violated civilized norms. The Allies, conversely, stood for "effective guarantees for the future security of the world," which included the nationality principle, the sanctity of international law, and the sovereign rights of small states.[62]

The failure of the peace initiatives in late 1916 led to a remobilization for war in 1917, but the escalation of violence was accompanied by further debates on the principles of an enduring peace. The secret French parliamentary debates in June 1917 provide perhaps the best illustration of this wider point. These took place within a national crisis occasioned by the mutiny of a number of French divisions in the aftermath of the horrific failure of the Nivelle Offensive of April 1917. Revolutionary rhetoric was prevalent in some units, and there were even threats to march on Paris.[63] Fears of a wavering of national resolve were exacerbated by a series of strikes in Paris in May and June 1917. The taboo against striking in wartime was pushed aside.

It was in this highly fraught context that the Petrograd Soviet announced a series of peace conditions and socialist deputies Marius Moutet and Marcel Cachin returned from St. Petersburg with information concerning very traditional territorial bartering that had taken place between France and the Tsarist regime in 1914–15. A delegation of socialist party officials visited Ribot to demand both a parliamentary discussion of war aims and passports for party officials to attend the international peace conference in Stockholm.[64] Ribot and his cabinet refused to grant passports to socialist delegates but accepted a secret session of parliament to debate the issue.[65] This session, which began on Friday 1 June and ran over to the following Monday, witnessed the most sustained parliamentary discussion of war aims and peace conditions of the entire war.

During this discussion, one socialist deputy after another hammered away at the contradiction between France's publicly stated commitment to national defence and upholding the rule of law, on the one hand, and the eighteenth-century-style horse-trading of territories and peoples that was going on in negotiations behind the scenes, on the other. They pressed the new French premier Alexandre Ribot repeatedly to renounce these agreements and to commit to a Society of Nations. Ribot replied that he was entirely supportive of such an international organization. This secret session of the Chamber ended only after three days of impassioned debate when deputies agreed on the following public statement: "Far removed from any thought of conquest or subjugation of foreign populations, [the French parliament] counts on the effort of the armies of the Republic and the Allied armies to provide, once Prussian militarism has been destroyed, durable guarantees of peace and independence for peoples, great and small, within an organization, to be prepared immediately, of the Society of Nations."[66]

Two aspects of these deliberations are of particular importance for the argument of this essay. The first is the prominence of Woodrow Wilson as a symbol of a new approach to international relations. Wilson was evoked no less than fifteen times during the secret session, always as a source of legitimacy in criticisms of traditional power politics. References were made to speeches by the American president while the United States was a neutral power as well as to his official justification of American entry to the war in April 1917. Secondly, the tone and substance of the secret parliamentary discussions reveal the increasing strength of internationalist conceptions of peace and security, which extended even to the French head of government.[67]

These discourses cannot be dismissed as disingenuous rhetoric by governing elites. The mere fact that politicians on all sides of the conflict felt compelled to assert and justify their claims concerning the purpose of the war within the language and logic of internationalist principles was testament to their growing power. While there was disagreement about their eventual implementation, the debates were a reflection of the changing normative environment of world politics brought about by the war. As French internationalist Antoine Pillet observed, one of the most interesting effects of the war was the "transport into the political arena of ideas that had long been confined to pure speculation."[68]

Crucial to this process of normative change was a mutually reinforcing dynamic between the constant intensification of the war, on the one hand, and ever-expanding conceptions of peace, on the other. The unprecedented human and material costs of the war underpinned growing calls for a transformative peace. At the same time, increasingly expansive visions of post-war transformation constituted justifications for continuing the conflict. The war became an existential struggle for survival as well as the necessary precondition for a new era in both international and domestic politics.

V

The effects of the normative transformation of 1916 and 1917 shaped peacemaking after 1918. This requires some explanation, given that the imperatives of wartime mobilization no longer applied, nor was there a necessity to win over neutrals once the armistice had been signed. Indeed, the election in the United Kingdom in December 1918 signaled popular support for a punitive peace settlement. Bruno Cabanes, meanwhile, has shown the extent to which the attitudes of returning French troops remained characterized by hatred of the vanquished foe.[69] In these conditions, one might have expected internationalist discourse to fade from prominence and more traditional power politics to re-assert itself. Had this happened, the treaty would have been more severe towards Germany. Diplomats, politicians, and generals within various Allied countries had proposed, at various points, the dismantling of the Reich.

Yet internationalism persisted in 1919 and by the mid-1920s became increasingly influential in shaping the construction of a European order.[70] This influence had several sources. First, Wilson was one of the central figures in the peace negotiations in the first half of 1919. Although his domestic political base had been eroded by his poor choice of American delegates and the Republican party's victory in the November 1918 mid-terms, his presence in Paris obscured his weakness from European leaders and diplomats. His principles, enunciated most clearly in the Fourteen Points speech, remained the touchstone for many controversies from the Rhineland to Fiume, and he was the driving force in prioritizing the Covenant of the League of Nations. Second, the Allies were divided over core issues and growing increasingly suspicious of one another. This led them to bargain, but the bargaining process was often structured by wartime promises and principles. Third, justification of outcomes was still a condition for any policy. While conventional arguments about security – defensible borders and the balance of power – remained part of the rhetorical armoury of politicians and diplomats, they also called on arguments derived from internationalist thinking and other sources of legitimacy that emerged strengthened by the end of the war.[71] The nationality principle, the rule of law, and minority rights were prominent in most configurations of a new world order.

The focus on the German question in the treaty of Versailles has long obscured important internationalist advances made during and after the Paris Conference. The establishment of the League of Nations, with a functioning bureaucracy, was an enormous achievement. Mocked for its failures in the 1930s, the League represented a revolutionary organization – it provided a permanent forum for states to negotiate as well as international machinery for settling political disputes peaceably. It also boasted an impressive range of technical experts dedicated to managing international cooperation of all kinds to improve the welfare and prosperity of peoples across the globe. Along with the International Labour Organization, also founded in 1919 (and including German representatives), the League provided eloquent testimony to the ways in which conceptions of peace had expanded. Peace had come to mean more than the absence of war, stable borders, and respect for sovereignty. Peace was now a complex and ever-expanding web of transnational and international social relations. Discrete areas of internationalist cooperation before 1914, such as communications and health, were now part of a thick social complex that underpinned international stability.[72]

Despite the innovations in the peace settlement – from free cities to the ILO – the immediate post-war period proved difficult for internationalists. Constructing peace was a process, and the years after 1918 witnessed violent conflict, particularly in central and eastern Europe. Lenin's consolidation of Bolshevik rule and Mussolini's seizure of power were significant blows to liberal internationalism, as was the move towards authoritarian governments in Eastern Europe. The Ruhr crisis threatened to overwhelm the Weimar Republic, yet it managed to survive. As a result of growing reflexes towards multilateral cooperation, exemplified most notably in the negotiations leading to the Locarno Accords, a measure of stabilization was achieved for European politics between 1924 and 1926. French, British, and German leaders were able to pursue policies of international cooperation following electoral shifts in their respective countries in 1923 and 1924. These shifts, and the stabilization that followed, were rooted in the cooperative prescriptions of wartime internationalist thinking.

Conclusion

Ian Clark has argued that "new principles of legitimacy tend to emerge most clearly in peace settlements at the end of major wars."[73] Paul Lauren, meanwhile, has judged that "[a]ll major international attempts to reduce racial discrimination and promote human rights … have come in the wake of wars and revolutions."[74] The experience of mass death, economic and social cataclysm, and political upheaval during the First World War similarly established contexts favourable to internationalism.

Wars of unprecedented scale and destruction tend to create new political space for alternative visions of international order. This is the case not only because they inflict enormous human suffering and material destruction on the populations of belligerent societies. This suffering is of course an important part of the story because it destroys the credibility of the political practices that produced the conflict in the first place. But there are other dynamics at work in such conflicts. Unlimited war creates conditions favourable to internationalism because it almost inevitably becomes imbued with ideological discourses of enduring peace. These discourses are deployed by political elites to justify sacrifices demanded of their societies and to sustain the conflict. The practice of justifying unlimited war as necessary for permanent peace opened up possibilities for new approaches to world politics based on cooperation and the creation of institutions beyond the state to promote peace and the rule of law. The terrible experience of the Great War in this way created the political conditions necessary for internationalist ideas to rise to new prominence. The processes would be repeated between 1939 and 1945. The result was the post-war "rules-based" international order that is now under threat as we enter the third decade of the twenty-first century.

NOTES

1 G. Kennan, *The Decline of Bismarck's European Order: Franco-Russian Relations, 1875–1890* (Princeton, 1979), p. 3; V. Berghahn, "Origins," in Jay Winter, ed., *The Cambridge History of the First World War*, vol. 1 (Cambridge, 2014), p. 16; J. Leonhard, *Pandora's Box: A History of the First World War* (Cambridge MA, 2018), p. 893.

2 D. Stevenson, *Cataclysm: The First World War as Political Tragedy* (New York); J.L. Gaddis, "The Long Peace: Elements of Stability in the International Postwar System," *International Security*, 10, no. 4 (1986), pp. 105–7.

3 A. Iriye, P.-Y. Saunier, eds., *The Palgrave Dictionary of Transnational History: From the Mid-19th Century to the Present Day* (Basingstoke, 2009).

4 An interesting partial exception to this state of affairs is Solomon Wank, ed., *Doves and Diplomats: Foreign Offices and Peace Movements in Europe and America in the Twentieth Century* (Westport CT, 1978); this collection has much more to say about peace movements than it does about diplomacy.

5 Two important recent studies of the problem of public debates and foreign policy are D. Hucker, "International History and the Study of Public Opinion: towards methodological clarity," *International History Review*, 34, no. 4 (2012), pp. 775–94 and P.P. O'Brien, "The American Press, Public, and the reaction to the First World War," *Diplomatic History*, 37, no. 3 (2013), pp. 446–75.

6 P. Anderson, "Internationalism: a breviary," *New Left Review*, 14 (March–April 2002), pp. 5–6; M. Geyer and J. Paulmann, *The Mechanics of Internationalism: Culture, Politics and Society from the 1840s to the First World War* (Oxford, 2001); G. Sluga, *The Invention of International Order* (Princeton, 2021), esp. pp. 27–56 and 221–34; P. Clavin, "Conceptualising Internationalism between the World Wars," in D. Lacqua, ed., *Internationalism Reconfigured: Transnational Ideas and Movements between the World Wars* (London, 2011) and G. Sluga, *Internationalism in the Age of*

Nationalism (Philadelphia, 2013); K. Fischer and S. Zimmerman, eds., *Internationalismen: Transformation weltweiter Ungleichheit im 19. und 20. Jahrhundert* (Vienna, 2008).

7 Quoted in G. Michon, *Robespierre et la guerre révolutionnaire, 1791–1792* (Paris, 1937), p. 38; see also D. Bell, *The First Total War: Napoleon's Europe and the Birth of Warfare as We Know It.* (New York, 2007), pp. 11–46.

8 Mulligan, *Great War for Peace*, pp. 6–9.

9 C. Schmitt, *The Concept of the Political*, trans. G. Schwab (Chicago, 1996), p. 36.

10 Bell, *First Total War*, pp. 316–17.

11 J.J. Ruedorffer, *Grundzüge der Weltpolitik in der Gegenwart* (Deutsche Verlags-Anstalt, Stuttgart, 1916), pp. 164–6.

12 J. Röhl, *Wilhelm II. Into the Abyss of War and Exile, 1900–1941* (Cambridge University Press, 2014); F. Fischer, *War of Illusions: German Policies from 1911 to 1914* (Chatto and Windus, 1975 edn).

13 J.J. Ruedorffer, *Grundzüge der Weltpolitik in der Gegenwart* (Stuttgart, 1916, 3rd edn.), pp. 151–2.

14 Q. Skinner, *The Foundations of Modern Political Thought*, vol. 1 (Cambridge University Press, 1978), pp. ix–xiii; id., Q. Skinner, *Visions of Politics*, vol. 1, *Regarding Method* (Cambridge University Press, 2002), p. 174.

15 There is a vibrant debate concerning the relationship between consent and coercion in the Allied war efforts. For the argument that the sacrifices made in France for the war effort were accepted within the context of a broad-based "culture de guerre," see especially Stéphane Audoin-Rouzeau and Annette Becker, "Violence et consentement: la 'culture de guerre' du premier conflit mondial," in J-P Rioux and J-F Sirinelli, eds., *Pour une histoire culturelle* (Paris, 1997), pp. 251–71; for the opposing position, see F. Rousseau, *La guerre censurée: une histoire des combattants européens de 14–18*, (Paris, 1999); see also the useful assessment in Antoine Prost and Jay Winter, *Penser la Grande Guerre: un essai d'historiographie* (Paris, 2004), pp. 140–3.

16 H. Bull and A. Watson, *The Expansion of International Society* (Oxford, 1984).

17 Geyer and Paulmann, eds., *Mechanics of Internationalism*; J. Boli and G.M. Thomas, *Constructing World Culture: International Nongovernmental Organizations since 1875* (Palo Alto, 1999); A. Iriye, *Global Community: The Role of International Organizations in the Making of the Contemporary World* (Berkeley, 2002), pp. 9–22; D. Held, A. McGrew, D. Goldblatt, and J. Perraton, *Global Transformation: Politics, Economics and Culture* (Stanford, 1999), especially pp. 39–81 and 154–7 and Sluga, *Internationalism*, pp. 18–32; Emily Rosenberg, "Transnational Currents in a Shrinking World," in Emily Rosenberg, ed., *A World Connecting, 1870–1945* (Cambridge MA, 2012), pp. 815–98; also still useful is F.S.L. Lyons, *Internationalism in Europe*

(Leyden, 1963); an interesting, if idiosyncratic, contemporary perspective is W.F. Crafts, *A Primer of Internationalism: With Special Reference to University Debates* (Washington [DC], 1908).

18 Sluga, *Internationalism*, p. 2; see also D. Laqua, "Transnational Endeavours and the 'totality of knowledge,'" in G. Brockington, ed., *Internationalism in Britain and Europe at the fin-de-siècle* (Oxford, 2009), pp. 247–71 and Mark Mazower, *Governing the World: The History of an Idea* (London, 2012), pp. 31–66, 94–115.

19 Quote from E. Keane, *Global Civil Society?* (Cambridge University Press, 2003), p. 44; see also W. Mulligan, *The Origins of the First World War* (Cambridge, 2010), pp. 133–76.

20 W.H. van der Linden, *The International Peace Movement, 1815–1874* (Amsterdam, 1987), p. 239; P. Brock, *Freedom from War: Nonsectarian Pacifism, 1814–1914* (Toronto, 1991); S. Cooper, *Patriotic Pacifism: Waging War on War in Europe, 1815–1914* (New York, 1991); M. Ceadel, *Thinking about Peace and War* (Oxford, 1987); Ceadel, *Semi-Detached Idealists: The British Peace Movement and International Relations, 1854–1945* (Oxford, 2000); D.S. Patterson, *Toward a Warless World, the Travail of the American Peace Movement, 1887–1914* (Bloomington, 1976); R. Chickering, *Imperial Germany and a World without War: The Peace Movement and German Society, 1892–1914* (Princeton, 1975); J. Bariéty and A. Fleury, eds., *Mouvements et initiatives de paix dans la politique internationale* (Berne, 1987); M. Abbenhuis, *The Hague Conferences and International Politics, 1898–1915* (London, 2018); Rémi Fabre, Thierry Bonzon, J.-M. Guieu, E. Marcobelli, and M. Rappoport, eds., *Les défenseurs de la paix, 1899–1917* (Rennes, 2018).

21 T. Imlay, *The Practice of Socialist Internationalism: European Socialists and International Politics, 1914–1960* (Oxford, 2018).

22 H. Hinsley, *Power and the Pursuit of Peace: Theory and Practice in the History of International Relations* (Cambridge, 1963), 20–3, pp. 164–5; M. Koskenniemi, *The Gentle Civilizer of Nations: The Rise and Fall of International Law, 1870–1960* (Cambridge, 2001), pp. 22–85; M. Mazower, *Governing the World: History of an Idea* (London, 2012), pp. 65–93; A. Fitzmaurice, "Liberalism and Empire in Nineteenth Century International Law," *American Historical Review*, 117, no. 1 (2012), pp. 122–40.

23 Rande Kostal, *A Jurisprudence of Power: Victorian Empire and the Rule of Law* (Oxford, 2005).

24 M. Howard, *War and the Liberal Conscience* (Oxford, 1989), p. 53; on the movement for arbitration generally, see Hinsley, *Power and the Pursuit of Peace*, pp. 126–33; C. Bouchard, *Le citoyen et l'ordre mondial (1914–1918): le rêve d'une paix durable au lendemain de la Grande Guerre* (Paris, 2008), pp. 48–50; Y. Zarjevski, *La Tribune des peuples: histoire de l'Union interparlementaire, 1889–1989* (Lausanne, 1989); Cecilie Reid, "Peace and

Law: peace activism and international arbitration, 1895–1907," *Peace & Change*, 29, nos. 3–4, (2004), pp. 521–48.

25 Guieu, "Les apôtres français de l'esprit de Genève: Les militants pour la Société des Nations dans la première moitié du XXe siècle," thèse de doctorat, Paris I, 2004, pp. 25–6; R. Fabre, "Un exemple du pacifisme juridique: Théodore Ruyssen et le mouvement de la paix par le droit," *Vingtième Siècle*, 39 (1993), pp. 38–54; M. Clinton, "Revanche ou Relèvement? The French peace movement confronts Alsace and Lorraine, 1871–1918," *Canadian Journal of History*, 40, no. 3 (2005), pp. 425–48. On the APD, see also Part I ("Pacifisme Ancien Style, Or the Pacifism of the Pedagogues") of Norman Ingram, *The Politics of Dissent: Pacifism in France, 1919–1939* (Oxford: Clarendon Press, 1991 and 2011), pp. 19–118.

26 J.-M. Guieu, *Le rameau et le glaive: Les militants français pour la Société des Nations* (Paris, 2008), p. 13.

27 P. Brock, *Pacifism in the United States from the Colonial Era to the First World War* (Princeton, 1968), pp. 892–924; S. Cooper, *Patriotic Pacifism*; Ceadel, *Semi-Detached Idealists*; Patterson, *Toward a Warless World*; C. Chatfield and P. van den Dungen, eds., *Peace Movements and Political Cultures* (Knoxville, 1988); P. Laity, *The British Peace Movement, 1870–1914* (Oxford, 2001); R. Chickering, *Imperial Germany and a World without War. The Peace Movement and German Society, 1892–1914* (Princeton, 1975).

28 Guieu, *Rameau et le glaive*, pp. 11–56; P. Jackson, *Beyond the Balance of Power: France and the Politics of National Security in the Era of the First World War* (Cambridge, 2014), pp. 60–84; F.A. Boyle, *Foundations of World Order: The Legalist Approach to International Relations (1898–1922)* (Durham, NC, 1999); S. Wertheim, "'The League that Wasn't': American designs for a legalist-sanctionist League of Nations and the intellectual origins of International Organization, 1914–1920," *Diplomatic History*, 25, no. 5 (2011), pp. 797–836; Benjamin Coates, "Transatlantic Advocates: American International Law and U.S. Foreign Relations, 1898–1919," (PhD diss., Columbia University, 2010).

29 L. Bourgeois, *Pour la Société des Nations* (Paris, 1910); see also Christian Birebent, *Militants de la paix et de la SDN: les mouvements de soutien à la Société des nations en France et au Royaume-Uni* (Paris, 2007), pp. 14–29.

30 Maartje Abbenhuis, *The Hague Conferences and International Politics, 1898–1915* (London, 2018).

31 Isabel V. Hull, *A Scrap of Paper: Making and Breaking International Law during the Great War* (Ithaca, 2014); Marcus Payk, *Frieden durch Recht: Der Aufstieg des modernen Völkerrechts und der Friedensschluss nach dem Ersten Weltkrieg* (Berlin, 2018), pp. 27–78; for a more pessimistic reading, see Jost Dülffer, *Regeln gegen den Krieg? Die Haager Friedenskonferenzen von 1899 und 1907* (Frankfurt, 1978).

32 Payk, *Frieden durch Recht*, pp. 79–148, esp. 123–8; Jackson, *Beyond the Balance of Power*, pp. 79–84 and 197–203.

33 "Il sacro egoismo per l'Italia," in Antonio Salandra, *I discorsi della guerra con alcune note* (Milan, 1922), pp. 1–8.

34 Diary entry in K. Riezler, *Tagebücher, Aufsätze, Dokumente*, K.D. Erdmann, ed., (Göttingen, 1972), 6 July 1916, p. 365.

35 H.G. Wells, *The War that Will End War* (New York, 1914), pp. 12–14, 97–100; see also Mulligan, *Great War for Peace*, pp. 82–3.

36 Manfred Berg, *Woodrow Wilson: Amerika und die Neuordnung der Welt* (Munich, 2017), pp. 81–116; J. Milton Cooper, *Woodrow Wilson. A Biography* (New York, 2009), pp. 307–33 and 362–89.

37 E.R. May, *The World War and American Isolation, 1914–1917* (Cambridge, Mass., 1959), p. 153; see also R.W. Tucker, *Woodrow Wilson and the Great War: Reconsidering America's Neutrality, 1914–1917* (Charlottesville, 2007), pp. 54, 104–6.

38 "Peace Without Victory Address," in A.S. Link et al., eds., *The Papers of Woodrow Wilson*, 69 vols. (Princeton, 1966–94), vol. 40, pp. 533–9; Knock, *To End All Wars*, pp. 111–13; Kennedy, *Will to Believe*, pp. 71–80 and 96–103.

39 See S. Audoin-Rouzeau and A. Becker, "Violence et consentement: la 'culture de guerre' du premier conflit mondial," in J.-P. Rioux and J.-F. Sirinelli, eds., *Pour un histoire culturelle* (Paris, 1997), pp. 251–71; see also "Représenter la guerre, 1914–1918," a special issue of *GMCC*, p. 171 (1993) and S. Audoin-Rouzeau and A. Becker, *14–18: retrouver la guerre* (Paris, 2000), pp. 129–230; This school of interpretation has been challenged in F. Rousseau, *La guerre censurée: une histoire des combattants européens de 14–18* (Paris, 1999). See also the discussion in Prost and Winter, *Penser la Grande Guerre: un essai historiographique* (Paris, 2004), pp. 140–3; Hew Strachan, *The First World* War, vol. I, *To Arms* (Oxford, 2000), pp. 1114–39.

40 Audoin-Rouzeau and Becker, *14–18*, p. 145.

41 S. Tison, *Comment sortir de la guerre: deuil, mémoire et traumatisme (1870–1940)* (Rennes, 2011), pp. 241–73.

42 Albert Sarraut, *Bulletin administratif du Ministère de l'Instruction Publique*, 3 October 1914, no. 2144, cited in J.J. Becker and S. Audoin-Rouzeau, *La France, la nation, la guerre: 185 – 1920* (Paris, 1996), pp. 297–8.

43 Balfour quoted in *The Scotsman*, "The Lord Mayor's Banquet," 10 November 1914.

44 Lloyd George, *War Memoirs* (London, 1938), pp. 504–12.

45 Mulligan, *Great War*, pp. 172–3, 207–13; Petronilla Ehrenpreis, *Kriegs- und Friedensziele im Diskurs: Regierung und deutschsprachige Öffentlichkeit während des Ersten Weltkrieges* (Innsbruck, 2005).

46 G.-H. Soutou, *L'or et le sang: Les buts économiques de la Première guerre mondiale* (Paris, 1989).
47 Charles Chatfield, *For Peace and Justice: Pacifism in America, 1914–1941* (Knoxville, 1971), Chatfield, ed., *Peace Movements in America* (New York, 1973), D. Cortright, *Peace: A History of Movements and Ideas* (Cambridge, 2008), pp. 14–71; Boyle, *Foundations of World Order*, p. 7–85; L.J. Rupp, *Worlds of Women: The Making of an International Women's Movement* (Princeton, 1997); S. Wertheim, *Tomorrow the World: The Birth of U.S. Global Supremacy* (Cambridge, MA, 2020), pp. 15–46; M. Siegel, *Peace on Our Terms: The Global Battle for Women's Rights after the First World War* (New York, 2019).
48 Ceadel, *Semi-Detached Idealists*, pp. 187–238; J. Wallis, *Valiant for Peace: A History of the Fellowship of Reconciliation, 1914–1989* (London, 1991), pp. 47–112; H. McCarthy, *The British People and the League of Nations: Democracy, Citizenship and Internationalism, 1914–1945* (Manchester, 2011), pp. 15–78.
49 Mulligan, *Great War*, pp. 204–6; Matthias Erzberger, *Völkerbund: Der Weg zum Weltfrieden* (Berlin, 1918).
50 Jackson, *Beyond the Balance of Power*, pp. 357–89.
51 On the impact of the Great War on international scientific cooperation, see Marie-Eve Chagnon, chapter 9 of this volume, p. 167–182.
52 Sluga, *Internationalism in an Age of Nationalism*, p. 36; see esp. Siegel, *Peace on Our Terms*, pp. 8–29.
53 C. Bouchard, "Projets citoyens pour une paix durable, en France, en Grande Bretagne et aux États-Unis (1914–1924)," thèse de doctorat, Université de Paris III and the Université de Montréal, 2004, pp. 129, 133–4, 138–41; see also the published version of this doctoral thesis: *Le citoyen et l'ordre mondial (1914–1918)* (Paris, 2008), pp. 114 and 121 respectively.
54 In 1929, for example, Pierre Cot argued that "For France, the heart of the problem is less to pronounce a solemn and platonic anathema against war than to work towards the organization of peace. The land of Descartes and of Voltaire prefers techniques to canticles ... The Anglo-Saxon, it has been said, tours the world with his Bible and the Frenchman with his Code. Let us not be ashamed by this natural and national penchant. We have a conception of peace which is more juridical than mystical. But justice, too, supposes an ideal. Pierre Cot, "La Conception française de la lutte contre la guerre," in *La Paix par le droit* 39/nos. 4–5 (April–May 1929), p. 164. Cited in Ingram, *Politics of Dissent*, p. 38.
55 Sluga, *Internationalism*, pp. 11–44; Birebent, *Militants de la paix*, pp. 13–58.
56 Imlay, *Socialist Internationalism*, pp. 22–34.
57 "Generalkommission der Gewerkschaften Deutschlands, 25 November 1917," BArch R 703/47, fos. 3–7.

58 The National Archives, Kew, FO 371, 2804, Sir R. Paget, W. Tyrrell, "Peace terms," fos. 405–14; Mulligan, *Great War*, 164–8.

59 Holger Afflerbach, *Auf Messers Schneide: Wie das Deutsche Reich den Ersten Weltkrieg verlor* (Munich, 2018), pp. 276–91.

60 "Deutschland und die europäischen Weltmächten," in Wolfgang Mommsen and Gangolf Hübinger, eds., *Max Weber. Zur Politik im Weltkrieg: Schriften und Reden 1914–1918*, series 1, vol. 15 (Tübingen, 1984), pp. 180–2, 188.

61 Cooper, *Wilson*, pp. 364–6.

62 Carnegie Endowment for International Peace, *Official Communications and Speeches, relating to Proposals, 1916–1917* (Washington DC, 1917), pp. 38–50.

63 G. Pédroncini, *Les mutineries de 1917* (Paris, 1967); L.V. Smith, *Between Mutiny and Obedience: The Case of the French Fifth Infantry Division during World War I*, (Princeton, 1994); Doughty, *Pyrrhic Victory*, pp. 361–5.

64 A. Kriegel, *Aux origines du communisme français*, tome I, 152–79. For the international dimensions of this issue, see J.-J. Becker, *1917 en Europe: l'année impossible* (Brussels, 1997), pp. 134–39.

65 A. Ribot, *Journal d'Alexandre Ribot et correspondances inédites* (Paris, 1936), pp. 138–41.

66 France, Assemblée nationale, *Journal officiel de la République française*, Chambre, Débats, 1925, "Comité secret du 1er juin 1917," 4 June 1917.

67 See also Jackson, *Beyond the Balance of Power*, pp. 149–55.

68 Antoine Pillet, *De l'idée d'une Société des nations* (Paris, 1919), pp. 18–19.

69 Bruno Cabanes, *La victoire endeuillée: La sortie de guerre des soldats français, 1918–1920* (Paris, 2004), pp. 72–6; Erik Goldstein, "Great Britain: the Home Front," in Manfred Boemeke, Gerald Feldman, Elisabeth Glaser, eds., *The Treaty of Versailles. A Reassessment after 75 Years* (Cambridge, 1998), pp. 147–66.

70 For a more detailed treatment of the relationship between diplomatic initiatives and domestic politics, see Jackson, *Beyond the Balance of Power* and Jonathan Wright, *Gustav Stresemann: Weimar's Greatest Statesman* (Oxford, 2002).

71 See the eloquent discussion of the way ongoing debates over war guilt reverberated through French politics during the war, the peace conference, and the post-war decades in Norman Ingram, *The War Guilt Problem and the Ligue des droits de l'homme, 1914–1944* (Oxford, 2019).

72 Several recent studies of the role of the League illustrate these claims very effectively: P. Clavin, *Securing the World Economy: The Reinvention of the League of Nations, 1920–1946* (Oxford, 2013); S. Pedersen, *The Guardians: The League of Nations and the Crisis of Empire* (Oxford, 2015) and the essays in Sluga and Clavin, eds., *Internationalisms: a twentieth century history* (Oxford, 2018); see also Zara Steiner's brilliant reconsideration of the place of the

League in post-war international relations in *The Lights that Failed: European International History, 1919–1933* (Oxford, 2005), pp. 349–86.

73 Clark, *International Legitimacy and World Society*, p. 37.

74 P.G. Lauren, *Power and Prejudice: The Politics and Diplomacy of Racial Discrimination* (New York, 1996), p. 19.

3 Setting Out on a Long Irenic Campaign: The Carnegie Endowment for International Peace Prepares the Construction of a Peaceful World Order, 1910–1920

ANDREW BARROS

The post-1919 world marked the arrival of non-governmental organizations (NGOs) as important actors on the world stage. In the vanguard of this movement was the Carnegie Endowment for International Peace (CEIP). The first American think tank, it was a unique organization. The CEIP's sole mission was to build a peaceful, American liberal internationalist, world order. This study examines the important evolution, over the course of the war and then of the peace conference, of the strategy that the CEIP developed to achieve this goal. Particular attention is paid to this period for two reasons. First, the CEIP's interwar approach to building a peaceful order was largely an application of this strategy. Second, the endowment's inability to understand and address some of the key issues that bedevilled the post-war international system, such as nationalism, was clearly exposed during the war. Laying out the strengths and weaknesses of the CEIP in this era helps explain why its influence was far greater than its political successes, a problem it shared with many nation-states, most notably the United States.

To deal with the disorder of the post-war world the CEIP adopted a strategy of building the expertise and networks needed to influence elites and publics, as exemplified by its epic series on the Economic and Social History of the War. This approach was adopted in late 1914, before the magnitude of the conflagration became clear, much less the problems of its post-war settlement. The war's intensification and globalization, not to mention the disappointments and hopes of the peace conference, the establishment of the League of Nations, and the subsequent failure of US President Woodrow Wilson to obtain the Senate's approval for American membership in the League, underscored the importance of its mission and the vacuum in American leadership that it did much to fill. This study lays out for the first time how the CEIP embarked upon the building of this order and some of the key shortcomings under which it laboured.

From the CEIP's inception in 1910 it sought to put in place a peaceful world system. Part of a large current of liberal internationalism, and one of its central financiers, the CEIP was as American as it was international. This was in large part thanks to its leadership and funding but also the increasingly important role the United States was coming to play in the world, and Europe in particular. Achieving its goal required a better understanding of how wars arose, a task that was primarily seen as the work of economists. However, within months of the outbreak of war in August 1914 its views had evolved, leading to the adoption of a fresh strategy, one that relied above all on history. It was seen as having the analytical and emotional power necessary to transform public opinion into a force that would defend the peace that needed to be won. As important as the diplomatic negotiations in Paris were for both Wilson and the CEIP, the latter's vision and policies for the post-war world were already well developed by the end of hostilities. As much as it depended on, and profited from, the creation of the League, the endowment's irenic march was focused on changing the public's understanding of the cost of war, most notably through education, and the research into armed conflict on which it needed to be based.[1] That was the force which would make nations, institutions like the League, and international law capable of ensuring the peace. In many ways this was a very non-state Anglo-American project which grew in the interstices between national calculations and interests. The CEIP played a key role in this process, one that remains largely underappreciated by historians.[2] Despite some similarities in hope and rhetoric, Wilson ended up on a very different path. He immediately called upon the public to support the peace treaty's passage through the American Senate only to find upon his return that neither was up to the task. Unable to win over the two-thirds of the senators required for the treaty's ratification the president appealed directly to public opinion in a fruitless effort to gain its passage.[3] One consequence of Wilson's failure was that in the years that followed it fell in part to the CEIP to defend the League and the liberal internationalist project. The endowment's search for order, in the form of lasting peace, thus often stands in stark contrast to that of the nations that negotiated the peace treaties, particularly the United States.

I

Founded in 1910 by the industrialist Andrew Carnegie the endowment was incorporated in 1911 by an act of Congress which was introduced by former Secretary of State and Secretary of War Senator Elihu Root. The CEIP's creation, and Root's role in it, underscored just how politically well-connected it was. In addition, the CEIP's financial strength was assured by the $10 million endowment provided by Carnegie at its founding. Root went on to become the organization's first president and was awarded the Nobel Peace Prize the following year. He was a member of the establishment and not the more politically radical peace movement. The endowment was very much an organization of the establishment whose international, and especially trans-Atlantic, ties and mission offered precious little place for women and minorities. Root's views were reflected throughout the CEIP and can be seen in its conception of its mission. As the act stated, the endowment was "to advance the cause of peace among nations, to hasten the abolition of international war, and to encourage and promote a peaceful settlement of international differences." A key task was to "promote a thorough and scientific investigation and study of the causes of war and of the practical methods to prevent and avoid it." Two other essential missions also need to be highlighted. The first was the importance to "aid in the development of international law" and promote its adoption by nations. The second was the need to increase public understanding of the dangers and cost of war as well as "cultivate friendly feelings between inhabitants of different countries and to increase the knowledge and understanding of each other."[4] At the first meeting of the trustees of the CEIP's precursor, the Carnegie Peace Fund, on 14 November 1910, Root was elected chairman, after which he outlined his vision for the organization. It needed to distinguish itself from other "enterprises" in this field "in one respect." "It must base its action on a careful, scientific and thorough study of the causes of war and the remedies which can be applied to the causes, rather than merely the treatment of symptoms."[5] This philosophy and strategy were embodied in the way the CEIP was organized. It consisted of three divisions: Economics and History, International Law, and Intercourse and Education.

Ultimately, the CEIP's mission depended on the results of the research it sponsored on the nature of war, which was seen as a disease. While the CEIP often found itself involved in treatments to alleviate war's symptoms, its fundamental mission was to eradicate it. What the endowment searched for was a cure, or more precisely a vaccine with which to inoculate the public and bring about war's end. In 1913 Carnegie himself upbraided the CEIP's Board of Trustees at their seeming inability to focus on this task. He spoke of being "amazed" to hear them discuss anything but "the most direct means of abolishing what I consider the greatest crime that man commits."[6] A similar research program and its underlying philosophy had already begun to emerge in some of the work carried out at the Carnegie Institution in Washington in the decade prior to the CEIP's creation. While the divisions of International Law and Intercourse and Education played important roles in this process, the CEIP's diagnostic efforts were primarily located in the division dedicated to the use of economics and history.

In 1911 the CEIP launched its first major effort to understand the nature and causes of war. The Division of Economics and History, led by the distinguished Columbia University economist John Bates Clark, organized a conference in Berne that helped lay the foundations for the CEIP's work in this area. Clark assembled a distinguished group of specialists from eleven countries that included the prominent economists Lujo Brentano from Germany as well as Paul Leroy-Beaulieu and Charles Gide from France. The gathering was not composed exclusively of academics, as was testified to by the presence of Belgian Senator Henri La Fontaine, whose work as the president of the International Peace Bureau would help lead to his being awarded the Nobel Peace Prize two years later, and Francis Hirst, the editor of the *Economist*.[7] As Clark noted immediately afterwards, their work had been strictly devoted to "plans for future investigations." The group had divided into three committees, each charged with a specific field of inquiry. The committees' immediate task had been to identify the key questions in their area that needed to be addressed. The CEIP's research taxonomy said much about its underlying philosophy. The first committee was in charge of dealing with questions of "actual war," i.e. issues dealing with how wars were fought, the second dealt with "armaments and preparations for war," and the third was responsible for "economic developments affecting the probability of war."[8]

The research program that emerged from the Berne conference reflected the CEIP's conception of the problem. Economic development, notably the Industrial Revolution, was bringing greater interdependence but also greater competition between states. Plumbing the depths of this struggle was clearly a central theme for the research that the CEIP was preparing to sponsor. Historical examinations of previous conflicts and economic assessments of their cost as well as the impact of their preparation on nations were all important topics that would have to be explored. To this end, the CEIP brought to bear what can already be described as its characteristic methodology and practice, one that can be seen in its prewar investigation into the situation in the Balkans.[9] First, there was the organization and stockpiling of the necessary resources, including a careful bibliographical enumeration of the relevant scholarly literature. Second, once outfitted, the work would begin and studies ordered, in part thanks to a growing network of specialists (academics, jurists, journalists, and others). Sponsored by the CEIP, the results of this research would be authoritative and would be published and distributed as widely as possible, often thanks to the endowment's generous financial assistance. A year after the gathering at Berne the Division of Economics and History had seventy-five studies under contract.[10]

As fate would have it the follow-up conference to the 1911 meeting was scheduled for early August 1914 in Lucerne. The first four days of the month saw the July Crisis transformed into a European war that included the continent's major powers and their empires. Yet some delegates did manage to make it to neutral Switzerland. They met from 5 to 6 August, with those present engaged in an at times surreal discussion of how best to pursue the CEIP's research program. This included approving the commission of new studies, including a rather esoteric and anachronistic examination of "the industrial effects of the Hundred Years' War on the population and industry of Paraguay." Reflecting the strong consensus on the importance of economics in fostering interdependence, and thus peace, the members underscored the need to support work which would "show what economic activities tend in the direction of international harmony."[11]

II

Just a few months later the CEIP had begun a dramatic change of course. In November, Clark, aided by his Columbia University colleague and eventual successor, the Canadian born and raised James T. Shotwell, submitted a proposal to the Board of Trustees. Entitled "Project of a History of the European War," the document started by acknowledging that the war's arrival had brought a dramatic change to the research then being undertaken. The conflict "will afford supremely important objects of study" necessitating an immediate program to collect the documentary sources required for this work.[12] Several weeks earlier, in a letter to the prominent jurist and head of the International Law Division, James Brown Scott, Clark admitted that he wished to go well beyond what had already been authorized, i.e. collecting documents for a solely economic history of the conflict. "We are in a position to produce a monumental work" that would take advantage of the fact that a truly neutral, presumably objective, history could only be written in the United States.[13]

The proposal contained three options for a history of the war. The first was the narrowest, to examine the economic impact of the conflict, notably on the belligerents. This would essentially be a study of the toll the war took on public and private finance, commerce, industry, and agriculture in order to properly measure its costs. In so doing it could avoid the thorny question of who was responsible for the conflagration. Underlining the CEIP's, and America's, impartiality at no time would it "pronounce moral judgment on the participants," leaving the facts to speak for themselves. When they pointed to terrible events "the bare statement of the fact of such a waste and an estimate of the approximate amount would suffice." By couching it in economic terms they hoped the project would benefit from the continued participation of the European members of the research committee that the division had struck in the aftermath of the Berne conference. During this period the endowment continued to oversee the studies that had been commissioned. In the late 1914 thinking of Clark and others, while the war had divided most of the participants along belligerent lines, the idea was that they could remain united in their work for the CEIP since economic history was a field in which the dangers of "national bias" were easier to minimize.[14]

The second proposal was for a more complete history of the war, one that could include political, diplomatic, intellectual, and "human" aspects, including its origins. Despite this greatly enlarged ambit the dangers of sliding into the impolitic remained manageable, and it would still be possible to "refrain from expressing judgments" regarding the comportment of various nations. Instead, the "facts revealed by the evidence" would do the talking. These might be given context by exposing the "obvious principles of ethics and international law" that would then allow the public to reach its own conclusions. The proposal would take the authors to the frontier of the political but still leave them safely on the right side of the divide. The third option would "abandon the effort to avoid approval and criticism" and where appropriate lay or apportion blame all the while maintaining "as far as possible" professional objectivity. It would begin with the war's origins, which were to be found in the period roughly ten to fifteen years before its arrival. Among the advantages of this approach was the wide readership it could attract.[15]

Behind the proposal was a rapid dawning on Clark, Shotwell, and others of the fact that the newly arrived war was a pivotal moment for the CEIP. This proposed history was on the way to becoming an almost total history of what had yet to become a total war. In its final form the over 130 volumes of the endowment's Economic and Social History of the Great War represented, in the words of Jay Winter and Antoine Prost, "the largest collective enterprise of its kind in history."[16] The immense contours of this study were already visible in late 1914. While the cost of war remained at the centre of the project, the scope, both geographical and thematic, of what that constituted had been pushed well beyond what until then had been imagined, much less considered. It is a terrible irony that the CEIP's history, in its accountancy of the war and its lessons for the peace, foreshadowed in ways it did not fully appreciate, the course the conflagration would take.

This new conflict was not simply the most recent example of the phenomenon; its contemporaneous nature offered unprecedented pedagogical and political support for the CEIP's message. This was encapsulated in Shotwell's November 1914 observation that "the importance of an authoritative survey of the present war in the moulding of opinion and further policies is too evident to require argument." While Clark had emphasized that the greater the scope of the history the more difficult it would be to take advantage of the research committee that the Division of Economics and History had established with the Berne conference, ultimately the reverse proved true. In the aftermath of the peace conference Shotwell would go on to perfect a system that commissioned not just scholars but prominent politicians and officials to contribute to the series. Their work obviated the considerable problems in gaining access to key government records and accounts and helped extend the CEIP's reach into political elites, especially in France. The pre-September 1914 CEIP approach of studying the economics of the past had given way to learning and advocating from the history of the present. This reorientation can be seen in the initial sum of $5,000 that was allocated by the Board of Trustees for the purchase of primary source material as well as the CEIP's on-going concern about remaining engaged with nations rather than risking their displeasure and having to pursue their work from the outside.[17]

In 1919 Shotwell was named the general editor of the series, and he would dedicate much of the next eighteen years to its completion. One can gain a sense of the enormous size of this project in the calculation done by the CEIP in 1950, thirteen years after the series had been completed. The total cost came in at $879,448.26, of which $373,890.36 had been provided by the CEIP and $505,575.96 from the Carnegie Corporation. The collection's authors included not only distinguished academics but thirty-five wartime cabinet members.[18]

In rapidly mobilizing to gather the documentary record of a war that had only just begun the CEIP was years ahead of the belligerent governments. Projects like the French Bibliothèque et Musée de la Guerre, the history of the war prepared by the Historical Section of the British Committee of Imperial Defence, and what became the Imperial War Museum, emerged around 1916–17 and were products of a much more mature conflict.[19] These national efforts stood in stark contrast to the CEIP's internationalist agenda and unprecedented deployment of contemporary history, focusing on the societies and economies rather than battlefields.

The endowment's hope to maintain the pre-war scholarly solidarity it had been building rapidly proved to be illusory, as was its ability to sustain both its impartiality and good relations with all of its collaborators. By the time Clark was drafting his proposal for the Board of Trustees the war had already divided those who had gathered at Berne. For example, Leroy-Beaulieu rapidly ended his participation with the CEIP. In summarizing the situation on 7 November 1914, Clark noted the economist's inability to work with Germans "in view of what Germany has and is doing." Yet he maintained a starry-eyed optimism that this would prove to be an unfortunate exception. Clark's somewhat tortured argument was that since his belligerent colleagues would pursue research projects only in consultation with the CEIP in New York and "without communication with each other" whatever animosities had risen would not encumber their work studying the conflict.[20] This was an unwise extension of the already flawed argument used to justify the CEIP's "neutrality."

By the end of 1914 the CEIP's strategy for the eradication of war, both its research into the disease and its eventual program of public inoculation, was centred on the recent conflict and its as yet uncertain evolution. This was starkly in evidence during the first wartime meeting of the CEIP's Board of Trustees on 13 November 1914. A key participant in the discussions there was the president of Columbia University, head of the CEIP's Intercourse and Education Division, and its future president and Nobel Peace Prize winner, Nicholas Murray Butler. He drew his colleagues' attention to how the war's arrival demonstrated that the CEIP needed to renew its efforts rather than accept the conflict with resignation. The conflagration demonstrated the poverty of international treaties and agreements in the absence of deep public support. Butler set the tone for the CEIP's change of course as he outlined how "history is being made now ... and the minds of men by force, by loss, by damage, by suffering ... are being opened to receive the gospel of international peace." His remarks reinforced and reflected the comments and thinking of Clark, Shotwell, and Scott. As Butler argued, once the war had physically and intellectually exhausted the combatants, they would be "ready to be shown some way" of avoiding a repetition of its horrors. If anything, the longer and more terrible the on-going conflict the greater its ability to pull up the roots of war which were so firmly ensconced in the "historic past, in the structure of nations, in the psychology of peoples, in the ambitions of rulers, in the strifes [*sic*] between languages, religions, and races." The corollary of this, as Butler admitted, was that the CEIP had been overly optimistic about its ability to rapidly understand and implement a program for peace in the face of such a powerfully entrenched foe. Events, not research, had shown that the nature of the current war, and its study, were going to be central to the CEIP campaign, one that would last much longer than the conflict that had so quickly become central to the CEIP's solution.[21]

III

For the next three years the CEIP held to its new course. Yet as in other aspects of the United States' implication in the growing conflict, geopolitics increasingly aligned it with Great Britain and France. Contacts with its Germans collaborators were strained and withered. The American entry into the war in April 1917 constitutes a short but very important chapter in the CEIP's peace program, one full of unappreciated lessons that recall an earlier insensitivity to the endowment's own failings and contradictions. This helps explain why Shotwell, Scott, and others saw no contradiction between their patriotic mobilization by the government and their work for peace at the CEIP. This complementarity of purpose was particularly ironic given their criticism of many European colleagues caught up in the vortex of the nationalism that the war's arrival had opened. Over the course of 1917–18 the CEIP gave itself over to winning the war. For example, among Shotwell's many duties, including "the Inquiry" into American peace policy, was his work as chairman of the National Board for Historical Service. This was a private organization, in part supported by the Carnegie Institution in Washington, with links to the government, involved in mobilizing history and historians and, via them, students and the broader public. David Kennedy has characterized their widely distributed "War Issues Course" as often constituting "hate propaganda."[22]

A little over two weeks after the United States declared war on Germany, on 19 April 1917, the CEIP's Board of Trustees decided unanimously to adopt a report by a specially constituted committee, one which embodied the organization's wartime patriotism. At the meeting the Board engaged in a revealing discussion of the dilemmas raised when a foundation devoted to peace supports a war. The gathering also provided a telling glimpse of the racism of the time, a factor that did little to bring about a better understanding of nationalism. This was exemplified by the remarks of Congressman and Board member James L. Slayden (Democrat, Texas). He stated that:

> I want to see the war prosecuted to a successful and speedy conclusion; but when it comes to the question of voting for universal military service, no matter by whom recommended, I can not go that far. It will have the effect of training and disciplining and organizing in the South several hundred

> thousand young negroes. It will threaten the social order of the South. It will threaten every woman in the South. It will put in the very heart of the South a body of disciplined, organized, trained men, who will be a danger, a menace; and I hope that this body will not commit itself and not go into the domain of politics, as this does, and commit itself to such a proposition as that.[23]

In the end the Trustees decided to "declare hereby their belief that the most effective means of promoting durable international peace is to prosecute the war against the Imperial Government of Germany to final victory for democracy, in accordance with the policy declared by the President of the United States."[24]

The November 1918 armistice and the peace negotiations brought a rapid demobilization of the CEIP as it reprised its pre-1917 strategy. The endowment's members, and close contacts, were very much a presence during the negotiations in Paris. The most notable of them was Shotwell, who played a key role in the creation of the International Labour Organization (ILO). As he explained to Butler shortly afterwards, his joining the committee involved in creating the ILO was "a natural outgrowth of my work in social history." He had taken up the position "with the subsequent work for the Carnegie Endowment in mind." His endeavours there had been "of immense benefit to me as a preparation for the [Economic and Social] History of the War," not simply in terms of learning about the "industrial history" of the conflict but becoming "acquainted" with the "men who can best help in forming an idea" of how "Labor" reacted to "governmental and non-governmental agents." Thanks in part to his involvement in establishing the ILO, Shotwell was also deeply implicated in the elaboration of article 312 of the peace treaty, which guaranteed social security rights for the population of regions which were to be placed outside of Germany, such as Alsace-Lorraine. As Shotwell outlined to Butler, "the part of the Treaty which I have had a hand in is one which contains in it the germs of constructive statesmanship." By advancing a social agenda in the peace treaty he felt he had found one possible front to open in a larger campaign to reunite a transnational popular opinion. Its corollary was that "despite the many things about the Treaty which I personally dislike," including the positions of "some of the territorial specialists," he felt the need to avoid being "drawn further from the field of the historian than the war has drawn me." Shotwell did not want to become embroiled in the "hot controversies of politics which will undoubtedly result from the Treaty." Yet he worked ceaselessly to stabilize the situation in Europe and integrate America into the League system. Shotwell was an important, if behind the scenes, player at key moments during the 1920s, stretching from the 1922 peace offer by German Chancellor Wilhelm Cuno through the 1928 Kellogg–Briand Pact and into the 1930s. Perhaps his central contribution to that effort was the American entry into the ILO in 1934. It was the only part of the League system of which the United States would become a member, in no small part thanks to Shotwell's work at Paris and afterwards. That success provides an important part of the context for his other diplomatic efforts during the 1920s.[25]

While many CEIP members and associates were to be found among the delegates to the conference, of far greater importance was their dissatisfaction, which echoed Shotwell's, with the treaty they had worked so hard to produce. This sentiment emerged with force in the spring as the conference entered the final stretch. On 30 May, the day after Shotwell's letter to Butler, he attended a dinner organized by a British delegate, Lionel Curtis, which included a number of distinguished members of the American and British delegations. They all harboured considerable doubts about the document they had helped negotiate. In the face of the impending signing of the treaty, Curtis proposed a continuation of their work on assuring a new peaceful system of international relations by repairing to a nascent, non-state, foundation. There they would remain in contact with each other, but outside the ambit of government. Well-informed and ready to give advice, the experts gathered at the dinner could continue their research and discussion of the wide range of problems raised by the war and its conclusion, attracting scholars, journalists, politicians, and others to their new forum. This became the Royal Institute for International Affairs (Chatham House) and led American delegates to help re-found the Council on Foreign Relations in New York.[26] It was but one step in the construction of a non-governmental system that would be connected to, but run parallel to, nation-states and the League. It was a system in which the CEIP, and people like Shotwell, would play a key role.

IV

The CEIP's post-1919 efforts to pursue the construction of a liberal internationalist order, and reinforce organizations like the League of Nations, were considerable. Yet it was badly handicapped by America's diplomatic disengagement from the rest of the world, and in particular the failure of Wilson to ensure the United States' participation in the League and the rest of the post-war order the American president had done so much to negotiate in Paris. Yet Shotwell's diplomatic success and influence with the ILO and at key moments during the 1920s highlighted the possibilities of the CEIP's diplomacy, particularly when it came to Europe.[27] The American government's diplomatic withdrawal created a vacuum that the CEIP, pushed by a desire to affect change and pulled by the need of other powers to find an effective American interlocutor, attempted to fill.

Throughout the 1920s the CEIP was active, both inside and outside the United States, promoting the League and international law as well as trying to raise public support for them. Shotwell's social and economic history of the war exemplified the vast network that the CEIP had built. Yet to fully take stock of the endowment's effort to construct this order one also needs to look at two important failings of the CEIP's vision and approach, factors that help explain the organization's continued struggle to attain its goal.

The first failure stems from a focus on everything but the actual practice of war, in particular those who fought it. As dramatic a change in course as the Economic and Social History of the War was in many ways it marked a continuity in the approach adopted early on by Clark. Both the Berne program and the Shotwell series focused on tallying up the civilian and economic costs of war in order to drive home to the public its tremendous burden and therefore its folly. What this left out was a central part of the war itself, i.e. combatants. The most dramatic example of this was the landmark study by Jean Norton Cru of the testimony of French soldiers during the war. Contracted as part of the Economic and Social History of the Great War the manuscript was ultimately rejected by the French editorial committee of the series and eventually Shotwell, forcing Cru to publish elsewhere, albeit with assistance from the CEIP.[28]

The decision not to publish Cru's study was a telling example of the CEIP's focus on the civilian costs of war, almost to the exclusion of the soldiers who served on the front. This extraordinary state of affairs was reflected in the relative absence of military officials, much less enlisted servicemen, in the CEIP, and their vast network of contacts. The jurist and future Nobel Peace Prize recipient René Cassin along with the distinguished historian Pierre Renouvin, are two important exceptions to this rule.[29]

The specialists that Shotwell convened over the course of this period to help formulate solutions to the vexing problem of disarmament included a few former officers, particularly the American General Tasker Bliss, but there was never a deep historical analysis of the way war had changed and the difficulties that new technologies presented in putting in place a viable disarmament system.[30] In comparison to the resources invested in studying the economic and social history of the belligerent powers during the First World War it was a frightfully small investment.

This problem had a second, post-1919, dimension. The CEIP also paid little attention to a key group in post-war society: veterans. As Antoine Prost and others have shown, and as the career of Cassin demonstrates, veterans were an extremely important group but never really integrated into the strategy developed by Shotwell and Clark in 1914. Labour meant workers and farmers, not soldiers.[31]

The second problem for the CEIP, which was a recurring one, highlighted in the numerous incidents outlined here, was the organization's inability to come to terms with nationalism, testimony to a remarkable lack of self-awareness. The CEIP put tremendous stock in the "objectivity" of scholarly disciplines like economics and history, whose research they depended upon, and likewise that of the endowment's country, i.e. the United States. It never questioned the assumptions of its mission and liberal internationalist philosophy, particularly when it came to education and public opinion. Perhaps the most telling example occurred right in front of Clark and Shotwell over the course of the last few months of 1914, as their own committee of experts was consumed by the conflict. Nor did Shotwell seem to have learned much from his mobilization in 1917.

Both of these problems would leave the CEIP, and the order it was attempting to establish and support, particularly ill placed to deal with the challenges of the 1930s. While the CEIP over the course of the 1920s had participated in diplomatic initiatives which assisted in developing the League, notably Germany's entry in 1926 following the Locarno accords, and the Kellogg–Briand Pact (1928), the essence of its strategy remained focused on public opinion. The ongoing Economic and Social History of the War, despite the massive efforts of Shotwell and his contributors, not to mention the endowment's financial outlay, did little if anything to change public opinion. Of great importance was the campaign for "moral disarmament." It focused not on the physical elimination of weapons, which any country could put into production, but the need to quench people's desire to use them by demonstrating the folly and cost of war, in which belligerent states undercut a shared humanity. The CEIP supported many groups involved in this global movement, whose accomplishments, like those of other parts of the liberal internationalist movement, failed the twin shocks of the Great Depression and the rising tide of political extremism that the latter helped bring.[32]

For the CEIP the First World War marked above all a weapon for peace, one whose destructive power they could not have fully appreciated when they first took hold of it in 1914. The Great War's interwar legacy, its ability to sustain disorder, proved stronger than that of those who, like the endowment, attempted to harness it in the construction of a liberal internationalist order. If that is in part the failure of the CEIP, its success comes from what happened next. At the end of the 1930s, with war on the horizon in Europe and already being waged in Asia, planning began for the next post-war order. The CEIP, and specifically Shotwell, were again to play a role in its formulation and diplomacy.[33] The geopolitics of this second attempt would prove, at least in the near term, to be more favourable if far from completely successful. Seen from 1910 or 1914 the strategy the CEIP pursued for a peaceful order was fairly consistent, despite the inevitable adaptations to circumstances. Over a century after the peace conference, the endowment and the order it fostered after 1919 remain very much works in progress.

NOTES

I would like to thank the archivist of the Carnegie Collections at Columbia University, Jennifer Comins, for her invaluable assistance in navigating the CEIP archives.

1 For the problematic role of public opinion in liberal internationalist thought, see Stephen Wertheim, "Reading the International Mind: International Public Opinion in Early Twentieth Century Anglo-American Thought," in Daniel Bessner and Nicolas Guilhot, *The Decisionist Imagination: Sovereignty, Social Science and Democracy in the 20th Century* (New York, 2018) ch. 1.

2 For the international history of this period, see Zara Steiner, *The Lights that Failed: European International History, 1919–1933* (Oxford, 2005); Ludovic Tournès, *Les États-Unis et la Société des nations (1914–1946). Le système international face à l'émergence d'une superpuissance* (Berne, 2016). Notwithstanding a few exceptions, such as Tournès, the CEIP is absent from much of the recent resurgence of scholarly interest in twentieth-century internationalism. For example, in the otherwise excellent recent study of the subject edited by Glenda Sluga and Patricia Clavin it is only mentioned once. See Glenda Sluga and Patricia Clavin, eds., *Internationalisms: A Twentieth-Century History* (Cambridge, 2016), p. 136.

3 See the classic study by Thomas Knock, *To End All Wars: Woodrow Wilson and the Quest for a New World Order* (Oxford, 1992) as well as John Milton Cooper, Jr., *Breaking the Heart of the World: Woodrow Wilson and the Fight for the League of Nations* (Cambridge, 2001).

4 H[ouse]. R[esolution]. 32084, 61st Congress, 3rd Session, 25 January 1911. For the history of the CEIP, see David S. Patterson, "Andrew Carnegie's quest for world peace," *Proceedings of the American Philosophical Society*, cxiv (1970), pp. 371–83; C. Roland Marchand, *The American Peace*

Movement and Social Reform, 1898–1918 (Princeton, 1972), ch. 4–5, p. 8; Michael A. Lutzker, "The Formation of the Carnegie Endowment for International Peace: A Study of the Establishment-Centered Peace Movement," in Jerry Israel, ed., *Building the Organization Society: Essays on Associational Activities in Modern America* (New York, 1972), pp. 143–62.

5 "Carnegie Peace Fund," Washington, DC, 14 November 1910, folder "Board of Trustees – Meetings 1910–1912," Box 12, Carnegie Endowment for International Peace Records, Rare Book and Manuscript Library, Butler Library, Columbia University [hereafter CEIP archives, RBML, CU].

6 "Meeting of the Board of Trustees of the Carnegie Endowment for International Peace, at the Board Room of the Carnegie Foundation for the Advancement of Teaching, No. 576 Fifth Avenue, New York, Friday, 14 November 1913, 11 A.M.," Folder 13.1, "Board of Trustees–Meetings 1913," Box 13, CEIP archives, RBML, CU.

7 "Liste des Économistes et Publicistes distingués qui doivent recevoir une invitation à la Conférence de Berne," Folder 2; Clark to North, 5 September 1911, Folder 2, Series II.A, Volume 3, Box 355, CEIP archives, RBML, CU, *Procès-verbaux de la conférence convoquée par la Division "Économie Politique et histoire"* (Berne, 1911).

8 CEIP, *Procès-verbaux de la Conférence convoquée par la Division "Économie Politique et histoire"* (Berne, 1911).

9 Nadine Akhund, "Une enquête internationale dans les Balkans. La commission Carnegie, de l'expédition au rapport de 1913–1914," in Catherine Horel, ed., *Les guerres balkaniques (1912–1913): conflits, enjeux, mémoires,* (Berne, 2014), pp. 201–18.

10 "Memorandum of the Sub-Committee of the Executive Committee regarding the proposals of the Berne Conference," 9 November 1911, Folder 5, Series II.A, Volume 3, Box 355; "Memorandum; On the Progress of Organization; Division of Economics and History," [1913], Folder 3, Series II.A, Volume 7, Box 359, CEIP archives, RBML, CU; CEIP, *Carnegie Endowment for International Peace: Report of the Director of the Division of Economics and History* [confidential print] (CEIP, 1911), pp. 68–76.

11 CEIP, *Carnegie Endowment for International Peace: Report of [the] Director of the Division of Economics and History* [Confidential Print] (CEIP, 1915), pp. 1–2, appendix III. For the complicated relationship between the CEIP and the crusading best-selling journalist Norman Angell during this period, see Martin Ceadel, *Living the Great Illusion: Sir Norman Angell, 1872–1967* (Oxford, 2009), ch. 4. Angell's personality and philosophy did not fully mesh with that of the CEIP, which helps explains why his work was not central to their efforts.

12 Clark, "Project of a History of the European War" [hereafter Project of a History], 13 November 1914; Le Coq to Tibbits, 3 December 1914; Tibbits

to Shotwell, 10 December 1914; Shotwell to Tibbits, 15 December 1915, Folder 2, Series II.A, Volume 9, Box 362, CEIP archives, RMBL. CU.

13 Clark to Scott, 3 October 1914, Folder 2, Series II.A, Volume 9, Box 362, CEIP archives, RMBL. CU.

14 Clark, "Project of a History," 1914.

15 Clark, "Project of a History," 1914

16 Jay Winter and Antoine Prost, *The Great War in History: Debates and Controversies, 1914 to the Present* (Cambridge, 2005), pp. 8, 12, 110–15, 123, 128, 152; John L. Harvey, "The Common Adventure of Mankind: Academic Internationalism and Western Historical Practice from Versailles to Potsdam" (PhD, Pennsylvania State University, 2003), ch. 5.

17 Project of a History; letter to members of the Executive Committee, 9 February 1915, Folder 6, Series II.A, Volume 10, Box 364, CEIP archives, RBML, CU; Harvey, ch. 5.

18 "Synopsis of History Timetable from Clark's and Shotwell's Reports Contained in the Yearbook"; letter to Fitch, 23 March 1950; *Economic and Social History of the War: Statement and Estimates* (Washington, 1922); CEIP press release, "Giant War History Planned 23 Years Ago Completed," 15 March 1937, File 8, Box 36, James Brown Scott papers, Lauinger Library, Georgetown University [hereafter LL, GU]; Katharina Rietzler, "The War as History; Writing the Economic and Social History of the First World War," in Thomas W. Zeiler, David K. Ekbladh, and Benjamin C. Montoya, eds., *Beyond 1917: The United States and Global Legacies of the Great War* (Oxford, 2017), pp. 36–53; Alain Chatriot, "Comprendre la Guerre. L'histoire économique et sociale de la Guerre mondiale, les séries de la Dotation Carnegie pour la paix internationale," in Jean-Jacques Becker, ed., *Histoire culturelle de la Grande Guerre* (Paris, 2005), pp. 33–44. For the 12 October 1916 confidential and at times critical report Scott prepared at the request of Root on the work of the Berne conference, see "Scott confidential report to Root on Admin. Of Div. II: excerpts," File 8, Box 36, Scott papers, LL, GU.

19 Andrew Green, *Writing the Great War: Sir James Edmonds and the Official Histories, 1915–1948* (London, 2003), pp. 1–20; Martin Conway, "Memorandum on the Scope of the National War Museum," 26 June 1917, and the covering memorandum to the war cabinet by Alfred Mond, 8 August 1917, GT 1650, CAB 24/22, The National Archives, Kew; Gaynor Kavanaugh, "Museum as Memoria: The Origins of the Imperial War Museum," *Journal of Contemporary History*, 23 (1998): pp. 77–97; Kavanaugh, *Museums and the First World War: a social history* (Leicester, 1994), ch. 10–11; *Le Temps* (Paris), 9 September 1916; France, *Journal officiel de la République française. Documents parlementaires. Chambre des députes*, Annexe no. 2817, 22 December 1916; Joseph Hue, "La Bibliothèque-Musée de la Guerre

dans les années vingt," in Robert Frank, Laurent Gervereau, and Hans J. Neyer, eds., *La course au moderne: France et Allemagne dans l'Europe des années vingt, 1919–1933* (Nanterre, 1992), pp. 169–75; Hue, "De la Bibliothèque-Musée de la Guerre à la BDIC," *Matériaux pour l'histoire de notre temps* 45–50 (1998): pp. 5–6; Bruno Van Doren, "La Bibliothèque de documentation internationale contemporaine," in Martine Poulain, ed., *Histoire des bibliothèques françaises: Les bibliothèques au XXe siècle* (Paris, 1992), vol. 4, pp. 131–3. The process was very different in Germany. For a compendium of German war collections, see A[lbert] Buddecke, *Die Kriegssammlungen. Ein Nachweis ihrer Einrichtung und ihres Bestandes* (Oldenburg, 1917). For the history of a key German collection, the Weltkriegsbücherei, see Jürgen Rohwer "50 Jahre Weltkriegsbücherei Bibliothek für Zeitgeschichte," in *50 Jahre Bibliothek für Zeitgeschichte 1915–1965* (Frankfurt, 1965), pp. 1–38.

20 Clark to Scott, 9 November 1914; Scott to Brown, 6 November 1914; [North] to Clark, 3 November 1914; Memoranda [November 1914], Folder 5, Box 320, Volume 8, Series II.A, CEIP archives, RBML, CU.

21 "Carnegie Endowment for International Peace; Meeting of the Board of Trustees; 13 November 1914," File 13.2, "Board of Trustees–Meetings–1914," Box 13, CEIP archives, RMBL, CU.

22 David Kennedy, *Over Here: The First World War and American Society* (New York, 2004), p. 57. The organization's "leadership came from the Department of Historical Research of the Carnegie Institution in Washington, where were located the editorial offices of the *American Historical* Review and the secretariat of the American Historical Association." See Waldo G. Leland, "Historians and Archivists in the First World War," *The American Archivist*, 4 (1942), p. 3.

23 CEIP, "Proceedings of the Special Meeting of the Board of Trustees," 19 April 1917, File 13.4 "Board of Trustees – Meetings – 1917," CEIP archives, RMBL, CU. For Carnegie's racial calculations as well as his views on Empire and peace, see Duncan Bell, *Dreamworlds of Race: Empire and the Utopian Destiny of Anglo-America* (Princeton, 2020), esp. ch. 2.

24 CEIP, "Proceedings," 19 April 1917, File 13.4. This is a classic example of Martin Ceadel's analysis of "crusading" in the peace/war debate. See Martin Ceadel, *Thinking about Peace and War* (Oxford University Press, 1987), pp. 43–71. The same phenomenon is also to be seen in France. See Norman Ingram, "The Crucible of War: The Ligue des droits de l'homme and the Debate on the 'Conditions for a Lasting Peace' in 1916," *French Historical Studies* 39 (2016), pp. 347–71.

25 Shotwell to Butler, 29 May 1919, File "Shotwell, James T.," Box 379, Nicholas Murray Butler Papers, RBML, CU. This aspect of Shotwell's career has received very little attention but see the place it occupies in the January 1952 draft of the nomination he received for the Nobel

Peace Prize (https://www.cia.gov/library/readingroom/docs/CIA-RDP80R01731R003100190074-1.pdf) as well as the recent but incomplete account of Shotwell's diplomacy in the 1920s, in many ways culminating in the Kellogg–Briand Pact of 1928. See Oona A. Hathaway and Scott J. Shapiro, *The Internationalists: How a Radical Plan to Outlaw War Remade the World* (New York, 2017), esp. ch. 5; Carl Bouchard, "Le plan américain Shotwell-Bliss de 1924: une initiative méconnue pour le renforcement de la paix," *Guerres mondiales et conflits contemporains*, 202–203 (2001), pp. 203–25.

26 L[ionel] C[urtis] undated note and the enclosed [30 May 1919] text of his speech and [Curtis and Shepardson], "Memorandum," no date [June, 1919]; Curtis to Biddle, 16 June 1919, Folder 2/1/2, archives, Chatham House; David Stevenson, "Learning from the Past: the relevance of international history," *International Affairs* 1 (2014), pp. 6–22.

27 For the United States, see Steiner, especially ch. 7.

28 Years, later, in 1945, Shotwell rejected the suggestion that the CEIP assist in the translation and publication of Cru's 1929 and 1930 studies of soldiers' accounts and testimony. See Fitch to Shotwell, 2 March 1945, and Shotwell to Fitch, 5 March 1945, Folder 87.4 "MSS Not Published, C," Box 87, CEIP archives, RBML, CU; Jay Winter and Antoine Prost, *The Great War in History: Debates and Controversies, 1914 to the Present* (Cambridge, 2005), pp. 14–15, 87, 106, 176, 199. For the CEIP's rejection, see Folder "Cru, Jean Norton, French Series," Box 66, Shotwell papers, RBML, CU. See also Frédéric Rousseau, *Le procès des témoins de la Grande Guerre: l'affaire Norton Cru* (Paris, 2003). I would like to thank Jay Winter for pointing out this example.

29 For the former, see Andrew Barros, "Turn Everyone into a Civilian: René Cassin and the UNESCO Project, 1919–1945," in Andrew Barros and Martin Thomas, eds., *The Civilianization of War: The Changing Civil-Military Divide, 1914–2014* (Cambridge, 2018), ch. 12. For the latter, see Andrew Barros, "L'internationalisme de Pierre Renouvin: le cas de la dotation Carnegie," in Laurence Badel, ed., *Histoire et relations internationals: Pierre Renouvin, Jean-Baptiste Duroselle et la naissance d'une discipline universitaire* (Paris, 2020), pp. 49–63.

30 For Shotwell's system of national committees for advice on disarmament, see the example of the early post-Locarno negotiations, including the contributions of Bliss. See "Compte-Rendu de la Séance tenue par le Comité de Désarmement, le Lundi 23 Novembre 1925 à 5h. ½ en l'Hôtel de la Dotation Carnegie," Shotwell to Fontaine, 1 February 1926; Tasker Bliss, "Désarmement. Le questionnaire de Genève et la commission préparatoire," File "Comité du Désarmement – 1926," 127.4, CEIP archives, RBML, CU.

31 For veterans, see the classic study by Antoine Prost, *Les Anciens Combattants et la société française: 1914–1939* (Paris, 1977), 3 vols.

32 For the moral disarmament campaign, see Barros, "Turn Everyone into a Civilian," pp. 254–7.

33 Shotwell's role in post–World War Two US planning has not yet been fully elucidated, but see the recent noteworthy study by Stephen Wertheim, "Instrumental Internationalism: The American Origins of the United Nations, 1940–3," *Journal of Contemporary History* 54, no. 2 (2019), pp. 1–19.

4 Three Visions of Internationalism: European Socialists after the First World War

TALBOT IMLAY

This chapter examines the efforts of European socialists in the wake of the First World War to reconstitute the pre-war socialist International and to revive the practice of cooperation between socialist parties on doctrinal questions and on more concrete issues. Four long years of war had strained this practice to the breaking point as socialist parties found themselves in competing belligerent camps and as the insatiable demands of modern war transformed politics within nations. The result was a splintering of socialism into three groups: national reformist, Bolshevik revolutionary, and non-Bolshevik revolutionary. Each group embodied a distinct vision of socialist internationalism – a vision that encompassed an approach to the post-war political order both between states and within them. If this splintering ultimately doomed efforts to recreate a single socialist movement, the emergence of multiple socialist internationalisms is worth considering, for it challenges the dominant view of post-war international politics as a struggle for predominance between liberal/Wilsonian internationalism and Bolshevik internationalism. Post-war socialists offered two alternative internationalisms, a national-reformist one, which would come to dominate interwar socialism, and a non-Bolshevik revolutionary one. This latter socialist internationalism, whose institutional expression was the short-lived Vienna Union, represented an intriguing attempt to forge a third way between the politics of revolution and the politics of reform within and between states.

This chapter is divided into several sections. The first section discusses the international socialist conference in Berne in February 1919, teasing out its historiographical implications for an understanding of post-war socialist internationalism. The next three sections explore the different versions of socialist internationalism that emerged from the wreckage of pre-war and wartime socialism: national reformist, Bolshevik revolutionary, and non-Bolshevik revolutionary. The final section makes a plea for treating interwar socialist internationalism as a distinct political phenomenon.

The February 1919 Berne Conference

In early February 1919, some eighty socialists representing twenty-one parties met in Berne, Switzerland. Unlike the peace conference that had recently opened in Paris to much fanfare, the Berne gathering brought together socialists from both sides of the belligerent divide. Remarking that the socialist conference involved "a meeting of enemies face to face for the first time," the British socialist Charles Roden Buxton described his arrival in Berne from Paris as "passing from darkness into light."[1] The overlap between the two conferences was not coincidental. No sooner had the armistice been announced in November 1918 than European socialists worked to organize an international conference. Taking the lead, Arthur Henderson, the British Labour Party leader, urged the Allied governments to permit an "ad hoc Conference" of socialists, preferably in Paris. Although the Allies rejected Paris as a venue, presumably because of the projected presence of German and Austrian socialists, they agreed not to place obstacles in the way of a conference in a country that had been neutral during the war.[2]

In organizing a conference, socialists hoped to place a socialist stamp on the emerging post-war European and international order. For Henderson, it was imperative that the socialist conference occur during the inter-Allied deliberations in Paris rather than after they had been concluded. Socialists, he explained privately in December 1918, must ensure "that the views of International Labour and Socialism shall have consideration at the Official Peace Conference before it is too late for protests or encouraging words."[3] On the opening day of the Berne conference, Henderson reiterated the point, defining its goal as follows: "to bring to bear upon the great problems of the world peace the fullest measure of working influence ... That there is a need for working class influence must be obvious to all, not only having regard to the difficulties involved in the international situation, but the possibility of securing for all those for whom we represent in the countries who have their delegates on the floor of this Conference proper settlements of the vast issues of life and death."[4]

Echoing Henderson, an editorial in *Vorwärts*, the principal newspaper of the majority German socialists (SPD), welcomed Berne as a sign of international socialist unity – a unity deemed indispensable if the "international proletariat" was to influence international politics.[5]

The idea that European socialists might have something to say about peacemaking and the post-war international order was not simply a socialist conceit. During the conflict, the monumental task of mobilizing resources had, in numerous belligerent countries, pushed national authorities into negotiating not only with workers and their trade union representatives but also with Socialist Party leaders whose apparent popular legitimacy among the masses governments hoped to harness to the war effort. This development, together with the growing appeal of revolutionary politics among trade unionists and socialists, meant that the Left in general emerged from the war as a powerful political force in the minds of many observers. As a result, the Berne conference received widespread media coverage in different countries; no less importantly, the conference was followed closely by various foreign ministries, even if their assessments differed. The German foreign ministry was perhaps the most enthusiastic, a position largely explained by the country's desperate need for political allies in 1918–19 calling for something other than a draconian peace. In Paris, meanwhile, Quai d'Orsay officials received worrying intelligence reports suggesting that the *Auswärtiges Amt*'s enthusiasm was justified – that German socialists might succeed in Berne in turning international socialism into an instrument of German foreign policy. It was British diplomats, however, who appeared the most alarmist, warning that the Berne conference could "mark the birth of a more dangerous [socialist] International ... which under the brilliant and irresponsible leadership of a few cosmopolitan intellectuals will aim at establishing in every land the dictatorship of a section of the proletariat."[6]

But whatever the precise nature of contemporary assessments, it is interesting to compare the attention the Berne conference garnered at the time with its relative absence in much of the recent scholarship on the post-war period. Neither Zara Steiner nor Patrick Cohrs, for example, even mention the conference in their richly detailed studies of post-war international politics, though both are admittedly state-centred. But Berne gets only the slightest of mentions in William Mulligan's *The Great War for Peace*, an innovative examination of wartime and post-war efforts at peacemaking that accords considerable space to non-state actors.[7] This scholarly neglect of the Berne conference mirrors a larger absence – that of socialism as an international movement. To be sure, scholars continue to examine post-war socialism within different European countries.[8] But socialism as something other than its national parts, as an aspiring international or transnational political force is almost nowhere to be seen.

There are several reasons for this relative neglect of the Berne conference and, more largely, of international socialism. One reason no doubt concerns the shift in geographical focus away from peacemaking in Western Europe, which dominated scholarship for so long, towards other regions – Eastern Europe, the Balkans, and the colonial world.[9] In almost all these regions, socialists figured less prominently as political actors than they did in countries such as Britain, France, and Germany. Another and related reason is the recent interest in political violence as a subject. If the armistice in November 1918 ended military operations on the Western Front, armed conflict continued across large swathes of central Europe, eastern Europe, and the Balkans as groups clashed over the question of what (or whom) would replace imperial rule, whether Russian, German, Austro-Hungarian, or Ottoman. In this "shatterzone" of imperial collapse, violence became endemic, reconfiguring and deepening pre-existing ethnic, linguistic, political and other divisions. A dangerous brew of polarization, radicalism, and racism would poison politics in many of the successor states, fragilizing the functioning of democratic regimes during the coming years. When socialists appear in this scholarship, they often do as victims of a reactionary wave that sought to crush the left in general.[10]

Still another reason for the neglect of post-war international socialism lies in the heritage of August 1914. This was the moment when European socialists supposedly chose national over class solidarities, demonstrating the hollowness of their internationalist pretensions. In 1914, as James Joll wrote, "[t]he life had gone out of the Second International" and "it was never to return." If pre-war socialist internationalism had proven to be a "sham," then there was no reason to study its post-war manifestations.[11] As a political phenomenon, European socialism was best approached in national or sub-national frameworks.

A final reason for the neglect of international socialism – and for this chapter perhaps the most pertinent one – stems from an understanding of post-war internationalism as dominated by two competing approaches: liberal or Wilsonian internationalism on the one hand, and Leninist or Bolshevik internationalism on the other. Arno Mayer's two magisterial studies of peacemaking published in 1959 and 1967 not only exemplify this binary understanding of the stakes involved but also contributed greatly to enshrining this perspective on post-war international politics in the scholarship.[12] While scholars continue to investigate the nature and working of Communist internationalism and its institutional expression, the Comintern, Mayer's enduring influence is perhaps most evident in the ongoing fascination with Woodrow Wilson, with his conception of international relations, and with his legacy for American foreign relations.[13] In this world marked by two competing visions of internationalisms, liberal and Bolshevik, other possible internationalisms all too easily get squeezed out. This is sometimes the case for anti-colonial internationalism, whose post-war history is integrated into the Comintern efforts to instrumentalize anti-colonialism as part of the Soviet Union's existential struggle against Western imperialist powers. But it also the case with the non-communist left. Thus, in Adam Tooze's imposing study of the making of global order during and after the war, the socialists who gathered at Berne in February 1919 could not escape a choice between the Bolshevik and Wilsonian visions.[14]

In light of this binary framework, the Berne conference is noteworthy for two related reasons. One is that the conference placed the issue of internationalism squarely on the agenda of socialist politics. The First World War had proved to be an extremely divisive experience for European socialists, with growing cleavages emerging both between and within parties concerning the nature and justification of the war. As the conflict dragged on, increasing numbers of socialists queried the wisdom of pursuing the war to victory, and by 1916–17 vocal and burgeoning minorities existed within the major parties pushing for international negotiations and a compromise peace. The Russian revolutions in 1917 further fueled tensions not simply because the Bolsheviks called for a peace without indemnities and annexations but also because they openly pursued the revolutionary overthrow of the existing order at home and abroad. For socialists, the issues of war, peace, and revolution fused together, forcing them to take a position on each and all of these three issues.

But if the war fostered fractures within the pre-war socialist movement, it also reaffirmed the urgency for socialists to cooperate across national borders. The result was attempts throughout the war to organize a conference of socialists and socialist parties from both belligerent camps. Considerable scholarly attention has been directed to the Zimmerwald movement and its two conferences, one in Zimmerwald in September 1915 and one held in Kienthal in April 1916. But the Zimmerwald movement quickly radicalized, placing it within the extreme left of the socialist movement.[15] More representative of the cross-currents of wartime socialism was the aborted Stockholm conference due to occur in September 1917. The failure to pull off the conference, however, did not spell the end of socialist efforts, and during the last year of the war, various European socialists continued to work towards a conference. Following the armistice in November 1918, these socialists redoubled their efforts, as the pressing aim now become to influence the post-war order.[16]

The Berne conference was thus both an end and a beginning: it marked the end of wartime efforts on the part of socialists to cooperate across the belligerent divide, and it marked the beginning of post-war efforts to develop socialism into a powerful force in international politics. To do so, though, required unity, and the Berne conference pointed to the difficulties involved, for not all pre-war socialists agreed to participate. Belgian socialists, for example, chose to stay away rather than meet in the same room with German socialists, while the Bolsheviks contemptuously denounced the entire proceedings as a reactionary enterprise. It was only in 1923 with the creation of a new International, the Labour and Socialist International (LSI), that some semblance of socialist unity was achieved. But if the Belgian party joined the new International, the Bolsheviks hunkered down in their own International, created soon after the Berne conference.

The post-war confrontation between pre-war socialists begun at the Berne conference possessed political implications that extended well beyond the socialist world. The immediate post-war years were a period of immense upheaval and flux but also of possibility. Writing about the European left in general, Geoff Eley has argued that large-scale war fosters "enabling indeterminacies" – situations in which people can conceive of political means and ends in ways that they could not before.[17] What seemed utopian and even unimaginable, now appears as feasible. This revolution in political expectations can be invigorating, and in 1918–19 many socialists fervently believed that a new and better world could be constructed from the wreck of world war. Equally pertinent, socialists were not marginal political actors but constituted a significant political force in almost all the principal European countries. Accordingly, the prolonged confrontation between European socialists on the nature of post-war international and national politics needs to be integrated into the larger story of how international and national politics were recast in the wake of war.

The National-Reformist Version of Socialist Internationalism

At the risk of simplifying a complex situation, it is possible to identify three different versions of socialist internationalism in the post-war years. One version consisted of a return to the pre-war period, often viewed as the heyday of socialist internationalism.[18] Grouped together in the Second International, European socialists before 1914 advocated a variety of policies aimed at reducing if not eliminating international tensions, among them disarmament, compulsory arbitration, limited support for the national aspirations of subject populations, and a reformed colonialism that would rein in exploitative practices while fostering the political and economic development of colonial possessions. To be sure, disagreement existed among socialists, not least regarding the fraught question of what socialist parties should do in the event of a major war – a possibility that increasingly preoccupied prominent socialists such as Jean Jaurès in the immediate pre-war years. Nevertheless, from a longer-term perspective, pre-war European socialists envisaged an increasingly inter-connected world of harmonious and mutually beneficial exchanges between states and regions in which empires would gradually evolve to allow for more and more autonomy (and perhaps even independence) to their members.

In this world, the sources of international tensions and war would disappear over time as international relations became more civilized thanks in no small part to institutions and practices such as compulsory arbitration. If the arena of civilized relations excluded for the time being much of the non-Western world, most socialists believed that this arena would be enlarged as the beneficial effects of a reformed colonialism helped to prepare colonies for membership. No less importantly, European socialists designated themselves as the guarantors of this emerging world. As socialist parties gained in electoral strength within the principal national and imperial powers, socialists would be in a position to influence and even to determine government policies. In this sense, the Socialist International, the institutional embodiment of socialist internationalism, amounted to a model of international relations in a world of states governed by socialists.

In the immediate post-war period, this national-reformist version of socialist internationalism manifested itself in the ambiguous response of some European socialists to the peace treaties and to the Versailles treaty in particular. On the one hand, these socialists decried the treaty as unacceptable – and indeed the major parties either voted against or refrained from ratifying it in their national parliaments. Speaking to French socialists in April 1919, Henderson denounced Versailles as a "violent peace."[19] That Henderson did so is not fortuitous: not only did Labour quickly emerge as a pillar of the national-reformist version of socialist internationalism, but within its ranks hostility towards Versailles was notable. An internal memorandum written by Norman Angell, a world-renowned internationalist, described the treaty as "defective" not in its details "but fundamentally, in that it accepts, and indeed is based on the very political principles or premises which were the ultimate causes of this war, and which must, if adhered to, produce not only other wars, but a perpetuation in peace time of those economic and social conditions which it is the object of workers to abolish." Similarly, another memorandum insisted that Versailles did not serve the interests of peace "but is concerned almost solely with the moment and with securing to the victors in the last war the immediate spoils of victory."[20] As evidence, Labour officials pointed to the treaty's territorial clauses, which did not respect the principle of national self-determination, to its economic clauses, which were one-sidedly punitive, and to the anticipated seizure of the defeated countries' colonies by France and Britain, which reflected the enduring hold of the disastrous power politics that were held responsible for the recent war.

The result was a generalized call for treaty revision. A report in 1919 from the Second International's bureau thus proposed that European socialists unite around a shared determination to undo the peace treaties – a proposal that found expression in the general resolution agreed to by the majority of socialist delegates at a meeting in Lucerne, Switzerland, in August of the same year. All member parties, the resolution declared, must "work with all their energy for a change in the [peace] treaties in a sense favourable to the reconciliation of peoples."[21]

Significantly, however, treaty revision was understood in reformist terms. Nowhere was this more in evidence than with the League of Nations, widely viewed as the lynchpin of the post-Versailles international order. Although socialists initially denounced the League as a victors' institution, more moderate positions soon prevailed. An undated Labour party memorandum circulated to European socialist parties, while recognizing the League's "many defects," nevertheless contended that the wisest policy was to work with rather than against the institution. "British Labour," it argued, "holds the League of Nations is a real beginning in international cooperation. With different governments in power, it is capable of being changed for the better both in form and spirit."[22] This argument resonated among continental socialists, prominently among them the majority German socialists (SPD), who, like Labour, constituted a pillar of the national-reformist vision of socialist internationalism. In its 1921 program, the SPD called on socialists to work for a reformed League of Nations, one representing the interests of peoples rather than states and capable of rectifying the numerous wrongs of the Versailles Treaty.[23] Working together, European socialists would transform the League into an instrument of their national-reformist-oriented internationalism.

In the meantime, an International reconstituted along much the same lines as the pre-war Second International would be the principal instrument of socialist internationalism. Taking the lead, Labour quickly sought to steer continental socialists towards an International that reflected its national-reformist version of internationalism: as with states, member parties would cooperate with one another on a voluntary basis in order to work out consensus positions on concrete international policies. As a proto international society, the International would point the way to a more harmonious, peaceful, and mutually beneficial practice of relations between the independent members of a community of states. As a circular in June 1919 explained, such an International would aim at the "development of a society of nations that is a reality comprising all nations and aimed at maintaining international peace." At a meeting in Geneva a year later, members of Labour, the SPD, and eleven additional parties agreed to constitute a new International along these lines.[24]

From this perspective, the reform of domestic politics constituted the flipside of the reform of international politics. It was not simply that as socialist parties gained in electoral strength they would presumably pursue more cooperative policies at the international level. It was also assumed that reform of the political system within states – better social provision, fairer tax policies, an enhanced political role for trade unions – would help to create the domestic underpinnings of more peaceful international relations. By reducing some of the domestic causes of inter-state tensions, which many socialists believed stemmed from the functioning of oligarchic and exploitative political regimes, socialist inspired and directed reforms within states would improve international relations.

Three points about this national-reformist version of socialist internationalism are worth making. The first is that it would infuse the reconstituted Second International (the LSI, created in 1923), becoming the primary political current within the institution and among its dominant member parties. The second and related point is that this internationalism resembled Wilsonian or liberal internationalism, which helps to explain the temptation of some scholars to conflate the two.[25] But this temptation, and this constitutes the third point, needs to be resisted. One reason is because important differences existed between the two internationalisms. For example, on the question of democracy, whereas liberal internationalists thought largely in limited political terms (parliamentary regime and elections), socialist internationalists of a national-reformist bent included an important social-economic element. Their reformist ambitions, in short, should not be ignored. But another, and perhaps more important, reason is that other versions of socialist internationalism existed during the post-war period.

The Bolshevik Version of Socialist Internationalism

In 1918–19, the national-reformist version of socialist internationalism faced powerful challenges from other groups that sought to claim the mantle of socialism. Probably the greatest challenge in this sense came from the Bolsheviks, whose roots were in the pre-war socialist movement but who broke definitively with the latter during the war. Bolshevik internationalism constituted not only a markedly determined and powerful version of socialist internationalism but also a foil against which other versions – the national reformists and non-Bolshevik revolutionaries – would define themselves.

From the outset, the Bolsheviks sought to impose their version of socialist internationalism on the left. Only two months after the armistice ended hostilities on the Western Front in November 1918, they issued an invitation to several parties and groups to gather in Moscow "to convene the first congress of a new revolutionary international." The resulting conference in March 1919 saw the creation of a communist International – the Comintern. That the Berne conference the previous month served as principal spur to the Bolsheviks is apparent from the resolution announcing the Comintern's birth: "The foundation of the Communist International is the more imperative since now at Berne, and possibly later elsewhere also, an attempt is being made to restore the old opportunist International and to rally to it all the confused and undecided elements of the proletariat. It is therefore essential to make a sharp break between the revolutionary proletariat and the social-traitor elements."[26]

The goal of the Bolsheviks, in other words, was to monopolize the left by framing the stakes in binary terms – as a contest between communist revolution and reaction. In pursuit of this goal, the Bolsheviks in 1920 drew up what became known as the "Twenty-One Conditions" for admission to the Comintern. The conditions envisaged the formation of communist parties on the Bolshevik model: highly disciplined, hierarchical, and centralized organizations under Moscow's leadership. No less importantly, these new parties were expected to purge "all elements which continue to act in the spirit of the Second International."[27] For Bolsheviks, the choice was between acceptance or rejection of this model – no third option existed.

As is well-known, the twenty-one conditions spurred impassioned and divisive debates within socialist parties about the aims and nature of socialism – and, of course, whether or not to seek admission to the Comintern. Probably the best-known case is that of the SFIO, which split in two at the Tours conference in December 1920, with the majority joining the newly created PCF and the minority remaining loyal, in Léon Blum's words, to socialism's "vieille maison."[28] No doubt some socialists harboured illusions about Bolshevist internationalism, maintaining that the Bolsheviks were more flexible and their conditions less imperious than appeared. That said, the Comintern's appeal among socialists in the immediate post-war years probably had less to do with the precise conditions for membership than it did with the aura surrounding the

Bolsheviks. Part of this aura stemmed from the reaction against national-reformist socialism, which stood accused of having irredeemably compromised itself through close association with the nation during the war. At a conference of independent German socialists in September 1919, Walter Stoecker spoke of the "*spiritual collapse* of international socialism" due to the wartime capitulation of socialist parties to nationalism. Several months later, the French socialist, Raoul Verfeuil, insisted that socialist parties had betrayed socialist internationalism by refusing to subordinate their "patriotic duty" to their "internationalist duty." A new International was accordingly needed that would prioritize "proletarian solidarity," making "it a crime for workers to shoot one another whatever the reasons invoked to push them to commit such a crime."[29]

But Bolshevism's appeal did not stem simply from a reaction to the alleged betrayal of socialist internationalism during the war. The Bolshevik success in seizing power in St. Petersburg and Moscow in 1917 provoked widespread admiration among socialists. As Marcel Cachin, who would soon join the French Communist Party (PCF), wrote in August 1920, the Bolsheviks "showed the way" for socialists and "to have [so] acted confers on them an immense prestige and legitimacy." Even someone as anti-Bolshevik as Ramsay MacDonald, the future Labour prime minister, privately expressed respect for the Bolsheviks' "views of revolution," especially compared to what he viewed as socialist internationalism's excessive prudence. "Fault of the International," he jotted in his diary in May 1919, "is that it has become too parliamentary & has no vision."[30] Reinforcing this admiration for the Bolshevik's decisiveness was the belief that Europe in 1919–20 confronted a revolutionary situation, one perhaps even more favourable than that facing Russia in 1917. The international civil war was close at hand, Stoecker announced in September 1920, and German (and European) socialists must prepare themselves for "the coming struggle, which will quite possibly break out in the next few months."[31] In this exceptional and highly charged atmosphere, Cachin and Stoecker contended, the Comintern alone was equipped to guide socialists.

But, more than anything, the attraction of the Bolsheviks stemmed from their program. At the national level, it can be summed up as revolution: the seizure and monopolization of political power by a disciplined and determined avant-garde (the communist party) using all means necessary, including violence. Some Comintern supporters among socialists sought to downplay Bolshevism's violent and coercive aspects, but neither in theory nor in practice did it prove easy to reconcile the "dictatorship of the proletariat" with democracy – a point socialist critics of the Bolsheviks seized upon. The doctrines of dictatorship and violence, observed a memorandum from the Independent Labour Party, a self-consciously left-leaning group affiliated with the Labour Party, "run through" Moscow's statement, warning that it would be mistaken to view them as "meaningless words."[32] For those socialists in favour of joining the Comintern, Bolshevism's appeal was that it seemed to provide a road map for revolution – for victory.

Beyond the revolutionary seizure of power, what Bolshevism meant at the national level remained unclear, in part because the Bolsheviks themselves were uncertain. With Russia engulfed in a murderous civil war, neither the Bolshevik leadership nor the Comintern had the luxury of gazing very far into the future. The only certain point is that Bolshevism would break decisively with national-reformist socialism.

At the international level, Bolshevism as a project was best encapsulated in the Comintern. As the twenty-one conditions made clear, from the beginning it was to be a top-down, highly centralized organization. In the military vocabulary that infused so much of post-war politics, the Comintern would act as the general staff directing the various divisions (communist parties) in the revolutionary war against the bourgeois order at home and abroad. The task of individual communists, as with soldiers, was to obey orders from above. For those socialists who voted to affiliate with the Comintern, it was precisely this understanding of the Comintern as an instrument of revolution that appealed to them. The pre-war Second International had seemingly failed, and the new International must, in the popular wording at the time, be "capable of action" (*aktionsfähig*). If this entailed an organization capable of providing collective direction and imposing its authority on member parties, it also meant an unquestioning obedience to the centre, which meant Moscow. Once again, Stoecker is a useful guide. For true socialists, he lectured the independent German socialists in 1920, "only one position is possible: solidarity with Soviet Russia in all situations."[33]

As mentioned, in the immediate post-war years, Bolshevism enjoyed considerable appeal among socialists, spurred by the widespread conviction that the pre-war International – and socialist internationalism more generally – had disastrously failed. The question of whether to affiliate with the Comintern proved especially difficult, dividing and even tearing apart several socialist parties as well as leaving long-lasting scars in some cases. This experience created a gulf between the socialist internationalism embodied in the LSI and the Bolshevik internationalism embodied in the Comintern. Not surprisingly, the Comintern's class-versus-class strategy during the late 1920s, which lumped socialists with fascists, did much to deepen this gulf, reinforcing the perception of a Left divided between reformist socialism (akin to liberalism) and Bolshevism.

For this reason, it is useful to recall that many socialists remained outside the Bolshevik fold from the beginning. One reason they did so, of course, is that the Bolsheviks would not have them. In their twenty-one conditions, the latter insisted that aspiring member parties must purge themselves of "opportunists" – of those socialists judged insufficiently committed to the cause. But another and more important reason is that some socialists struggled to elaborate a compromise between Bolshevism and reformist socialism – between the Third International and a reconstituted Second International.

Non-Bolshevik Revolutionary Internationalism

In the immediate post-war years, socialists from several countries sought to avoid choosing between the Bolsheviks and the reformist socialists, between communist and socialist internationalism. For these socialists, a return to the pre-war Second International was simply anathema. Writing in 1921 to Ramsay MacDonald, who had become Labour's point man in negotiations with foreign socialists, Friedrich Adler, the Austrian socialist, denounced the Second International's "Social Patriotism," adding that it "has more and more become the select group of those unrepentant sinners who even now refuse to see and still more to confess the terrible mistakes committed by them during the war." Yet despite his contempt for reformist socialists, Adler refused to be hustled into the Comintern, even though he clearly sympathized with the Bolsheviks more than with the reformist socialists. Lenin's project, he avowed to MacDonald, constituted "one of the most fateful experiments for Labour, not only in Russia, but of [sic] the whole world."[34] For Adler and others of a similar bent, the Bolsheviks were too prone to violence, too intransigent, and perhaps even too German. In arguing the need for a third option, another Austrian socialist castigated the Comintern's "Ludendorff methods" and its attempts to impose them on the Western European proletariat.[35]

The desire for a compromise between Bolshevism and national-reformist socialism crystallized in February 1921 with the creation of another international socialist organization. That the founding conference occurred in Vienna was no coincidence, as Adler and the Austrian socialist party (SPÖ) had been at the forefront of efforts to define a socialist third way. After consultations with European socialists and following divisive votes on Comintern affiliation, the SPÖ took the initiative of inviting several parties to Vienna, most prominently among them the USPD, the French socialist party (SFIO), and the Independent Labour Party, the self-consciously leftist grouping affiliated with Labour. In Vienna, the delegates agreed to create the "International Working Union of Socialist Parties" – or the Vienna Union.[36]

Identifying the Vienna Union's version of socialist internationalism is not easy, partly because of its brief existence. Founded in early 1921, the Vienna Union would be absorbed into the reconstituted Second International two years later. During much of its short lifespan, moreover, the Vienna Union, with Adler as its secretary, preoccupied itself with negotiations with the Bolsheviks and with the reformist socialists on the question of unity – of how to construct a single socialist International.[37] The Bolsheviks famously dismissed the Vienna Union as the 2 and ½ International, but Adler from the beginning conceived of the organization not as an International but as a "provisional shelter" for socialist parties during a transitional period. Thus while conducting talks with the Bolsheviks, among others, Adler repeatedly preached patience, maintaining that the Vienna Union's purpose was to provide time for the emergence of a genuine internationalist spirit not only among its member parties but even more so, as he made clear to MacDonald, among the parties of the Second International that had betrayed socialist internationalism.[38] Whatever one thinks of Adler's reasoning – and the Bolsheviks and reformist socialists both grew increasingly frustrated with what they perceived to be his delaying tactics – the Vienna Union's transitional character arguably hampered the elaboration of a clear-cut political program.

Yet despite these obstacles, it is possible to discern the rudiments of a revolutionary non-Bolshevik socialist internationalism, however inchoate it remained. Perhaps the most notable feature of this internationalism was its systemic perspective. Rhetorically, this approach manifested in repeated references to the class struggle against international capitalism and imperialism and thus in the need for a "revolutionary proletarian united front" stretching across national borders. As one resolution declared: "The International Socialist Conference in Vienna calls on all workers for the unity of the socialist movement in the individual countries and in the International. It is determined to work hard, on the basis of its decisions and resolutions, to achieve this unity. It calls on the socialists of all countries to support their efforts by energetically endeavoring to establish a revolutionary proletarian united front against capitalism and imperialism both in their own country and in the bosom of the international proletarian class organization."[39]

Beyond such rhetoric, the Vienna Union's systemic perspective was evident in its position on more specific subjects. One was treaty revision. Whereas the reformist socialists generally criticized the peace treaties, and especially the Versailles Treaty, as one-sided and even contradictory in the application of its principles, the Vienna Union socialists dismissed the treaties as a symptom of a larger problem: the continued domination of international capitalism and imperialism. Only by defeating these enemies could socialists create a better world. This did not mean, however, that socialists could do nothing in the meantime. In fact, the Vienna Union socialists strove to find practical solutions to problems stemming from war and peacemaking, most notably perhaps the fraught issue of reparations. Under the Vienna Union's aegis, European socialists met during 1921–22 to work out a "socialist" solution to reparations – a solution, it is worth noting, that resembled the one later worked out by European governments and American bankers and known as the Dawes Plan. In addressing concrete issues, the Vienna Union sought to demonstrate both the pertinence of socialism to post-war international politics and the compatibility between revolutionary transformation and practical politics.[40]

A systemic perspective also shaped responses to the League of Nations, which the Vienna Union castigated as a tool of bourgeois class warfare. Reflecting this view, the *Socialist Review*, an ILP publication, insisted in 1919 that "[t]he wrong kind of League is worse than no League at all." The remedy was not to reform the League, as reformist socialists proposed in order to help it fulfill its promise as defined by its American, British, and French founders, but to transform the institution into an instrument of revolutionary change, one equipped with wide-ranging authority in the realms of international politics and economics.[41] Similarly, in the colonial realm, the Vienna Union refused to echo the call of reformist socialists for a reformed colonialism that would reduce if not eliminate abuses but instead considered the colonial world in the larger context of the relations between under-developed and developed regions – relations structured by the violence and exploitation inherent in capitalism. If this approach drew on pre-war socialist debates on the "colonial question," and especially on Karl Kautsky's contributions, Vienna Union socialists sought to update the analysis for the post-war world. In the case of Middle Eastern (Mesopotamian) oil, for example, the ILP lobbied for more equitable policies, contending that "[if] Economic Imperialism is to be ended, Socialist Governments must boldly challenge the exploitation of the natural resources of subject peoples by capitalist groups."[42]

For the Vienna Union, the socialist International that would eventually emerge would direct the systemic transformation of international relations. For this reason, Alder ruled out a simple fusion of the pre-war Second International and the Vienna Union, insisting that the Bolsheviks must be included. Adler hoped to mobilize the Bolsheviks' revolutionary zeal against the limited ambitions of the reformist socialists (once they had been cured of their "social patriotism"), while using the latter to help tame the Bolsheviks' dictatorial proclivities. Adler described this strategy in terms of a productive tension between social reform and social revolution, but unfortunately for him its viability was never tested because of the combined intransigence of the Comintern and the Second International.[43] Adler also made it clear that he wanted to avoid the pitfalls of the pre-war International, and especially its inability to impose a common line on member parties. Accordingly, the Vienna Union's statutes declared its resolutions to be binding on all parties, even if Adler also recognized the importance of ensuring the autonomy of each member party. All told, the projected socialist International would very much be a compromise between the pre-war Second International and the Comintern.

At the national level, compromise also figured as an essential feature of the Vienna Union's socialist internationalism. For Adler and others, the goal was to combine revolution with democracy. As the Vienna Union's emphasis on the class struggle against capitalism suggests, revolution implied profound changes to the social and economic order at home. The USPD's 1919 "program of action," for example, called for state control over food distribution, the collectivization of health care and education, the privatization of religion, legal equality for women, and a reorganization of the legal system. The program, one USPD leader wrote to the ILP, should be taken as proof of the party's commitment to the "proletarian class struggle."[44]

When it came to democracy, the Vienna Union socialists appeared less interested in its parliamentary forms, though they did not necessarily oppose them, than in its potential local and sectoral expressions. The wartime and post-war soldiers and workers' councils in various countries provided one possible model; other models included coops and bipartite (workers and employers) or tripartite (with state officials) corporatist arrangements at the factory and industry levels. More generally, some sense of the Vienna Union's socialist vision comes from the Austrian party's (SPÖ) administration of "Red Vienna" up to 1934, which included an ambitious program of social provision and education.[45] A common thread in these examples was a practical emphasis on grassroots activity and on mobilization from below, an emphasis that reflected a suspicion of hierarchical and centralized authority. In some ways, the Vienna Union socialists envisaged the widening and deepening of democracy through multiple and multi-faceted experiments. The role of socialist parties was to encourage and facilitate these experiments but also to draw inspiration and guidance from them. No less importantly, the assumption was that these experiments would occur simultaneously in several countries, fusing together into a transnational process from which a truly socialist revolutionary democracy would be forged. And here the International was important not so much as a formal institution but as the embodiment of this process. As an editorial in the USPD's newspaper explained: "we must do everything in our power to revolutionize the new organization of the proletariat from within, in concert with our like-minded friends in the other countries."[46]

There was a good deal of wishful and vague thinking in all of this. Adler, for example, endorsed the "dictatorship" of the proletariat, a concept dear to Bolsheviks; he sought to side-step the problem of authority through an almost mystical faith in the revolutionary and democratic potential of the "people."[47] Nevertheless, the Vienna Union should not be dismissed too quickly. Various elements of its project to carve out political space for a revolutionary non-Bolshevik socialism arguably merit further study, whether it be the quest for non-violent yet far-reaching change to the social-economic order or the willingness to experiment with local, grassroots forms of democracy. To be sure, the Bolsheviks and the national reformist socialists succeeded in quickly closing off this political space on the Left, leaving the majority of the Vienna Union socialists little choice but to re-integrate into reformist socialist parties in which, often enough, they found themselves marginalized.[48]

Conclusion

The existence of the Vienna Union and the project of a revolutionary non-Bolshevik socialism suggests that post-war politics on the Left offered more options than simply a choice between Bolshevik and national-reformist (liberal) internationalism. However fleeting its existence and under-developed its program, the Vienna Union embodied intriguing possibilities. If nothing else, its efforts to fuse political transformation with practical cooperation on international issues distinguished the Vienna Union from its two rivals, as did its emphasis on political experimentation at the local levels. European socialists and social democrats today might well benefit from revisiting this promising political experiment as they struggle to remake socialist parties and socialism.

In 1923, the Vienna Union disappeared into the LSI, the reconstituted Second International. From his position as LSI's secretary down to 1940, Adler laboured as best he could to keep alive the Vienna Union's promise of a socialist third way, with the help of groups within the different member parties. Although his ultimate success is questionable, and Adler was bitterly disillusioned with the LSI by the late 1930s, he and his allies did provide something of a counter to reformist and national-rooted tendencies within interwar European socialism. And this function of a counter offers one reason to resist temptation to view socialist internationalism after 1923 – an internationalism infused with national reformism and institutionalized in the LSI – as a variant of interwar liberal internationalism. The temptation to do so is understandable: after all, the two shared many positions or, perhaps more accurately, dispositions – a hostility to power politics (however defined), a suspicion of nationalism as prone to excess, support for disarmament in principle, etc. But there are at least two good arguments against conflating liberal and socialist internationalism during the interwar years. One concerns the practice of socialist internationalism, which can be defined as the well-established and ongoing routine of consultation and cooperation among socialist parties and socialists on international issues. This practice remained an exclusively socialist affair. Non-socialists did not participate.

The second and related reason is that, however national reformist it was, the practice of socialist internationalism fostered a posture of critical opposition towards the reigning methods of international relations. Working together, socialists created a vibrant site of informed debate and criticism on various concrete subjects – disarmament, treaty revision, reparations, and colonialism, among others. To be sure, differences existed between socialists, and consensus could be elusive. Nevertheless, taken as a whole, the critical opposition of socialists represented something more coherent than the various strains of liberal internationalism, which tended to splinter into movements devoted to single issues. In other words, even when it most resembled its liberal variant, socialist internationalism arguably remained something distinct.

NOTES

1 Bodleian Library of Commonwealth and African Studies, Oxford University, Charles Roden Buxton, MSS Brti. Emp. S 405, box 2/5, "The Berne Conference," 1919, Buxton.
2 National Museum of Labour History [hereafter NMLH], Labour Party Archives [hereafter LPA], LSI 2/2/18, Henderson to Emile Vandervelde, 18 November 1918.
3 Ibid, LSI 2/2/19, Henderson to Vandervelde, 6 December 1918.
4 "Arbeiter- und Sozialistenkonferenz in Bern, 3. bis 10. Februar 1919," reproduced in Gerhard A. Ritter, ed., *Die II. Internationale 1918/1919. Protokolle, Memoranden, Berichte und Korrespondenzen* vol I (Berlin, 1980), Henderson, p. 192.

5 "Die Wiedererstehung der Arbeiterinternationale," *Vorwärts*, no. 77 (11 February 1919), p. 1.

6 The National Archives, Kew Gardens, PRO FO 608/237, "A Note on the Berne Conference," Sadler, 26 February 1919. Also see Centre d'archives diplomatiques du Ministère des affaires étrangères, La Courneuve, Série Y International 1918–1949, vol. 395, Min. de la Guerre (2e Bureau) to MAE, 17 February 1919; and Politisches Archiv des Auswärtigen Amts, Berlin, vol. 833, "Bericht ueber die allgemeine Lage," undated but February 1919.

7 Patrick Cohrs, *The Unfinished Peace after World War I: America, Britain and the Stabilisation of Europe, 1919–1932* (Cambridge, 2006); Zara Steiner, *The Lights that Failed: European International History, 1919–1933* (Oxford, 2005); and William Mulligan, *The Great War for Peace* (New Haven, CT, 2014), pp. 286–8.

8 For example, see Thierry Hohl, *À Gauche! La gauche socaliste, 1921–1947* (Dijon, 2004); and David Howell, *MacDonald's Party: Labour Identities and Crisis, 1922–1931* (Oxford, 2002).

9 For a useful overview, see Jay Winter, "The Second Great War, 1917–1923," *Revista Universitaria de Historia Militar* 7 (2018), pp. 160–79; and for the colonial world, see Erez Manela, *The Wilsonian Moment: Self-Determination and the International Origins of Anticolonial Nationalism* (New York, 2007).

10 Paul Hanebrink, *A Specter Haunting Europe: The Myth of Judeo-Bolshevism* (Cambridge, MA, 2018); Robert Gerwarth, *The Vanquished: Why the First World War Failed to End, 1917–1923* (London, 2016); and Omer Bartov and Eric D. Weitz, eds., *Shatterzone of Empires: Coexistence and Violence in the German, Habsburg, Russian, and Ottoman Borderlands* (Bloomington, IN, 2013).

11 James Joll, *The Second International 1889–1914* (London, 1968 edn.), pp. 1, 183.

12 Arno J. Mayer, *Political Origins of the New Diplomacy, 1917–1918* (New Haven, 1959); and *Politics and Diplomacy of Peacemaking: Containment and Counterevolution at Versailles, 1918–1919* (New York, 1967).

13 For a recent example, see Trygve Throntveit, *Power Without Victory: Woodrow Wilson and the American Internationalist Experiment* (Chicago, 2017). Also see the H-Diplo roundtable on the book, available at: https://networks.h-net.org/node/28443/discussions/2493309/h-diplo-roundtable-xx-4-trygve-throntveit-power-without-victory. For the Comintern, see Alexander Vatlin, *Die Komintern. Gründung, Programmatik, Akteure* (Berlin, 2009).

14 See Oleksa Dracewych and Ian McKay, eds., *Left Transnationalism: The Communist International and the National, Colonial, and Racial Questions* (Montreal, 2019); and Adam Tooze, *The Deluge: The Great War, America and the Remaking of the Global Order, 1916–1931* (New York, 2014), pp. 241–4.

15 For this reason, the Zimmerwald movement is often treated as an element in the origins of the Comintern. For example, see R. Craig Nation, *War on War: Lenin, the Zimmerwald Left, and the Origins of Communist Internationalism* (Durham, 1989); and Horst Lademacher, *Die Zimmerwalder Bewegung. Protokolle und Korrespondenz.* Vol. 1 *Protokolle* (The Hague, 1967).

16 See Talbot C. Imlay, *The Practice of Socialist Internationalism: European Socialists and International Politics, 1914–1960* (Oxford, 2018), pp. 28–56.

17 Geoff Eley, "Europe After 1945," *History Workshop Journal* 65 (2008), pp. 207–8.

18 For a classic study, see Joll, *The Second International 1889–1914*. For a more critical perspective, see Sebastian D. Schikl, *Universalismus und Partikularismus: Erfahrungsraum, Erwartungshorizont und Territorialdebatten in der diskursiven Praxis der II. Internationale 1889–1917* (St. Ingbert, 2012).

19 "Ententesozialisten gegen Gewaltfrieden," *Vorwärts*, no. 204 (22 April 1919), p. 1.

20 NMLH, LPA, Advisory Committee on International Questions, memoranda: 1918–1920, untitled note, Angell, May 1919; and "Memorandum on the Draft Treaty of Peace," May 1919.

21 International Institute of Social History, Amsterdam, Bureau socialiste internationale, 103, "Report on the General Situation," undated but 1919; and "Resolution über die allgemeine Politik," reproduced in Ritter, ed., *Die II. Internationale 1918/1919*, vol I, pp. 655–6.

22 IISH, LSI London Secretariat, 73, Draft Reports for the International Socialist Conference. "I: The League of Nations and Disarmament," undated.

23 Bundesarchiv-SAPMO, Hermann Müller NL, N 2200/194, *Programmentwurf der S.P.D. Ein Kommentar* (Stuttgart, 1921), pp. 79–80.

24 Arbetarrörelsens Arkiv och Bibliotek, Stockholm, Hjalmar Branting Papers, 91/4/1/3, untitled circular, 10 June 1919; and "Statuten der Internationale," reproduced in *Kongress-Protokolle der Zweiten Internationale. Ergängzungsheft: Bericht vom zehnten Internationalen Sozialistenkongress in Genf 31. Juli bis 5. August 1920* (Berlin/Bonn, 1979 reprint), pp. 49–55.

25 For example, see Daniel Laqua, "Democratic Politics and the League of Nations: The Labour and Socialist International as a Protagonist of Interwar Internationalism," *Contemporary European History* 24 (2015), pp. 175–92.

26 "Platform of the Communist International, adopted by the first congress," 4 March 1919, reproduced in Jane Degras, ed., *The Communist International 1919–1943*, vol. I (London, 1971), pp. 17–24.

27 "Theses on the basic tasks of the Communist International adopted by the Second Comintern Congress," 19 July 1920, reproduced in Jane Degras, ed., *The Communist International 1919–1943*, vol. I (1971), pp. 113–27.

28 For a good overview, see Arthur S. Lindemann, *The 'Red Years': European Socialism versus Bolshevism, 1919–1921* (Berkeley, CA, 1974).

29 *Bericht über die Reichskonferenz der Unabhängigen Sozialdemoktratischen Partei Deutschlands am 9. und 10. September 1919 im Abgeordnetenhaus zu Berlin* (Glashüten im Taunus, 1975), Stoecker, pp. 23–15; and Verfeuil, "L'unité révolutionnaire," *Le Populaire de Paris*, 5 February 1920, p. 1.

30 Denis Peschanski, ed., *Marcel Cachin. Carnets 1906–1947*. Tome II *1917–1920* (Paris, 1993), 8 August 1920, p. 637; and The National Archives, Kew Garden [hereafter TNA], James Ramsay MacDonald Papers, PRO/30/69/1753/1, 2 and 22 May 1919.

31 *Protokoll über der Reichskonferenz vom 1. bis 3. September 1920 zu Berlin* (Glashüten im Taunus, 1976), Stoecker, pp. 67–9.

32 British Library of Political and Economic Science, London [hereafter BLPES], ILP papers, ILP 5/1920/18, "The Independent Labour Party and the International (A Memorandum for Members," undated.

33 Stoecker, untitled editorial, *Die Freiheit*, no. 381 (13 September 1920), pp. 1–2.

34 TNA, James Ramsay MacDonald Papers, PRO/30/69/1165, Adler to MacDonald, 10 February 1921.

35 A. Stein, "Die Internationale Arbeitsgemeinschaft," *Der Sozialist*, 7, no. 9, (5 March 1921), pp. 197–9.

36 The best history of the Vienna Union remains André Donneur, *Histoire de l'Union des partis socialistes pour l'action internationale (1920–1923)* (Sudbury, 1967).

37 For a concise history of these negotiations, see Robert Sigel, *Die Geschichte der Zweiten Internationale, 1918–1923* (Frankfurt, 1986).

38 IISH, Pietre Jelles Troelstra Papers, 485, "The Reconstruction of the International. Conference ... October 19th and 20th, 1921, between the Bureau of the International Working Union of Socialist Parties (Vienna Union) and the Executive Committee of the British Labour Party," undated.

39 *Protokoll der internationalen sozialistischen Konferenz in Wien vom 22. bis 27. Februar 1921* (Vienna, 1921), "Zum Punkt: Methoden und Organisation des Klassenkampfes," p. 115.

40 See "Sozialistiche Wiedergutmachung," in *Nachrichten der Internationalen Arbeitergemeinschaft Sozialistischer Parteien: Organ der II ½ Internationale* (Glashüten im Taunus, 1973), no. 1 (April 1921), pp. 1–5.

41 "The 'Socialist Review' Outlook," *Socialist Review*, July–September 1919, p. 200. Also see Leo Liebschütz, "Der Völkerbund," *Der Sozialist*, no. 48 (4 December 1920), pp. 968–72.

42 BLPES, ILP Papers, 5/1920/7, Fenner Brockway, "How to End War: I.L.P. View on Imperialism and Internationalism," undated pamphlet, pp. 7–11.

43 *Protokoll der Verhandlungen des Parteitages der Sozialdemokratischen Arbeiterpartei Deutschösterreichs … in Wien vom 25. bis 27. November 1921* (Vienna, 1921), Adler, pp. 200–5.

44 BLPES, ILP Papers, Frances Johnson Correspondence, 1919/97, series II, reel 17, Crispien (USD) to Johnson (ILP), 15 December 1919.

45 For Vienna, see Helmut Gruber, *Red Vienna: Experiment in Working Class Culture, 1919–1934* (Oxford, 1991); and Werner Michael Schwarz et al., *Das Rote Wien 1919–1934: Ideen, Debatten, Praxis* (Vienna, 2019).

46 "Das Problem der Internationale," *Die Freiheit*, no. 505 (19 October 1919), pp. 1–2.

47 IISH, Friedrich Adler Papers, 5, Adler to Karl Kautsky, undated but probably 1919.

48 A good example is Jean Longuet, who played a prominent role in wartime French socialist politics but faded from view during the 1920s. On Longuet's activities, see Gilles Candar, *Jean Longuet (1876–1938): Un internationaliste à l'épreuve de l'histoire* (Rennes, 2007).

Between Order and Disorder: The Case of France

5 Historical Dissent and the Contested Peace of 1919 in France

NORMAN INGRAM

The Great War was the *Ur-Katastrophe* – the mother of all disasters – of the sanguinary twentieth century. Ezra Pound wrote in 1920, in what today are taken to be misogynistic terms, of the First World War as a disillusion, a waste, in which a "myriad" died "For an old bitch gone in the teeth, For a botched civilization."[1] At virtually the same time, John Maynard Keynes, a brilliant economist and member of the British delegation to the Paris Peace Conference, was writing his damning book, *The Economic Consequences of the Peace*, which called the Versailles Treaty with Germany a "Carthaginian Peace."[2]

What are we to make of this "botched civilization," of this "old bitch gone in the teeth" and of the notion of a "Carthaginian Peace"? The words of both Pound and Keynes were portentous. At the very dawn of the interwar period, before the Ruhr Crisis, before Locarno and the Great Depression, long before the triumph of the Nazis and Europe's descent into another war even worse than the first, there was already a sense that the Great War had ended badly, that it had perhaps been fought under false pretences, and that the aftershocks of the cataclysm and of the peace that ended it were going to be severe.

Historians are divided on the impact of the Peace Treaties of 1919, even if there seems to be some recent consensus that more good came of them than bad. Zara Steiner rejects out of hand the idea that Versailles was a "Carthaginian peace," although she admits that it "was, nevertheless, a flawed treaty."[3] Even if it was a victor's peace, she writes that "it was also meant to create a legitimate post-war order that the defeated as well as the victor nations could accept." The legitimization of the post-war order was to occur with the establishment of the League of Nations (LoN), which, "whatever the reservations of the victor powers, held out the promise of a more just international regime which the excluded could join one day."[4] In this sense, 1919 is said to herald a new day in international relations with the development of international law and the creation of the LoN, which for the first decade or so of its existence was a positive force for good. Susan Pedersen and Erez Manela have demonstrated that the LoN's impact on the non-European world was great, albeit perhaps unintended.[5] With regard to Germany and the contentious Versailles Treaty which ended the war with France and the Entente, historians now argue that objectively speaking the Treaty was not nearly as negative for Germany as contemporaries on both sides of the belligerent divide once claimed.[6] Indeed, as Steiner points out, the Treaty of Versailles was much more lenient than the treaties with the other belligerent powers "which were far harsher and more vindictive than the one with Germany."[7]

Other historians continue to argue, however, that the Paris Peace Treaties, and perhaps especially the Versailles Treaty, had an enormously negative impact on the post-1919 European world. Timothy Snyder, for example, blames the violence of the "bloodlands" between Nazi Germany and Stalinist Russia on the fallout from the Great War, and singles out the French for particularly critical treatment, writing that the "Treaty of Versailles indeed contradicted the principle for which the Entente Powers had claimed to fight the war: national self-determination."[8] In Snyder's view, "because the treaty was drafted by moralizing victors, it could easily be attacked as hypocritical." This was the case because the "Entente Powers had declared themselves to be supporters of the liberation of the nations of central Europe."[9]

Robert Gerwarth, too, has been critical of the effect of the Treaties themselves. He examines "Europe's transition from world war to a chaotic 'peace'" and posits that "Even if one deems the recent scholarly 'rehabilitation' of the pre-war land empires exaggerated or overstated, it is difficult to suggest that post-imperial Europe was a better, safer place than it had been in 1914."[10] For Gerwarth, the essential problem in the post-war years was the spread of violence across the vanquished nations. He writes, "In the vanquished states of the Great War, the direction and purpose of internal violence was further guided by the widely held belief that the outcome of the war had remained open until 1918, and that the defeat of the Central Powers was nothing but the result of treason on the home front".[11] Even though he posits 1923 as a kind of end point for this orgy of post-war violence, he writes that after a brief respite from 1923 to 1929, despite many encouraging signs, "by 1929, Europe was already plunging back once again into crisis and violent disorder."[12] The aftershocks of 1914, according to Gerwarth, have continued all the way down to our day in the Arab world and, until recently, in the former Yugoslavia.[13]

Missing from all of this recent analysis of the Peace Treaties of 1919, however, has been a consideration of the impact they had within the victorious nations themselves, as opposed to the vanquished. In the case of France, it is usually argued that the 1920s were about a return to "normalcy" and that France was interested above all in "security" – against Germany, of course.[14] But the provisions of the Versailles Treaty were not universally accepted in France. As Sebastian Döderlein has recently demonstrated, the end of the war in Alsace-Lorraine was anything but a universally acclaimed French victory.[15] In a broader sense, the impact of the Great War and of the treaties which attempted to end it was negative and long lasting in France; the effects of the war and the Paris Peace Conference of 1919 continued to wreak havoc in French politics into the next war. This was largely a function of profound disagreement within the French intellectual and political elite on the origins of the Great War and the attendant questions of war responsibilities and war guilt. The debacle of the Ruhr occupation destroyed the Weimar German economy, but it also came close to inflicting severe damage on the French, too.[16] After the Ruhr, France entered a period of détente with Germany called the Locarno era. This came to a grinding halt with the Nazi seizure of power in January 1933. Seven years later, France fell to the Nazi army and endured four years of the humiliating Vichy regime. In this narrative, France was the hapless victim of German aggression both in 1914 and in 1940. The years from 1919 to 1939 were merely an inter-bellum. One war is linked with the other, and the *fil conducteur* between the two is German aggression.

There is no doubt that one war was intimately connected to the next but perhaps not in the passive sense understood by the analysis above. In some respects, France was the author of its own misfortunes. French political society had just as much trouble dealing with the victory of Versailles as the vanquished nations had in dealing with defeat.

Part of the problem is that the question of the impact of the Treaty of Versailles is *mal posée* in historiographical terms. The analysis of Versailles seems almost to occur in a parallel universe, as something separate and different from an appreciation of the impact of the Great War on European society, almost as if one could objectively deal with it in isolation from the event which brought it into being. From a strictly internationalist viewpoint, one might thus argue that 1919 represents a great triumph for civilization, a tremendous step forwards in the regulation of international affairs, most notably through the creation of the LoN. All of that is true on one level. Viewed in isolation, 1919 represents the enfranchisement of millions of people in central and eastern Europe, the end of empires, the advent of ostensibly democratic regimes in some if not all corners of Europe, and the creation in the LoN of an international body that, in theory at least, was meant to guarantee the peace and bring order to the chaos of international relations. The old-style pacifists rose up as one to congratulate Europe for choosing the Wilsonian path.[17] Charles Richet, Nobel Prize winner in medicine, and Théodore Ruyssen, who was to go on to become the secretary general of the Union internationale des associations pour la Société des Nations – both of them eminent old-style pacifists – exulted in November 1918 as the war ended, writing "Yes, this war is revolutionary. It achieves the work of our ancestors of '92, compromised by Napoleon. In all of central Europe crowns are falling in cascades: stunned, the sovereigns are fleeing the popular wrath."[18] This was the same Republican Ruyssen who, less than three short years earlier, had defended France's alliance with Imperial Russia and the British Empire by arguing that "all things considered, the group of Allied Powers represents, in their struggle against the empires of force, the continuity of the liberal tradition to which the newly-enfranchised nationalities owed their liberation in the course of the nineteenth century ... There is hardly a national movement to which, separately or together, France, England and Russia have not lent the support either of their political influence or of their arms."[19]

Lost in all of this, however, is the fact that 1919 cannot be understood in isolation from 1914. In our rush to periodize, we have a tendency to do just that: to view 1919 and the dawn of the post-period as completely separate from what went before. What went before was four and a half years of appalling blood-letting on various fronts. Our periodization does not end there, however. We also attempt to view the pre-1914 period as somehow conceptually separate from both the war and what followed, even if this is changing gradually with the passage of time and a desire on the part of historians to broaden the focus away from the war itself.[20]

This is why Article 231 of the Versailles Treaty was so important. Unlike much of the treaty, and especially the linkage with the Covenant of the League of Nations, which looked forwards and attempted to create something new and positive, Article 231 looked backwards. The forward-looking components of the treaties, and especially the creation of the LoN, were rendered nugatory by Article 231. The latter opened a twenty-year wound which would not close and which ended up vitiating much of the good that could have come of the Paris Peace Treaties. The past trumped the present and the future; the past could not be transcended.

The linchpin between the two wars is Article 231 of the Versailles Treaty, the famous "war guilt" clause of the treaty. The profound impact of the question of war responsibilities affected French society in general. These effects are to be seen most clearly in a precise, illustrative example, that of the Ligue des droits de l'homme (LDH). The LDH was affected in three notable and portentous ways by the debate on war guilt.

The first effect is that the debate on war guilt and Article 231 almost destroyed the LDH, an organization of enormous political and moral significance in interwar France because it lay at the very heart of the French Republican enterprise. It did this by 1937, long before the Nazi invasion of 1940; this is not a comforting argument to French historians who view the collapse of 1940 as a key moment for the Ligue.[21] The LDH was the locus of the debate on war origins, war guilt, and Article 231. The LDH has suffered from an almost total historiographical neglect until relatively recently.[22] Emmanuel Naquet's massive doctoral thesis at Sciences Po, defended in 2005 and published in book form in 2012, went a long way to rescuing the Ligue from the dustbin of history. Naquet's knowledge of the Ligue is encyclopaedic, but his examination is long on detail and occasionally short on critical analysis. A far more nuanced and critical look at the Ligue is contained in William Irvine's 2007 book which argues that the LDH was as much about venal small-town politics in France as it was about high-flown human rights principles.[23]

Whichever position one ultimately takes on the Ligue, both Naquet and Irvine agree that the LDH was absolutely central to French Republican politics in the period of the two world wars. The Ligue had been founded in 1898 at the very height of the Dreyfus Affair in an attempt to defend the rights of the individual against the miscarriage of justice represented by the French state's conviction of Alfred Dreyfus for treason. From its very inception, it was an organization dedicated to the rights of the individual. By the outbreak of the Great War in August 1914, the LDH had already become an important political and moral voice in French politics. That influence was only to grow during the interwar years. It is difficult to overestimate the importance of the Ligue in the 1920s and 1930s; hardly a government was formed without the significant and sometimes substantial participation of Ligue members as ministers and présidents du Conseil. Irvine reminds us that fully 85 per cent of Léon Blum's first Popular Front government were members of the LDH, and the Popular Front itself might never have been formed had it not been for the unstinting activity of the LDH and especially of its president, Victor Basch.[24] The Ligue was central to the Republican enterprise and Republican self-consciousness in this period. Its story is thus that of the Radical Republic from one war to the next. To use a consciously ironical metaphor, it was the Republican Establishment at prayer.

Secondly, the debate on war origins and war guilt created an on-going, festering historical dissent which led at the end of the 1920s to the emergence of a new style of French pacifism; it was its *fons et origo.* I argued in my book on interwar French pacifism that historical dissent was one of the constitutive elements, an essential catalyst, for the emergence at the very end of the 1920s of what I called *pacifisme nouveau style*, a pacifism which was absolute and sectarian in its relationship with French political society.[25] Unlike its "harmonious" British cousin, to use Martin Ceadel's word, the new style of French pacifism was profoundly riven by debates over the question of unique German war guilt during the Great War.[26] One pole of the debate on the aetiology of French pacifism has been to see it as essentially an elitist proposition originating from the pen of Romain Rolland, whose iconic 1914 essay, "Au-dessus de la mêlée," defined the revolt of the French generation of 1914 well into the 1930s until Rolland himself broke with the new-style pacifism in 1936. The new pacifism owed its advent more, however, to the debates within the LDH on how to end the blood-letting of the Great War during the hecatomb itself than to the impact of Romain Rolland's seminal – and still important – September 1914 article.[27] It was the 1916 debates on "The Conditions for a Lasting Peace" at the Ligue's first wartime congress that laid bare the growing divergences between the erstwhile pacifists-turned-*jusqu'au boutistes* on the one hand, and the incipient new-style pacifists, at this point still in the larva stage, on the other.[28] Unlike its homologue across the Channel in Britain, French pacifism was therefore anything but placid; rather, it was the site of sustained, often acrimonious debate centring on the question of war origins and war guilt in the Great War. The *locus in quo* of these debates, and hence the progenitor of the new pacifism, was the LDH. The LDH was thus the origin of what became the new pacifism by the beginning of the 1930s. Pacifism lay at the very heart of French Republican political society and not on the anarchist and syndicalist fringes, even if these were strongly represented in it. Having said that, pacifism did not kill the LDH as Simon Epstein has argued;[29] rather it was the war guilt debate that hobbled the Ligue. The LDH was transfixed by the debate on war origins and war guilt. The emergence of the new pacifism was a collateral effect of this debate, albeit a fundamentally important one.

Finally, the emergence of this new style of French pacifism, based as it was on a dissenting view of the historical record, had as its collateral effect the creation of an apparently pro-Vichy political position during the Second World War. The motor behind this "apparently" pro-Vichy sentiment was an absolute commitment to peace, making of it an "ethic of ultimate ends" to use Martin Ceadel's explanatory model of British pacifism, as opposed to philo-fascist collaboration or Philippe Burrin's "accommodation."[30] The two wars are thus intimately linked. In the eyes of these quintessential dissenters – "troublemakers," to borrow A.J.P.

Taylor's term, in the British context[31] – the sins of the fathers in 1914 were visited onto the sons in 1940. The war guilt debate provoked a deep suspicion of Russian motives as profound in 1939 as it had been in 1914. The distrust of, and dislike for, Russia is one of the constitutive elements which explains the "drift," to use Philippe Burrin's metaphor, of some parts of the LDH towards support for Vichy during the Second World War. Thus, the evolution of putatively pro-Vichy sentiment also has its origin in the debates on war origins and war guilt in the 1914 war. Just as Robert Gerwarth argues that the Great War did not end in 1918 for the vanquished nations, in like manner, one can argue that the war was also never really over for the French – in 1918 or in 1923 or in 1939. It continued.[32] In many respects, the issues came full circle. Was this the result of philo-fascism or antisemitism on the part of the minority within the LDH? Not really. It was, however, an expression of their political convictions in 1939, their attachment to peace and their by now rock-solid belief that the Second World War was the poisoned fruit of the First.

The Treaty of Versailles thus became the site of intense debate within the LDH, with a strident minority calling repeatedly for revision, especially of Article 231, and a majority which claimed to be opposed to the form of Article 231 and the way it had been arrived at, but which essentially believed it to be substantively correct. The opposition to Versailles had its origin in the debate on war responsibilities within the Ligue from the earliest days of the Great War. The majority did not question the belief that Germany was responsible for the outbreak of the war, while the minority, for its part, believed that responsibilities for the war were shared by all of the belligerents. The minority's position hinged around a highly sceptical view of the Franco–Russian alliance of 1894 coupled with an analysis of the order of general mobilizations during the July Crisis, which seemed to put the lie to the assertions of Raymond Poincaré up to 1921 that the Russian general mobilization was in response to the Austrian mobilization.[33] The following year, Poincaré was obliged to recognize that in fact it was Russia which had been first to order general mobilization.[34] That notwithstanding, the majority within the Ligue, largely under the leadership of Victor Basch, steadfastly maintained that no treaty revision was necessary because the good outweighed the bad by a significant measure in the Versailles Treaty.

Part of the problem was that the French Ligue was cosseted in a particular view of German appreciations of the treaty. These were articulated by the Deutsche Liga für Menschenrechte (DLfM), and especially its president, Hellmut von Gerlach, who maintained that all left-wing, Republican Germans were unanimously agreed on the need to pay reparations and therefore believed in the validity of Article 231. No treaty revision was necessary because the DLfM agreed with the LDH's view of things and claimed that all right-thinking German republicans did as well. The eminent German historian and a man apparently close to the Deutsche Liga at the outset in 1914 (according to Otto Lehmann-Russbüldt),[35] Hans Delbrück, responded that nothing could be further from the truth. It was not just "Hitler and the reactionaries" who were opposed to Versailles, but the "vast majority of the German people." Delbrück wrote that von Gerlach's "assertion" to the contrary was "not merely an error, but an error of pernicious consequences."[36] The error was compounded by the LDH's acceptance of its validity, a position completely at variance with the truth of what was actually happening in Germany.[37] French political society was thus lulled into the comforting, but mistaken, belief that all of left-wing, Republican Germany accepted the French view of war origins and war guilt.

The extent to which positions taken during the Great War continued to inform Ligue views in the 1920s can be seen with regard to other issues as well. The Polish question is a good example. Until the Russian Revolution of 1917, it had been virtually impossible for good French Republicans to express criticism of Russian policy in Poland because to do so would have been to criticize the conduct of France's ally, the Russian Empire. Some French Republicans were quite conscious of this intellectual anomaly, or of what some might call a glaring political inconsistency. The problem of Poland was debated at length at the first wartime congress of the LDH in November 1916. Many were the voices which condemned French hypocrisy on the Polish question in 1916. None of that prevented the Ligue's secretary general, Henri Guernut, from continuing to claim in 1928, long after the war's end, that the LDH had always fulsomely and courageously defended Poland, even (and especially) against France's Triple Entente ally, Imperial Russia.[38] This was clearly not the case, and in 1916 the best the Ligue could do was follow the sage advice of the feminist journalist Séverine and simply hold its nose.[39] After 1917, and especially with the entry of the United States into the war, it became possible to frame the fight as one to "make the world safe for democracy," rather than a crusade to rid the world of Prussian militarism, which is what it had been at the outset.[40] After the end of the war, in the wake of the Paris Peace Treaties, the Ligue liked to comfort itself with the illusion that it had always defended Polish independence, but this was clearly not the case.

Victor Basch was already complaining by 1922 that at every Ligue congress since 1916 the members of the minority had managed to get the question of war responsibilities discussed.[41] That remained the case for the rest of the interwar period. Repeated attempts at Ligue congresses to get the LDH to come out in favour of treaty revision all failed, but by increasingly small margins, until finally, at its December 1932 congress, the Ligue debated explicitly the issue of the controversy over the treaties. The Jesuitical (pardon the irony) approach of the majority is to be seen in Victor Basch's statement that "If we admit that Germany and Austria are guilty and solely guilty, the guilty plea that was torn from Germany under the threat of renewed hostilities constitutes a flagrant injustice. It is because it is unjust that we have opposed article 231. And we have not waited until today's session to declare that France would do the honourable thing if it took the initiative of erasing from the peace treaty an article that does no honour to those who imposed it on a vanquished enemy."[42]

It was the *forme* and not the *fond* of Versailles to which Basch and the Ligue's majority objected, whereas for the minority it was an article of faith that responsibilities for the outbreak of war in August 1914 were shared and that much of that responsibility lay with the Franco–Russian alliance. Basch and the Ligue's majority steadfastly refused to countenance any deviation from the interpretation of war origins first enunciated by Basch in the pages of the *Bulletin officiel de la Ligue des droits de l'homme* in 1915; the short book that came out of these articles became the Ligue's *vade mecum* on the war guilt question right through the interwar period.[43] From 1915 down to 1924 and the aftermath of the Ruhr debacle, the Ligue's minority struggled to make its voice heard. It was disdainfully dismissed because its leading lights were by and large not card-carrying intellectuals. As Basch wrote in the summer of 1922, "how does one even discuss with men who, visibly, are moved only by passion, and who lack an elementary preparation for this sort of research?"; in his view, it was a "waste of time."[44] By the end of the 1920s, however, Basch and the majority could no longer ignore the rising tide of criticism directed at the Ligue from within by men and women who were every bit as "intellectual" as Basch. People such as Félicien Challaye, Léon Emery, Georges Pioch, and René Gerin led the charge, providing leadership to a second wave of dissenters who demanded outright revision of the Treaty of Versailles in the name of truth and France's honour. René Gerin, in particular, brought the war guilt/war origins issue to broad public attention with the publication of a forensic debate on war origins with Raymond Poincaré, the president of the Republic during the war years.[45]

Two years later, Challaye, Pioch, and Gerin all heaped scorn on the "new" interpretation of Article 231 that was articulated in November 1931 by Pierre Renouvin and Camille Bloch; according to Renouvin and Bloch, Article 231 was nothing more than a limited civil law recognition by Germany of its obligation to pay reparations for damages caused to France by virtue of Germany's aggression.[46] Challaye excoriated the Renouvin/Bloch thesis at a meeting of the Ligue's central committee, saying that it was just "a way of jettisoning some ballast now that research by all impartial historians has established the responsibilities of all of the statesmen leading the peoples in July 1914."[47] The debate spread far and wide, with an essay by René Gerin published in the house journal of the German Foreign Office's war-guilt section.[48]

The minority did not win the day in 1932. It came much closer in 1935 when it received over 40 per cent of the vote in a debate on the general orientation of the Ligue. In 1935, even Victor Basch seemed prepared to use the term "revision" rather than merely "adjustment" of the treaties. By this point, however, the Nazis had been in power for well over two years. Two years later, in 1937, the Ligue foundered on the shoals of how best to defend democracy and peace in a debate that was deeply coloured by memories of 1914. After that, the Ligue went into a freefall so that when the Nazi barbarians arrived at the gates in May 1940, they found a Ligue half dead by its own hand. Informing the Ligue's perceptions of the crisis affecting France and Europe in the late 1930s was the memory of the Great War. Georges Pioch, a prominent member of the pacifist minority, justified his political stance of opposition to the Ligue majority's position on the Moscow Purge Trials and the Spanish Civil War by direct reference to the Great War and the peace that ended it. The majority believed that from a legal standpoint there was nothing untoward about the show trials and as far as Spain was concerned that France should intervene in the Civil War in support of the Republican side. Pioch's political position of 1938 found its justification through the lens of 1914:

> And I say that equally for the 51 million men who, from August 1914 to November 1918, exhausted themselves against one another in order finally to leave 12 million cadavers on European soil. How were they rewarded for their enormous sacrifice? When I look at what has become of this Europe twenty years after they slaughtered one another, this Europe for which many of them thought they were giving liberty, law, justice and real peace, I say that they fell to their deaths drunk with the idea that they were serving what they believed to be – and they were right – the highest and clearest virtues. In reality, they died for nothing ... Yes, died for nothing, since the peoples prove today through their folly and their docility that they do not merit the monstrous sacrifice made for them.[49]

If the members of the Ligue's by now genuinely pacifist minority could not see the enormous danger posed by Hitler at the end of the 1930s, equally the LDH's majority could not see how its positions before 1933 had helped to neuter the Ligue's understanding of the German situation after the Great War. An impermeable memory membrane prevented the majority from seeing that its policies towards Germany from 1914 to 1933 were part of the problem; for it, the Nazi seizure of power and especially the politics of the Popular Front were all that counted. The majority could not see that its political positions to some extent had helped to create Nazism. For the minority, on the other hand, there was no understanding of 1933 as a profound political caesura. They could not understand that while their political positions might have had some validity up to January 1933, the same could not be said thereafter.

Since 1915, and increasingly after the Paris Peace Conference of 1919, the LDH's minority was of the clear belief that the Great War had been anything but a morally pure and intellectually coherent crusade. The minority had argued that case in France with the war in full swing. The Great War had never been one based on principles in the critical view of the minority – despite the pious handwringing over the violation of Belgian neutrality. Rather, it had been a war based on great power, strategic considerations, dynastic rivalries, and competing economic interests. The problem with the minority's analysis was that it failed to take into account the meaning and impact of the Nazi seizure of power in January 1933. Hitler was no "ordinary German," and thus, even if the minority position might have been right in the 1920s, the advent of Hitler rendered that political position irrelevant in 1933. The end of the war created disorder, rather than order, in European politics, as much for the victorious as for the vanquished.

How are we to understand this obstinate refusal to see that the post-1933 years were dangerously different from the 1920s? It is because the same *fil conducteur* – the war guilt problem – unites them. Mathias Morhardt wrote to his dissenter colleague Georges Demartial in 1936, in a letter which was published under a title explicitly linking Versailles, Locarno, and the Rhineland crisis of 1936: "For the past twenty-two years, you and I have suffered an unspeakable moral and intellectual martyrdom. The atmosphere of imposture in which we live has poisoned all our joys. And we no longer have before us the hope of seeing the fog of hatreds dissipate, in which minds and spirits are so furiously agitating. This is because we are expiating the honour of belonging to a class of Frenchmen that is far too small. We are those, in effect, who suffer more from an injustice committed by France than from an injustice committed against her."[50]

NOTES

1 "Hugh Selwyn Mauberley," in Ezra Pound, *Selected Poems*, edited with an introduction by T.S. Eliot (London: Faber and Faber, 1928), p. 176. It is open to question whether Pound was referring here to a female dog, which would be consonant with the usage of "bitch" at the time in the United Kingdom, or whether he meant something more inflammatory. In a 1934 letter to the British classicist Dr. W.H.D. Rouse, he ruminated on the tendency in America to take umbrage at the use of certain terms such as "bitch" and "cock." See Ezra Pound to W.H.D. Rouse, Rapallo, 30 December 1934, in *The Selected Letters of Ezra Pound, 1907–1941* (New York: New Directions, 1971), pp. 262–4.

2 See John Maynard Keynes, *The Economic Consequences of the Peace* (New York: Harcourt, Brace and Howe, 1920).

3 Zara Steiner, *The Lights that Failed: European International History, 1919–1933* (Oxford: Oxford University Press, 2005), pp. 67–8. See also Carole Fink, "The Peace Settlement, 1919–1939," in John Horne, ed., *A Companion to World War I* (Chichester: Wiley-Blackwell, 2010), pp. 543–57.

4 Steiner, *Lights*, p. 69.

5 Erez Manela, *The Wilsonian Moment: Self-Determination and the International Origins of Anticolonial Nationalism* (Oxford: Oxford University Press, 2007), and Susan Pedersen, *The Guardians: The League of Nations and the Crisis of Empire* (Oxford: Oxford University Press, 2015).

6 A particularly trenchant expression of this thesis may be found in Gerhard L. Weinberg, "The Defeat of Germany in 1918 and the European Balance of Power," in Gerhard L. Weinberg, ed., *Germany, Hitler and World War II* (Cambridge: Cambridge University Press, 1996), pp. 11–22. Steiner agrees with Weinberg. See Steiner, *Lights*, pp. 67–70, 606. Weinberg's conclusions find an echo in a rather tendentious book by Jürgen Tampke, *A Perfidious Distortion of History: The Versailles Peace Treaty and the Success of the Nazis* (Melbourne: Scribe, 2017). Dissenting French voices which condemned the Versailles Treaty are examined at length in Norman Ingram, *The War Guilt Problem and the Ligue des droits de l'homme, 1914–1944* (Oxford: Oxford University Press, 2019).

7 Steiner, *Lights*, p. 608.

8 Timothy Snyder, *The Bloodlands: Europe between Hitler and Stalin* (New York: Perseus Books, 2010), p. 8. Snyder's very first sentence (p. 1) reads "The origins of the Nazi and Soviet regimes, and of their encounter in the bloodlands, lie in the First World War of 1914–1918." Steiner agrees that the application of the principle of self-determination "never clearly defined, was selectively applied." It was "violated or compromised when the strategic interests of the victor powers were engaged, and was not applied to the defeated nations." See Steiner, *Lights*, p. 607.

9 Snyder, *Bloodlands*, 7–8.
10 Robert Gerwarth, *The Vanquished: Why the First World War Failed to End, 1917–1923* (London: Allen Lane, 2016), p. 7.
11 Gerwarth, *Vanquished*, p. 255.
12 Gerwarth, *Vanquished*, p. 249.
13 Gerwarth, *Vanquished*, pp. 266–7.
14 This leitmotiv continued into the 1930s. See Maurice Vaïsse, *Sécurité d'abord: la politique française en matière de désarmement, 9 décembre 1930–17 avril 1934* (Paris: A Pedone, 1981). For the earlier period, cf. Peter Jackson, *Beyond the Balance of Power: France and the Politics of National Security in the Era of the First World War* (Cambridge: Cambridge University Press, 2013).
15 See Sebastian Döderlein, "Un pivot de l'histoire? – La société alsacienne-lorraine et les sorties ambiguës de la Première Guerre mondiale (1918–1919)," PhD thesis, Concordia University, Montreal, 2016.
16 See, for example, Sally Marks's comments in her essay "Poincaré-la-Peur: France and the Ruhr Crisis of 1923," in Martin S. Alexander and Kenneth Mouré, eds., *Crisis and Renewal in Twentieth-Century France* (New York and Oxford: Berghahn Books, 2002), p. 38.
17 What I call the "old style pacifists" were those for whom pacifism was a liberal, juridical, internationalist proposition. Their roots (in France at least) stretched back to the 1880s (if not earlier). See Part I ("Pacifisme ancien style: or the Pacifism of the Pedagogues") of Ingram, *The Politics of Dissent: Pacifism in France, 1919–1939* (Oxford: Clarendon Press, 1991 and 2011), pp. 19–118.
18 Charles Richet and Théodore Ruyssen, "La Fin de la guerre," *La Paix par le droit* 28/21–22 (November 1918), p. 330. Less than three months later, however, Richet seemed a little doubtful about the long-term effects of the end of the war. In a letter addressed to Woodrow Wilson, he wrote "il faut que vous reveniez bientôt, le plus tôt possible [emphasis in the original], pour que votre idéal, qui est le nôtre, malgré l'opposition de la routine et des vieilles théories, triomphe enfin. Revenez pour faire régner cette paix bienfaisante et juste." Charles Richet to Woodrow Wilson, Paris, 13 February 1919 in Woodrow Wilson Papers, Library of Congress, Series 5D, Reel 331. I am indebted to Carl Bouchard for drawing this letter to my attention.
19 Théodore Ruyssen, "Le Problème des nationalités I. La Guerre mondiale et le principe des nationalités," *Bulletin* 16, no. 1 (January 1916), p. 6.
20 In this regard, see the essays in Robert Gerwarth and Erez Manela, eds., *Empires at War, 1911–1923* (Oxford: Oxford University Press, 2014).
21 For a taste of the reaction to the views of Ingram, Cylvie Claveau, and Simon Epstein on the Ligue, one can do no better than to consult Emmanuel Naquet, "Le Péril et la riposte," in Gilles Manceron and

Emmanuel Naquet, eds., *Être Dreyfusard, hier et aujourd'hui* (Rennes: Presses universitaires de Rennes, 2009), pp. 301–28.

22 Witness John Sweets's comments on a paper on the Ligue des droits de l'homme which I gave at the 2005 Stanford meeting of the Society for French Historical Studies. Sweets said that he had no compunction at all in admitting that he had never heard of the Ligue.

23 See Emmanuel Naquet, "La Ligue des droits de l'homme: une association en politique (1898–1940)," Thèse de doctorat, Institut d'Etudes Politiques de Paris, 2005, 5 vols.; Emmanuel Naquet, *Pour l'Humanité: La Ligue des droits de l'homme de l'affaire Dreyfus à la défaite de 1940* (Rennes: Presses universitaires de Rennes, 2014); and William D. Irvine, *Between Justice and Politics: the Ligue des droits de l'homme, 1898–1945* (Stanford: Stanford University Press, 2007).

24 See Irvine, *Between Justice and Politics*, p. 164, n. 10. Cf. Emmanuel Naquet, "Ligue des droits de l'homme," iv., Annexe 20 "Liste des Ligueurs parlementaires sous la Troisième République," pp. 1076–107, and Annexe 21 "Liste des Ligueurs ministres sous la Troisième République," pp. 1108–31. See also Irvine, "Politics of Human Rights: A Dilemma for the Ligue des Droits de l'Homme," in *Historical Reflections/Réflexions historiques* 20, no. 1 (Winter 1994), p. 11.

25 See Ingram, *Politics of Dissent*, pp. 122–5.

26 Cf. Martin Ceadel, "The Peace Movement between the Wars: Problems of Definition," in Richard Taylor and Nigel Young, eds., *Campaigns for Peace: British Peace Movements in the Twentieth Century* (Manchester: Manchester University Press, 1987), p. 75.

27 Romain Rolland, "Au-dessus de la mêlée," *Journal de Genève*, 15 September 1914.

28 See Norman Ingram, "The Crucible of War: the Ligue des Droits de l'Homme and the Debate on the 'Conditions for a Lasting Peace' in 1916," *French Historical Studies* 39, no. 2 (April 2016), pp. 347–71. The stenographic record of the Ligue's 1916 debates on the contours of the future peace may be found in *Le Congrès de 1916 de la Ligue des droits de l'homme. Compte-rendu sténographique. 1er et 2me Novembre 1916* (Paris: Ligue des droits de l'homme, 1917), especially pp. 45–239.

29 See Simon Epstein, *Les Dreyfusards sous l'occupation* (Paris: Albin Michel, 2001).

30 See Norman Ingram, "Pacifism, the Fascist Temptation, and the Ligue des droits de l'homme," in Samuel Kalman and Sean Kennedy, eds., *The French Right between the Wars: Political and Intellectual Movements from Conservatism to Fascism* (Oxford and New York: Berghahn Books, 2014), pp. 81–94. For Ceadel's analysis of British pacifism, based on Max Weber's philosophy of religion, see Martin Ceadel, *Pacifism in Britain, 1914–1945: The Defining of a Faith* (Oxford: Clarendon Press, 1980).

31 See A.J.P. Taylor, *The Troublemakers: Dissent over Foreign Policy, 1792–1939* (London: Hamish Hamilton, 1957).

32 On the French "sortie de guerre," see particularly Bruno Cabanes, *La Victoire endeuillée. La sortie de guerre des soldats français (1918–1920)* (Paris: Seuil, 2004).

33 See Raymond Poincaré, *Les Origines de la Guerre (Conférences prononcées à la Société des Conférences en 1921)* (Paris: Plon, 1921), p. 261.

34 Raymond Poincaré to Ferdinand Buisson, Paris, 9 August 1922 in La Contemporaine/Archives de la Ligue des droits de l'homme [ALDH]/ FΔRés 798/9 Commission des Origines de la Guerre Folder 1.

35 See Otto Lehmann-Russbüldt, *Der Kampf der Deutschen Liga für Menschenrechte (vormals Bund neues Vaterland) für den Weltfrieden, 1914–1927* (Berlin: Hensel & Co Verlag, 1927), p. 6.

36 Despite the fact that Delbrück was clearly on the side of those Germans who were opposed to Article 231, the conversations he had in 1922 with the then vice-president of the Ligue Victor Basch were of great interest to the Gestapo and the Einsatzstab Reichleiter Rosenberg (ERR) when they seized the Ligue's papers in June 1940 after the fall of France. Dr. Gerd Wunder of the ERR wrote: "In den Akten des Juden Victor Basch befinden sich auch Papiere und Briefe, die die Diskussion zwischen Victor Basch und Hans Delbrück über die Kriegsschuldfrage am 12.6.1922 betreffen. Die beiderseitigen Niederschriften und die Manuskripte der späteren Veröffentlichungen über die Diskussion liegen dem Material bei. Delbrück gehörte zu jenen 'nationalen' Historikern des wilhelminischen Deutschland, die nach dem Umsturz sehr rasch den Anschluss an die liberale Demokratie fanden. In diesem Zusammenhang mag der herzliche Ton seines Briefwechsels mit dem Juden von Interesse sein." See Dr. Gerd Wunder, "Aktennotiz: Betr. Unterredung Basch-Delbrück," Paris, 17 February 1941, in La Contemporaine/ALDH/FΔRés 798/9 Commission des Origines de la Guerre Chemise 2.

37 Hans Delbrück's comments are contained in a letter to the Ligue, dated 9 September 1923. See Hans Delbrück and Hellmut von Gerlach, "Correspondance: sur les responsabilités de la guerre," in *Cahiers* 23/21 (10 November 1923), p. 504.

38 In 1928, the Ligue's secretary general, Henri Guernut, was still proclaiming to anybody who would listen that during the Great War France had been "la première, et un moment la seule, pour soutenir contre toutes les timidités la thèse de l'indépendance [polonaise]." See Henri Guernut, "Pour la Pologne. Ce qu'a fait la Ligue pendant la guerre," *Cahiers* 28, no. 21 (30 August 1928), p. 483.

39 See the comments by Séverine in the debate on "Les Conditions d'une paix durable," in *Le Congrès de 1916 de la Ligue des droits de l'homme. Compte-rendu*

sténographique. 1er et 2me Novembre 1916 (Paris: Ligue des droits de l'homme, 1917), p. 214. The entire debate extends from page 72 to 239.

40 See Norman Ingram, *The War Guilt Problem and the Ligue des droits de l'homme, 1914–1944* (Oxford: Oxford University Press, 2019), pp. 33, 48–51, 67–8. The issue of Poland remained a concern for the Ligue right through the interwar period.

41 Victor Basch, "Les Responsabilités de la guerre: discussion Delbrück-Basch," in La Contemporaine/ALDH/FΔRés. 798/9 Chemise 1, n.d. (1922), p. 2.

42 Victor Basch in *Le Congrès national de 1932. Compte-rendu sténographique. Paris, 26–28 Décembre 1932* (Paris: Ligue des droits de l'homme, 1933), p. 216.

43 See Victor Basch, "La Ligue des droits de l'homme et la guerre," *Bulletin officiel de la Ligue des droits de l'homme* 15, no. 2 (1 May 1915), pp. 65–175; and Basch, *La Guerre de 1914 et le droit* (Paris: Ligue des droits de l'homme, 1915).

44 See Victor Basch, "Les Responsabilités de la Guerre: Discussion Basch-Delbrück," p. 3, typescript in La Contemporaine/ALDH/FΔRés 798/9 Chemise 1, Commission sur les origines de la guerre. This is a long memorandum written by Basch after his meeting with Professor Hans Delbrück in June 1922.

45 See René Gerin and Raymond Poincaré, *Les Responsabilités de la Guerre: Quatorze questions par René Gerin, ancien élève de l'Ecole normale supérieure, agrégé des lettres, Quatorze Réponses par Raymond Poincaré de l'Académie Française* (Paris: Payot, 1930).

46 Camille Bloch and Pierre Renouvin, "Libres opinions. A propos des réparations. L'article 231 du Traité de Versailles," *Cahiers* 32, no. 15 (20 June 1932), pp. 339–45. This article was originally published on 15 November 1931 in *Le Temps.* It was published in Berlin even before it had been reprinted in the Cahiers. See Pierre Renouvin and Camille Bloch, "Die Entstehung und die Bedeutung des Artikels 231 des Versailler Vertrages," in *Die Berliner Monatshefte für internationale Aufklärung,* IX (December 1931), pp. 1166–87. Alfred von Wegerer, the director of the *Berliner Monatshefte,* responded to Bloch and Renouvin in a long essay. See Alfred von Wegerer, "Bemerkungen zu dem Aufsatz im 'Le Temps' vom 15. November 'Le Traité de Versailles et les Réparations' von Camille Bloch und Pierre Renouvin," in *Die Berliner Monatshefte für internationale Aufklärung,* IX (December 1931), pp. 1188–209.

47 "Comité central. Extraits," *Cahiers* 32, no. 17 (10 July 1932), p. 401.

48 See René Gerin, "Les Professeurs de la Sorbonne et l'Article 231 du Traité de Versailles," in *Die Berliner Monatshefte für internationale Aufklärung,* IX (December 1931), pp. 1210–12.

49 Georges Pioch, intervention in the debate on the Rapport moral, in "Le Congrès national de 1938," Avignon, 16–18 July 1938, unpublished and incomplete minutes in La Contemporaine/ALDH/FΔRés 798/16 Avignon 1938, typescript p. 227.

50 Mathias Morhardt to Georges Demartial, Capbreton, 19 March 1936, in La Contemporaine/ALDH/FΔRés 798/7 Correspondance Morhardt. This letter was published under the title "Le Respect des traités" in *Le Barrage*, 26 March 1936.

6 Not So Republican after All? The Ambiguous End of the Great War in Alsace-Lorraine, 1918–1919

SEBASTIAN DÖDERLEIN

When in November and December 1918, victorious French troops entered Alsace-Lorraine, the "lost provinces" were restored to France. Official French propaganda immediately pointed to the joy among the population that had remained faithful to the motherland during forty-seven years of German occupation. The reason for this was obvious: any possible French scepticism about the Alsatian-Lorrainers and the "bochisme" (a derogatory term for German culture) that had supposedly been injected into them had to be eliminated. Propaganda showed French troops being greeted enthusiastically by the local population and peddled the slogan "unforgettable moments for Alsace-Lorraine," focusing on the terms "return," "deliverance," and "liberation."[1] Seven months later, at the signing of the Treaty of Versailles, the Allies confirmed the return of the lost provinces to the motherland and therefore the definitive end to the war in Alsace-Lorraine.

Since then, this image has remained both in historiography and in collective French memory and has virtually never been challenged. The end of the war in Alsace-Lorraine is, in this sense, clearly the story of a *liberation* and therefore purely and uniquely a French story. At first glance, this idea seems problematic. The differing interests, the differing approaches, and the lack of communication between schools of historiography – particularly German and French – are what has led to this distorted perspective. In studying public opinion in Alsace-Lorraine both before and after the armistice, I will argue that we need to rethink the end-of-war experience, lending nuance to its unanimous, unequivocal character. Contrary to the enduring view, in terms of the local population, widespread hatred of German immigrants and general euphoria about the liberation hardly existed.

Separate Histories of Alsace-Lorraine

Although libraries are filled with literature about the history of Alsace-Lorraine since 1870/1871, in France, in Germany, and elsewhere, approaches and interests fundamentally differ.

In German historiography, Alsace-Lorraine disappeared completely from the scientific lens after 1945. With a few exceptions, such as a 1961 article by Hans-Ulrich Wehler,[2] research on the history of the *Reichsland* (1871–1918) developed essentially beginning in the 1980s, in particular with the work of Hermann Hiery and Michael Essig. Against the backdrop of German reunification in 1990 and until the present day, German scholars have mainly been concerned with the constitutional status of Alsace-Lorraine and the debate around its incorporation in the *Reich.*[3] And only recently did cultural history discover Alsace-Lorraine and its traditions as a field of study, emphasizing the regional identity of the *Reichsland* – both unique and torn between France and Germany.[4] In almost all of this work, 11 November 1918 represents a veritable break. German historiography of Alsace-Lorraine does not consider the interwar period, nor the civilian experience of the end of the war.[5]

It is different in France because French historiography looks only at the post-war period. Particularly since the fiftieth anniversary of the armistice, new studies, such as by Robert Heitz, Job de Roince, and Jacques Granier, reinforce the image of the jubilant welcome reserved for French troops by the population of Alsace-Lorraine in November and December 1918.[6] In 1969, Christian Baechler was the first to argue that, while the joy of liberation was real and universal, that changed quickly when Paris imposed a centralized French administration on the former *Reichsland*, increasing the impetus for an Alsatian independence movement.[7] Since then, Alsace-Lorraine's difficult transition to France in the 1920s has been at the centre of French historiography,[8] with many local and hyperlocal studies conducted to date. With the 100th anniversary of the armistice, it has been almost exclusively Alsatian and Lorrainer historians who have shown an interest in the provinces, resulting in broader and multidisciplinary approaches, such as *Les Alsaciens-Lorrains dans la Grande Guerre* by Jean-Noël and Francis Grandhomme.[9] But despite certain multidisciplinary approaches and recent cross-border projects, both sides of the Rhine continue to work pretty much in a vacuum. The new *Historial* at Hartmannswillerkopf, which opened in 2017, appears to be more of a Franco-Alsatian institution than a Franco-German one.[10] And in 2018, a conference in Strasbourg entitled "From awe for the French flag to Alsatian discomfort – the reversion of Alsace to France (1918–24)" ("De l'éblouissement tricolore au malaise alsacien: Le retour de l'Alsace à la France [1918–24]") showed yet again that, in French historiography, 11 November and the unanimous joy of the population is a starting point.

In fact, the "memorable moments" and the photos of soldiers marching into cities in Alsace-Lorraine are a clear site of French memory, as Jean-Marie Mayeur points out in *Lieux de mémoire* by Pierre Nora. However, Étienne François and Hagen Schulze did not include Alsace-Lorraine as a site of German memory in their *Deutsche Erinnerungsorte.*[11]

This is in addition to Anglo-American historiography, where the issue of Alsace-Lorraine nationalism and regional identity – at once unique and ambivalent – has been attracting the interest of researchers since the 1970s, following the example of Dan Silverman.[12] In the past 20 years, many important studies have been published, among them by Stephen Harp, Elizabeth Vlossak, and, recently, Alison Carrol.[13] This is understandable, given that Alsace-Lorraine holds a unique place in European history and more importantly in the French national psyche. Between 1871 and 1945, the dominant nationalism in the region would change four times, following victories and defeats in a succession of wars, making Alsace-Lorraine a symbol and a victim of nationalist rivalries. The Anglo-American approach is particularly interesting, to the extent that it emphasizes the complex reality of Alsatian-Lorrainian society. However, by concentrating on the issue of identity over a long period (1871–1939/45), it falls rather short in providing a response to the end-of-war experience. Laird Boswell's important article on the purge trials between 1918 and 1920, and Tara Zahra's article on national classification in post-war Alsace-Lorraine and Czechoslovakia contribute a lot to our understanding of the difficulties of restoring peace in these provinces. While both authors argue rightly that parts of Alsace were not overwhelmingly enthusiastic about the return to France, they do not engage with the question of the end-of-war experience in detail. No larger study has yet analysed in detail the complex ways the *sortie de guerre* was actually perceived by the inhabitants of this highly contested region.[14]

At first glance, the idea of an entire population drunk on joy about the armistice seems simplistic. But our understanding of the Alsace-Lorraine population is biased by the French policy of assimilation following the armistice. Starting at the end of 1917, Jules Jeanneney, deputy secretary of state and radical socialist figure with a Jacobin and anti-clerical reputation, assumed responsibility for affairs in Alsace-Lorraine. With no knowledge of the particularities of the region, his ultimate goal was the unconditional assimilation of the provinces to the French nation.[15]

Yet the months following the armistice would show how reuniting the lost provinces with the motherland was a complicated, painful process. Elated by the novels of René Bazin and Maurice Barrès,[16] the French wanted to reunite with Hansi's Alsace-Lorraine[17] and expected to welcome two martyr provinces frozen in time, grateful to their liberators. While propaganda continually emphasized the patriotism of the Alsatian-Lorrainers, military reports suggested that once liberated, the provinces should be occupied by French rather than American troops, who might be surprised by the Germanic character of the region. They also held that the occupation should begin immediately following the armistice to prevent any calls for a referendum by citizens.[18] This was justified because an American intelligence service report recognized the real possibility that a referendum could favour Germany and show opposition against French annexation.[19]

Based on the concept of the "single, indivisible nation," the French policy of rigorous assimilation and massive expulsions of a large part of the German population immediately after the armistice must be understood against the principle of self-determination propagated by the American president Woodrow Wilson: with the provinces reverting to France, the question of Alsace-Lorraine would not be the topic of international discussion during the Paris Peace Conference.[20]

According to words attributed to a French bureaucrat upon arriving in Strasbourg, the French government sought simply to align the reunited provinces with the rest of the country: "we closed the book of 1870, and we open it on page 1918."[21] And indeed they followed what medievalist Charles Haskins recommended: "The restoration of Alsace-Lorraine to France, with the boundaries of 1870, may be assured as settled by the acceptance of President Wilson's eighth point and of the terms of the Armistice of 11 November. No discussion necessary."[22]

With the signature of the Treaty of Versailles, the fate of the provinces – vital for France since 1871 and confirmed by the American president's Fourteen Points on 8 January 1918 – was sealed: Alsace-Lorraine was French – and so were its people. However, a closer look at the population of Alsace-Lorraine at the beginning of the twentieth century shows that the simplified vision that has been advanced to date does not hold up to scrutiny.

The Population of Alsace-Lorraine during the Great War

Following the annexation of 1871, the Treaty of Frankfurt allowed Alsatian-Lorrainers to leave and settle in France. Some 5 per cent of the Alsatian population, particularly members of the wealthy intellectual and industrial bourgeoisie, professors, jurists, and military men, left the *Reichsland*.[23] At the same time, the *Altdeutsche* (Germans from other parts of the Reich) immigrated: first German military men and bureaucrats, then doctors, dentists, lawyers, etc., mainly from the neighbouring Rheinland, where customs and behaviour were similar to those of the Alsatian-Lorrainers. This immigration would stop only on the eve of the First World War. According to the regional bureau of statistics – the Office de statistique d'Alsace et de Lorraine – around 200,000 *Altdeutsche* (12 per cent of the population) settled in Alsace-Lorraine.[24] In parts of annexed Lorraine that were home to major garrisons (Metz, Bitche), the influx was particularly strong. In 1905, a quarter of the population was German – 50 per cent of the population of Metz and even 53 per cent of the population of Thionville. In Alsace, 46 per cent of German immigrants settled in Strasbourg. On the eve of the conflict, a third of the city's population was of German origin.[25]

At the same time, the integration of Germans who immigrated after 1871 to Alsatian and Lorrainer society seems to have been much more widespread than traditionally believed. According to François Uberfill – along with Alfred Wahl, one of the only scholars to take an interest in the German population of Alsace-Lorraine – mixed marriages were common. From 1871 to 1914, they represented between 18 per cent and 25 per cent of all weddings celebrated in a given year in the *Reichsland.*[26]

At the time of the armistice, over 300,000 citizens of German origin lived in the Imperial Territory, many of them born there. Many Alsatian-Lorrainers had family ties on the other side of the Rhine. After almost fifty years of cohabitation, the native population and German immigrants mixed much more than French historiography suggests. Over the years, annexation had become a reality, and people grew accustomed to it. According to a report from the local postal censorship service, the Contrôle Postal de Strasbourg, even Francophile Alsatians noted that the "German yoke was dragging on: one had to keep living; there were many mixed marriages."[27] Particularly among the younger generations of Alsatians, Lorrainers, or *Altdeutsch*, many had no ties to France, a country to which they had never been.

Anticipating the End of the War

French historiography, constructed primarily from private pro-French sources, generally suggests that Alsatian-Lorrainian society was clearly divided along national lines: while the Germans feared the end of the war, native-born Alsatian-Lorrainers eagerly awaited French victory. Aptly illustrating this disparity, on 5 September 1918, Jeanne Haas noted in her diary: "it is raining and grey, almost as grey as the immigrants' faces that grow longer as ours relax and attempt to hide the boundless joy bursting from our hearts for the past few weeks."[28]

Yet a detailed analysis of public opinion, including official and private German sources often ignored by French historians, reveals more nuance. It appears that clear preferences based on nationality were barely detectable. According to Rudolf Schwander, the former mayor of Strasbourg and as of October 1918 the *Statthalter* of the *Reichsland Elsaß-Lothringen*, opinions expressed by the public were very much divided: while some were convinced of a German victory, others were betting on France. But everyone remained cautious and adopted a wait-and-see approach.[29] The same month, Auguste Zundel, a committed Francophile Alsatian, was preparing to celebrate, "while others were showing … scepticism about a French victory and the ensuing return of Alsace-Lorraine to France." Of course, one must assume that towards the end of the conflict, the majority of *Altdeutsche* supported Berlin's statements regarding the independence or neutrality of the *Reichsland.* But, as Zundel suggests, even some natives, particularly in urban areas, welcomed the possibility, "the financial advantages of this solution being fairly attractive."[30] At the end of October, the Mulhouse German military secret police noted that "the workers don't care about the political future of Alsace-Lorraine. The desire for peace was more important. Most believed that their situation would not change under a French government."[31] In Metz, on the other hand, most workers seemed to have been convinced that Alsace-Lorraine would become independent.[32]

Among members of the clergy, the debate about the future of the provinces was obviously dominated by a fear of state secularism.[33] During the final months of the war, an increase in these concerns could be detected, leading to a reinforcement of the campaign in defence of denominational schools.[34] People in the small communes were particularly sensitive to the religious question and concerned about the position the French government would adopt with respect to the clergy. Virtually every week, the Contrôle Postal de Belfort noted "religious fears."[35] Once again, opinions varied. French intelligence services, which also had an interest in public opinion among religious circles, would point out in October – rather simplistically – that "in Strasbourg, the protestant clergy would be won over to the German cause, while the Catholic clergy would remain attached to France."[36] However, in an article in the *Straßburger Post,* the priest of Rountzenheim (Basse-Alsace), Father Siegwalt, warned his fellow clergymen three days before the armistice that "the prospect of being united with a state and an atheist people requires Catholic Alsace to oppose such a misfortune with all of its might. The clergy must be the judge."[37]

In addition to diverging expectations about the end of the war, these sources also show that it is important to contextualize the idea of widespread hatred among the Alsatian-Lorrainers for the Germans – an idea that developed in French collective memory. Amongst themselves, Alsatian-Lorrainers often talked about the presence of the "Boches" or the "filthy Prussians." However, as Nicolas Stoskopf points out, it was just a manner of speaking: "What people hated about the Boches was the emperor, Hindenburg, Ludendorff, Prussian militarism, the military dictatorship, the foolishness of certain measures, the corrupt gendarme; but not any of their long-time friends."[38] This was how it was for artist Joseph Sattler, Charles Spindler's Bavarian friend, whom Spindler consoled in October 1918 over his dashed hopes for victory. For a man like Spindler, founder of the *Revue alsacienne illustrée* and friend to German officers whom he considered good people, the essential division was more political than national.[39] In the same vein, only once in his diary did Jean Obrecht make a distinction between the Alsatians and the *Altdeutsche*, whom he called "our fellow citizens of German origin."[40] In their letters, civilians also confirmed the peaceful coexistence of the two communities. "I passed along a message to the Flunemacher woman," one Lorrainer woman wrote to her mother. "It's sad. They have to leave next week for Germany."[41] A number of reports from the Contrôle Postal noted similar letters in which Alsatian-Lorrainers expressed sympathy for the Germans – and not just those they knew personally. "Everywhere the Germans are withdrawing to the other side of the Rhine. It was truly a difficult fate that hit them, and they inspire a great deal of pity."[42]

While many Germans and Germanophile Alsatians left the *Reichsland*, plenty wanted to stay, whether for personal or professional reasons. It is not surprising that in the final weeks of the war, a number of voices expressed fear at being expelled. On 11 November 1918, one German wrote to a loved one: "We no longer feel secure about our lives, because we are German. We may end up on the other side of the river within the next four weeks. If I had money, I would stay, but without money, nothing can be done."[43] At the same time, it would be wrong to imagine the German population was virtually immobilized in fear and desperation. Plenty of immigrants did indeed leave the *Reichsland* during this period, but a large proportion of them stayed; mixed couples in particular did not seem to be thinking ahead to the future that the French victory would hold for them and saw no reason to leave. In fact, they had a much greater chance of escaping the purges between 1918 and 1920 – 75 per cent of couples with an Alsatian husband and German wife and 55 per cent of couples with a German husband and Alsatian wife would remain in Alsace after the armistice.[44] In the fall of 1918, close to 30,000 Germans (out of a total of 60,000) were forced to leave Strasbourg. However, on 18 January 1919, the military governor of

Strasbourg, General Hirschauer, informed the Marshal of France that at least 40,000 still remained in the city.[45] These numbers are important because they clearly call into question the French claim that the Alsatian-Lorrainers had always lived apart from the Germans but also that post-war Alsace-Lorraine had been scoured of immigrants. What is even more surprising is that in addition to mixed couples, 21 per cent of German couples remained in the *Reichsland.* For these Germans, many of whom were probably born in the Imperial Territory, Alsace-Lorraine, and not the *Altreich,* was their homeland. "A lot of people think the French will be arriving soon and that we will probably all be required to leave," wrote one German. "Dr. Lehmann of Herlisheim thinks that Alsace will become French. But he will stay regardless. In the meantime, he let it be known to the *Franzosenköpfe* [French heads] that he has already taken out his French flag."[46]

But aside from the debates in the *Landtag* and in the newspapers, it seemed that people were not overly concerned about the political future of the *Reichsland.* It was their personal future, the economic situation, and issues of supply that were top of mind for the entire population, whether bourgeoisie or labourers, *Altdeutsch* or native born. Many diaries and letters that even in November made no mention of the war and its imminent end, discuss food almost exclusively. Faced with economic and food supply issues, Fritz Maisenbacher recalled that military and political events played only a secondary role.[47] And in his diary, Alsatian industrialist Alfred Ungerer made little mention of politics but meticulously noted his meals almost every day: "October 5: Prince Max v. Baden is named Chancellor of the German Empire and forms a new government ... We had eel for dinner. Very good."[48] These diaries point to the importance of the food situation. On top of her own comments about the food situation in the *Reichsland,* Elisabeth-Ester Lévy began adding to her journal excerpts from the press, official notices, posters, and price lists for food. She complained that "the rich can buy anything."[49] Remarking on the same conflict, Colmar's *Kreisdirektion* noted in a report that "due to difficulties of supply, discontent can be felt in angry comments against the more affluent population."[50] As the report emphasized, while the population had not yet been spurred to action, class hatred was growing increasingly intense: "it is war only for the poor; we are suffering and hungry, the rich are growing fatter and want the war to go on."[51]

In fact, people were hoping for rapid peace and a return to normalcy. This was the case for teacher Philippe Husser, who said, not without a certain amount of pragmatism: "whether we are neutral, or independent, or French, all we ask for is peace. Calm! Something to eat! That is what we all want."[52]

Post-war Disappointment

The Armistice of 11 November 1918 sealed the return of Alsace-Lorraine to France, which took possession of the territory in only fifteen days. Stationed outside the old border, the troops were preparing for the liberation. On 17 November, the first army unit entered the territory of the former Imperial Territory and, that very day, the city of Mulhouse, then Metz, and Strasbourg. By 22 November, the French army controlled the entire territory. The French press kept publishing articles about the "liberation," closely tracking the progress of French and Allied troops.[53]

But the enthusiastic reception of France in November 1918 calls for more nuance. Reports from the police, the military, and Commissions du Contrôle Postal as well as private accounts reveal that the celebrations did not always reach proportions evoked by unofficial descriptions. A report from Colmar noted that "a few entire villages seem to have maintained Germanophile feelings [although we have noted] half-hearted Francophile sentiment in others. Wary peasants rallied tentatively around the new regime."[54] As a general rule, small towns in Lorraine and the countryside had a decidedly more favourable attitude towards the French. However, in the industrial parts of Lorraine, particularly along the German border, the reception troops received seems to have been "fairly reticent, at times almost hostile."[55] There was unadulterated, sincere joy in some areas, and slightly stiff timidity in the expression of French feeling in others. Viticultural settings were also more hesitant. War journals of French soldiers regularly featured comments about the reserved welcome in some communes, where citizens were growing less pleasant. For example, Second Lieutenant Pierre Thiriet remembered having found a closed door from Alsatian civilians who were supposed to house him, while Captain Pierre Chaurand noted that "civilians looked uncomfortable and timidly saluted."[56]

Not everyone took part in the celebration – far from it. Georges Wolf, the liberal democratic leader and former editor-in-chief of the *Straßburger Zeitung*, reported that "the French received an enthusiastic reception in most Catholic villages and a reserved one in most Protestant villages."[57] In large cities as well, the French presence sometimes created hostile feelings, as a police report from Strasbourg noted, lamenting that "our troops in Alsace-Lorraine are being harassed. There are attacks everywhere." In Strasbourg, the report said, "sentries are being thrown in the water."[58]

French reports often suggest a difference in attitude among the population depending on age. While "the younger generations raised in Prussian schools are completely won over to German ideas," the military administrator of Wissembourg reported, "older people have maintained some sympathy for France, which they feel is still the land of liberty."[59] This explains once more why, when the French troops arrived, the reception committees in the communes often put young girls in traditional costume up front and why the propaganda from the 1920s insisted that it was young Alsatian and Lorrainer boys who, in November 1918, were responsible for toppling German statues. Faced with Alsatian-Lorrainer youth far from France, the connection between the generations had to be maintained. But action was also required given that there was no guarantee that the population had unconditional, uniform love for the motherland. The deputy in the Alsatian-Lorrainer *Landtag* and leader of the *Zentrum*, Charles Hauss, had already understood that one should not confuse possible anti-German sentiment with ardent attachment to France.[60]

Through an order of 14 December 1918, French authorities introduced to the reunited provinces a system of ID cards to indicate the residents' background. The local townhalls received instructions to distribute four types of cards (A–D) that could be used as passports and that held surprises for some:[61]

CARD A: given to Alsatian-Lorrainers who were (or whose two parents or grandparents were) French citizens before the 1870 annexation.
CARD B: given to people with one parent with an A card and another not native-born French and of foreign origin (from an enemy, neutral, or allied country).
CARD C: given to people with both parents native to an allied or neutral country.
CARD D: reserved for immigrants from an enemy country and their descendants, even if the descendants were born in Alsace-Lorraine.

In total, 1,082,650 A cards, 183,500 B cards, 53,050 C cards, and 513,800 D cards were distributed to adults and children over sixteen.[62] In Strasbourg, of an estimated population of 165,523, 125,729 cards were distributed between December 1918 and January 1919, of which 77,401 were A cards (61.6 per cent), 14,733 were B cards (11.7 per cent), 2,457 were C cards (2 per cent), and 31,138 were D cards (24.8 per cent).[63]

Then arose the fundamental problem of French republicanism and its policy of assimilation, which was unable (or reluctant) to understand the complex reality of the heterogeneous Alsatian-Lorrainer population, which did not correspond to a clear separation between *German* and *Alsatian-Lorrainers*. In fact, the existence of these cards contradicted French statements that any imperial attempt to Germanize the provinces had not had an impact on a native population in the previous forty-seven years. Obviously, eliminating the German element and categorizing residents according to ethnic purity was not enough; they also had to identify and pursue Alsatian-Lorrainers who had committed moral or social crimes by collaborating with the imperial regime. As a result, classifying the population according to national belonging was just one step in a policy of purging.

To accomplish this, an order from the Prime Minister's Office of 2 November 1918, one week before the armistice, required the creation of triage commissions – Commissions de Triage – immediately after the troops entered the territory. While the stated pretext was ensuring military security in accordance with Article 9 of the law of 9 August 1849, the commissions were pursuing a different goal altogether. Inspired by the words of the Abbé Wetterlé,[64] along with the ID card system, commissions were meant to identify the "good" from the "bad" Alsatian-Lorrainers, classify them according to their degree of patriotism and their activities under the German regime, then purge the undesirable elements.[65] By 1920, these Commissions had ejected some 200,000 Germans and Germanophile Alsatian-Lorrainers.[66]

It is hardly surprising that this atmosphere occasionally resulted in German hunting. In Strasbourg, Alfred Ungerer noted that signs with violent messages were posted in the night of 1 December: "Alsatians! 5 francs for every dead *Schwob*! – so: kill at will!"[67] In the windows of some stores, posters called for the boycott of German shops: "Alsatians! Remember 47 years of repression and tyranny! Buy from Alsatian stores!"[68] Obviously, the reasons for this behaviour were not necessarily patriotic. In many cases, Alsatian-Lorrainers were also trying to eliminate the competition.

But not everyone was "pleased to see the dirty Boches leave." On the contrary, plenty of Alsatian-Lorrainers criticized "this shameful and pathetic spectacle."[69] The ID cards had a negative impact on people's lives, creating frustration, disillusionment, and hatred among those who had not obtained an A card (around 41 per cent). Holders of B cards had difficulty keeping public service positions. And in March 1919, faced with growing discontent, Captain Quinchez, administrator of Metz-Campagne, was required to rein in the zeal of certain gendarmes who, at the Gare de Metz, were turning away arrondissement residents who held B and C cards.[70] Since it was origin and not national sentiment that determined the type of card assigned, a French nationalist could be refused an A card because of a German parent, while another who had possibly collaborated with the Germans received one. Tara Zahra and Laird Boswell both have demonstrated how this policy entailed disputes about what it meant to be French or German and who had the authority over this question.[71] According to Pierri Zind, "this racist segregation was fundamentally loathsome,"[72] and it was particularly problematic in the case of mixed marriages: while French children legally carried their father's citizenship, this was denied to children in Alsace-Lorraine who had a French father but a German mother. "What is becoming difficult is the triage of pure-blood Alsatians with mixed marriage Alsatians. To be the former, you need to have had Alsatian parents and grandparents on both sides, something few families have. In Strasbourg, of 180,000 habitants, it is said that only 22,000 [*sic*] are of pure blood. If all the others have to leave, what will become of our city? Let's hope that the French become less strict. Otherwise this will cause problems in a lot of families."[73]

In fact, during the first half of 1919, the German Armistice Commission (the *Waffenstillstandskommission*) received many letters from those expelled who were trying to return to join their families. There were many cases where spouses stayed in Alsace-Lorraine to protect the family property from seizure with their physical presence.[74]

Despite these tensions, the rigid policy of French assimilation did not clearly separate Alsatian-Lorrainer society and establish a decisive dichotomy between so-called faithful patriots and undesirables. Ties between fellow citizens, formed over almost half a century, remained stable. Many native-born Alsatian-Lorrainers were concerned about the precarious situation of their German friends and loved ones and came up with ways to prevent their departure. "We cannot accept the idea that you must leave even though you are legally German; this is why we need to see to it that you stay."[75] Plenty of people asked for help (in the form of a word in their favour) from Alsatian-Lorrainers, ideally holders of A cards. Winegrower André Hugel recalled a fellow citizen who "wrote a letter to the *Kreisdirektor* [of Riquewihr] begging Mr. Weber to certify that he never denounced anyone."[76] And in a letter addressed to the Commission de Triage, a German included a list of five of her husband's friends of Alsatian origin who were prepared to vouch that he was "a good guy in favour of Alsatians."[77] In fact, faced with the threat of expulsion, people, regardless of national origin, helped each other more often and more naturally than French historiography has generally maintained. This was most notable in the case of exiles. In the months after the Treaty of Versailles was signed, many individuals, along with the *Hilfsbund für die Elsass-Lothringer im Reich*, would address the German *Waffenstillstandskommission* (WSK) to find out how expelled Germans or Alsatian-Lorrainers whose goods had been sold could recover them and have them sent to Germany. "Many people expelled by the French and denied the right to take their furniture with them transferred it through these so-called sales to people they trusted, mainly of Alsatian origin. True Alsatian-Lorrainers bought the goods of expelled Germans to protect them from French bailiffs."[78]

This request from the *Hilfsbund* and the response from the WSK showed that many Alsatian-Lorrainers helped their expelled German loved ones buy back their property and that this was a widespread practice. Having received many requests, the WSK would advise people to request a temporary travel permit to go to Alsace-Lorraine and buy back their property, providing a specific application form for this purpose.

Beginning in December 1918, a new section appeared in the French Contrôle Postal reports: *Opinion about the French regime* or *Opinions about attachment to France.* While agents still highlighted excerpts of patriotic letters, that did not hide the real reason for this section: French authorities realized that France's image of the unanimous elation among Alsatian-Lorrainers with the liberation was incorrect. Complaints against the French administration, the ineffective supply of goods, and the behaviour of soldiers and bureaucrats had clearly become important issues for Paris, as well as for the military and civilian leaders on the ground. From that point on, people noted public discontent with the French regime. The end of the war in Alsace-Lorraine was not black and white. In fact, the civilian experience was multi-faceted. In addition to those who experienced it as a true liberation, attention needed to be paid to the growing number of negative comments, some of which criticized the very essence of the French war effort, the liberation of the lost provinces.

Also beginning in December, the Commission de Contrôle Postal in Metz noted complaints on all sides. "It's funny, since the French have been in Metz, life has become twice as expensive; prices are practically out of reach."[79] Exhausted, the president of the commission even noted that "people almost regret having become French again, and I fear they are not wrong."[80] In fact, Alsatian-Lorrainers started to compare their situation unfavourably with that under the German regime. Some even argued that while the situation was particularly bad during the final years of the war, it was no worse than the current situation in Alsace-Lorraine now liberated and under French organization: "I already miss the Boches' organization. Not *the* Boches. Heaven forbid! But their organization."[81] The *Journal d'Alsace-Lorraine* addressed this issue on a number of occasions, pointing out that if high prices prevented people from buying what they needed, the responsibility lay with Paris. "In German times, people might say, prices were the same or even higher in a sense. That is true. But their organization worked. There were cards for necessities, maximum prices for the rest, and above all they were German, we knew what to expect from them. We thought it would get better once French soldiers were here and, good lord, what a disappointment. And disappointment is an important factor in such circumstances."[82]

In a long article published in a number of newspapers, the president of the Union of the Reformed Churches of France – the Union des Églises réformées de France – Jules Pfender, revealed the privileged situation Alsatian-Lorrainer pastors and priests enjoyed in the German era, drawing the conclusion that there should be no surprise if some Protestant pastors now greeted France with a certain mistrust. They would only be won back to the cause of France, he insisted, "if France knows how to take them, i.e., if it changes nothing for the moment with the organization."[83] This argument was supported by the Chief Rabbi of Strasbourg, Émile Levy.[84]

Given the transitional period of relief and joy, and also of discontent, disappointment, sadness, and uncertainty, Alsatian-Lorrainers wanted the peace treaty signed and normalcy to be restored. In June 1919, the police chief of Strasbourg remarked critically that "excellent Alsatians (son of an Alsatian father and a Swiss or Luxembourgish mother) obtained a B card, while the *Elsässer Franzosenfresser* received an A card. In B and D circles, we impatiently await an option that would get things back to normal, which is currently impossible for a large number of people."[85] In this tense atmosphere, slow peace treaty negotiations bothered the population, which started pointing the finger at "the weakness of the French government and its clumsy diplomacy."[86] While the city of Mulhouse was decked with flags, Philippe Husser noted in his journal on 29 June 1919 that the announcement of the signature of the treaty led to only "a little more activity in the streets … The odd drunk. But there is no outburst of joy strictly speaking, no delirious enthusiasm: it's already too chilly."[87] Of course, Alsatian-Lorrainers were relieved that peace was finally signed and the war ended. Overall, the press approved of the clauses of the treaty regarding Alsace-Lorraine. But some newspapers, such as the *Lorrain*, were critical: "Are Lorraine and Alsace satisfied? No!"[88]

The details of territorial, financial, and political decisions made in Versailles did not seem to play a major role in public opinion. The residents of the two provinces barely discuss them in their letters. What dominates is a return to normal – and, therefore, particularly among Germans and mixed couples – the issue of naturalization. In fact, due to Wilson's pressure, Article 79 of the Treaty of Versailles set out that in the year following its coming into force, Germans living in Alsace-Lorraine could, under certain circumstances, request French citizenship through the naturalization process.[89] This also applied for Germans married to an Alsatian or Lorrainer. By 1921, French authorities had received some 95,893 applications for naturalization, particularly from Germans in mixed marriages.[90] Of those, 77,064 were granted. And while many Alsatian-Lorrainers were in favour of naturalization for personal and family reasons, they also thought the country's economy – and therefore society in general – depended on it. As was noted by the priest Louis Hackspiel, editor of the *Lothringer Volkszeitung*, most applications were not motivated by pro-French sentiment, but rather by family and economic factors.[91] As such, it is no surprise that seven months after the war, despite the strong criticism from Francophile Alsatian-Lorrainers, plenty of others had applauded the naturalization policy. "I will opt for naturalization," wrote a German expelled in December 1918. "If the League of Nations is formed, it could fix everything. I don't care where I live."[92]

As a general rule, the restoration to French sovereignty of territories which had been ceded to Germany under the Treaty of Frankfurt of 10 May 1871 was not, in Alsace-Lorraine, unexpected or questioned. In fact, the weeks and months that followed the armistice were an effective preliminary to the territorial and political decisions made in Versailles – a taste in December 1918 of what would come in June 1919. In this sense, the French policy of complete assimilation and the expulsion of many Germans was a success.

However, it was another story when it came to the integration of the population. Of course, beginning in January 1919, Wilson's directive suggested settling the question of Alsace-Lorraine by applying the people's right to self-determination. But this was not set out in the policy of Clemenceau and Jeanneney. As early as 9 December 1918, President Raymond Poincaré had proclaimed definitively in Strasbourg, faced with the public's approval: "The referendum is done!" As a result, the simple return of the provinces – supposedly by general popular consent – allowed France to erase the humiliation of 1871 and to justify the sacrifices of war while conforming to the Wilsonian principle.[93] Article 51 of the treaty officially restored Alsace and Lorraine to France, setting their return for 11 November 1918.[94] In this sense, Versailles marked the "definitive" end of the war, while pointing to the armistice which highlighted the end of the war and the return of the lost provinces – a date that would be forever etched in collective French memory. But for Alsace-Lorraine, the events around 11 November 1918 marked the end of the "real" war, the ambiguity of which has been discussed above.

During the legislative elections of November 1919 – one year after the triumphant entry of French soldiers – Alsatian-Lorrainers confirmed their attachment to France. French historians did not stop emphasizing this fact. Yet, this return did not automatically mean consent for complete reintegration to France. Alsatian-Lorrainers did not stop defending what made them unique. Very soon, the "Alsatian malaise" would make itself felt.[95]

Conclusion

The story of the end of the war in Alsace-Lorraine is clearly a French story, told from a victor's point of view and approved by the Allies at Versailles. As a result, not only are Alsatian-Lorrainers seen as a homogenous group, but also the events of 11 November 1918 seem to be taken for granted.

Of course, in Alsace-Lorraine, there were eruptions of joy at the armistice. Like elsewhere in France, the population expressed its joy with the end of the war and the difficulties of the military occupation. But unlike what French historiography suggests, these moments – and therefore the end-of-war experience – must not be understood as an undivided collective experience. As the case of this border region between France and Germany with its heterogeneous population shows, an overly generalizing approach is insufficient to understand public opinion at the end of the Great War. A detailed analysis of public opinion, both before and after the armistice, not only provides a better understanding of how people truly experienced the *sortie de guerre* – a moment when tremendous joy was intermingled with profound grief – but also gives voice to those who are often forgotten by a history based on specific chronological events while ignoring the complex reality in Alsace-Lorraine.

One could certainly also not dispute that 11 November is a foundational event. But this foundational event – this fulcrum – has been constructed in an historical French imaginary without any anteriority. It is based on a collective memory that is exclusively French. And yet, 11 November has a past – as it has a future. In Alsace-Lorraine, they are both shared by Francophile and Germanophile communities. By studying the experience of the Alsatian-Lorrainers at the end of the war and taking into consideration what came before and after the armistice, 11 November 1918 does not seem simply to have separated the so-called native and German populations but also Francophones and Germanophones, Catholics and Protestants, urban and rural, bourgeois and workers, young and old.

The order re-established by the Treaty of Versailles says nothing of this reality which, of course, had collided with the French goal of regaining full control of Alsace-Lorraine. Therefore, it was through national classification and expulsion that the government sought to re-establish order in the lost provinces. In the long term, and despite the *malaise alsacien* which spread after 1919, the post–World War I French peacemaking process proved successful.

But if national classification was certainly common in Europe after 1918,[96] the situation in Alsace-Lorraine, with its long and complex history between France and Germany and its heterogeneous population, was particular. It provoked uncertainty amongst the inhabitants about what it actually meant to be French or German, as many had become German or French only through the force of law. There was thus no genuine, deep-seated hatred by Alsatians and Lorrainers of the German inhabitants of the former *Reichsland*. Rather, the card system and the merciless expulsions encouraged many, troubled by the abrupt switch to French rule after half a century, to denounce neighbours in order to prove their patriotism to the French administration, thus "generating the very forms of local ethnic conflict that classification claimed to redress"[97] and ultimately threatening the cohesiveness of local communities.

The indifference of German historiography and the ignorance of French historiography have led to an overly simplified vision. For Alsace-Lorraine, there was no single end-of-war experience but, rather, several ambiguous end-of-war experiences, which then took tangible and concrete form through the provisions of the peace treaty. In this sense, Versailles would offer permanent, legal shape to how Alsace-Lorraine emerged from the Great War.

NOTES

1 See Martin Béhé, *Heures inoubliables – recueil des relations des fêtes de libération, des discours prononcés dans plus de 80 villes et villages d'Alsace et de Lorraine en novembre et décembre 1918 et des impressions personnelles des maréchaux et des généraux* (Strasbourg: Le Roux & Cie, 1920).

2 Hans-Ulrich Wehler, "Elsaß-Lothringen von 1870 bis 1918. Das 'Reichsland' als politisch-staatsrechtliches Problem des zweiten deutschen Kaiserreichs," *Zeitschrift für Geschichte des Oberrheins*, 109 (1961), pp. 133–99.

3 Hermann Hiery, *Reichstagswahlen im Reichsland. Ein Beitrag zur Landesgeschichte von Elsaß-Lothringen und zur Wahlgeschichte des Deutschen Reiches 1871–1918* (Düsseldorf: Droste, 1986); Michael Essig, *Das Elsass auf der Suche nach seiner Identität* (Munich: Eberhard, 1994).

4 Günter Riederer, *Feiern im Reichsland: Politische Symbolik, öffentliche Festkultur und die Erfindung kollektiver Zugehörigkeiten in Elsaß-Lothringen* (Trèves: Kliomedia, 2004).

5 Markus Evers, *Enttäuschte Hoffnungen und immenses Misstrauen. Altdeutsche Wahrnehmungen des Reichslandes Elsaß-Lothringen im Ersten Weltkrieg* (Oldenburg: BIS-Verlag, 2016).

6 Jacques Granier, *Novembre 18 en Alsace* (Strasbourg: Dernières Nouvelles d'Alsace, 1968); Job de Roince, *Le Livre de l'Armistice: l'Allemagne à genoux – novembre 1918* (Rennes: Imprimerie Les Nouvelles, 1968); Robert Heitz, *Souvenirs de jadis et de naguère* (Woerth, 1963).

7 Christian Baechler, "L'Alsace entre la guerre et la paix. Recherches sur l'opinion publique (1917–1918)," doctoral thesis (Université de Strasbourg, 1969).

8 Geneviève Baas, *Le malaise alsacien, 1919–1924* (Strasbourg: Alsagraphic, 1972); Pierre Brasme, *Moselle 1918: le retour à la France – délivrance, bonheurs, désenchantements…* (Sarreguemines: Pierron, 2008).

9 Jean-Noël and Francis Grandhomme, *Les Alsaciens-Lorrains dans la Grande Guerre* (Strasbourg: La Nuée Bleue, 2013).

10 http://www.memorial-hwk.eu.

11 Jean-Marie Mayeur, "Une mémoire-frontière: L'Alsace," in Pierre Nora, ed., *Les lieux de mémoire, vol II: La Nation* (Paris: Gallimard 1986), pp. 63–95; Etienne François and Hagen Schulze, eds., *Deutsche Erinnerungsorte*, 3 vol. (Munich: Beck, 2001).

12 Dan Silverman, *Reluctant Union: Alsace-Lorraine and Imperial Germany, 1871–1918* (University Park: Pennsylvania State University Press, 1972); John Craig, *Scholarship and Nation Building: The University of Strasbourg and Alsatian Society, 1870–1939* (Chicago: University of Chicago Press, 1984).

13 Stephen Harp, *Learning to Be Loyal: Primary Schooling as Nation Building in Alsace and Lorraine, 1850–1940* (DeKalb: Northern Illinois University Press, 1998); David Allen Harvey, *Constructing Class and Nationality in Alsace, 1830–1945* (DeKalb: Northern Illinois University Press, 2001); Christopher Fischer, *Alsace to the Alsatians? Visions and Divisions of Alsatian Regionalism, 1870–1939* (New York: Berghahn, 2010); Elizabeth Vlossak, *Marianne or Germania? Nationalizing Women in Alsace, 1870–1946* (Oxford: Oxford University Press, 2011); Alison Carrol, *The Return of Alsace 1918–1939* (Oxford: Oxford University Press, 2018).

14 Laird Boswell, "From Liberation to Purge Trials in the 'Mythic Provinces': Recasting French Identities in Alsace and Lorraine, 1918–1920," *French Historical Studies*, 23/1 (2000), pp. 129–62; Tara Zahra, "The 'Minority Problem' and National Classification in the French and Czechoslovak Borderlands," *Contemporary European History*, 17/2 (2008), pp. 137–65. Cf. Sebastian Döderlein, "Un pivot de l'histoire? La société alsacienne-lorraine et les sorties ambiguës de la Première Guerre mondiale (1918–1919)" (PhD thesis, Concordia University, Montreal, 2016).

15 Joseph Schmauch, "Novembre 1918: l'administration française s'établit en Alsace-Lorraine," *Revue d'Alsace*, 139 (2013), pp. 259–76.
16 René Bazin, *Les Oberlé* (1901); Maurice Barrès, *Au service de l'Allemagne* (1905).
17 Jean-Jacques Waltz (1873–1951), better known by his artistic name Hansi, was a staunch opponent of annexation and German immigration. He criticized and ridiculed the "German invaders," particularly through his images, which are still symbols of Alsace-Lorraine. See Benoit Brunant, *Hansi, l'artiste tendre et rebelle* (Strasbourg: La Nuée Bleue, 2007).
18 Archives of Service Historique de l'Armée de Terre, Vincennes (SHAT), 6 N 70, Clemenceau holdings: Conditions d'Armistice, 28 October 1918.
19 Lawrence E. Gelfand, *The Inquiry: American Preparations for Peace, 1917–1919* (New Haven, 1963), p. 140, quoted in William R. Keylor, "Versailles and International Diplomacy," in Manfred F. Boemeke, Gerald D. Feldman, and Elisabeth Glaser, eds., *The Treaty of Versailles: A Reassessment after 75 Years* (Cambridge: Cambridge University Press, 1998), pp. 469–506, 491.
20 For a detailed analysis of the political strategies behind the regain of French territory and identity in Alsace-Lorraine after World War I, see Volker Prott, *The Politics of Self-Determination: Remaking Territories and National Identities in Europe, 1917–1923* (Oxford: Oxford University Press, 2016).
21 Bernard Vogler, *Histoire politique de l'Alsace* (Strasbourg: La Nuée Bleue, 1995), p. 214.
22 Gelfand, *Inquiry*, p. 140.
23 Alfred Wahl, *L'Option et l'émigration des Alsaciens-Lorrains en 1871–1872* (Paris: Orphyrs, 1974).
24 Office de statistique d'Alsace et de Lorraine (OSAL). Report (Strasbourg, 1920).
25 Alfred Wahl, "L'immigration allemande en Alsace-Lorraine, 1871–1918," *Recherches germaniques* 3 (1973), pp. 202–17.
26 François Uberfill, *La société strasbourgeoise entre France et Allemagne (1871–1924)* (Strasbourg: Société Savante d'Alsace, 2001).
27 SHAT 16 N 1450, Bulletin de Quinzaine, Strasbourg, 4 February 1919.
28 Quoted in Pierre Brasme, *Metz, une ville dans la guerre 1914–1918: La vie quotidienne à Metz à travers le Journal de Jeanne Haas* (Metz: Paraiges, 2016), p. 145.
29 Erich Matthias and Rudolf Morsey, *Die Regierung des Prinzen Max von Baden. Quellen zur Geschichte des Parlamentarismus und der politischen Parteien* (Düsseldorf: Droste, 1962), p. 213.
30 Auguste Zundel, *1914–1918 – Journal de la Grande Guerre vécue à Mulhouse* (Colmar: Jérôme Do Bentzinger, 2004), p. 190.
31 Hauptstaatsarchiv Stuttgart (HStAS), M 30/1 Bü 49, Geheime Feldpolizei Mühlhausen, 25 October 1918.

32 HStAS, Geheime Feldpolizei Metz, 31 October 1918.
33 Like the Chief Rabbi of Strasbourg during the war, Germanophile Émile Levy, his successor, Isaïe Schwartz, noted in 1919 that no religious leader could tolerate the introduction of secular laws in Alsace, since "all religions will suffer." Vicki Caron, *Between France and Germany: The Jews of Alsace-Lorraine 1871–1918* (Stanford: Stanford University Press, 1988), pp. 184–6.
34 Harp, *Learning to Be Loyal*, pp. 160–83; David Hopkin, "Identity in a Divided Province: The Folklorists of Lorraine 1860–1960," *French Historical Studies*, 23/4 (2000), pp. 639–682.
35 SHAT, 16 N 1450, Grand Quartier Général, 2e Bureau, Contrôle Postal (CP) Belfort.
36 SHAT, 16 N 1311, Information provided by a French captain interned in Switzerland, Berne, 18 October 1918.
37 *Straßburger Post*, 7 November 1918.
38 Nicolas Stoskopf, "'L'Alsace pendant la guerre' de Charles Spindler – Le journal d'un artiste alsacien," in Grandhomme, *Boches ou Tricolores*, pp. 217–29, 225.
39 Charles Spindler, *L'Alsace pendant la guerre* (Strasbourg, 1925), facsimile edition (Nancy: Place Stanislas, 2008), p. 696.
40 Jean Obrecht, *Vivre à Mulhouse à la fin de la Première Guerre mondiale. Journal d'un Instituteur*, excerpts presented by André Studer and Marie-Claire Vitoux, *Annuaire historique de Mulhouse*, 19 (2008), pp. 25–48, 41.
41 SHAT, 16 N 1450, CP Belfort, report of 12–27 September 1918.
42 Obrecht, *Vivre à Mulhouse*, p. 43.
43 SHAT, 16 N 1312, Grand Quartier Général, 2e Bureau, Service de Renseignement de Belfort.
44 Uberfill, *La société strasbourgeoise*, p. 235.
45 SHAT, 16 N 1558, lettre.
46 HStAS, M 30/1 Bü 20, Postal Censor Office of the 15th Army corps, report to the Postüberwachungsstelle des XV. Armeekorps an das stellvertretende Generalkommando XV, 26 September 1918.
47 Fritz Maisenbacher, *Ein Strassburger Bilderbuch. Erinnerungen aus den Jahren 1870–1918* (Strasbourg, 1931), p. 157.
48 Archives Départementales du Bas-Rhin, Strasbourg (ADBR), 193 J 5, Alfred Ungerer, Kriegstagebuch, vol. III, p. 313.
49 Elisabeth-Esther Lévy, *Tagebuch einer Colmarerin während des Weltkrieges 1914–1918*, 4 volumes (Colmar, N/O), volume 1918/I, 14, entry of 14 January 1918.
50 Archives Départementales du Haut-Rhin, Colmar (ADHR), 3 AL 1 / 1477, Kreisdirektion Colmar.
51 HStAS, M 30/1 Bü 50, Überwachungsstelle Colmar, Stimmungsbericht, 19 April 1918.

52 Philippe Husser, *Un Instituteur alsacien entre France et Allemagne, journal, 1914–1951*, presented by Alfred Wahl (Paris: Hachette, 1989), p. 117.
53 See Béhé, *Heures inoubliables*, op. cit.
54 SHAT, 16 N 1464, CP Colmar, report of 8–15 December 1918.
55 Archives nationales françaises, Paris (AN), F7 13377, Reports of the Territorial High Command in Lorraine: État d'Esprit, November 1918.
56 Jérôme Troester, "22 novembre 1918: les Français à Strasbourg," *La Grande Guerre Magazine*, 38 (April 2003), pp. 9–15, 11; Baron Chaurand, *Cinq siècles de chronique familiale* (Lyon: Audin, 1986), pp. 327–34.
57 Georges Wolf, *Vom zweiten zum dritten Reich. Siebzig Jahre Elsässischer Geschichte 1871–1914* (Saverne, 1941), p. 18. For the problem of confession, see Alfred Wahl, *Confession et comportement dans les campagnes d'Alsace et de Bade, 1871–1939* (Strasbourg: Coprur, 1980).
58 AN, F7 12951, Notes Jean, report of 13 December 1918.
59 SHAT, 16 N 1450, Bulletin de Quinzaine, 27 November to 12 December 1918.
60 Rossé et al., *Das Elsass von 1870–1932*, I, p. 401.
61 Archives Départementales de la Moselle, Metz (ADM), 304 M 325, Instruction on the application of the order of 14 December 1918 from the Governor General of Metz. "Pense donc que j'ai appris aujourd'hui, à mon grand étonnement, que, parce que mon père descend d'un allemand, notre argent ne peut être changé. Il nous faudra donc quitter la Lorraine. J'en suis stupéfaite." SHAT, 16 N 1464, CP Metz, 8–14 December 1918.
62 *Journal d'Alsace et de Lorraine*, 15 December 1919.
63 Uberfill, *La société strasbourgeoise*, p. 217.
64 Émile Wetterlé, *Têtes de Boches* (Paris, 1917), p. 279. Colmarian by birth, Émile Wetterlé was appointed curate in Mulhouse in 1893. Yet he mainly handled journalism and politics. From 1898 onwards, he was a pro-autonomy deputy in the Reichstag from which he was expelled in 1915 because of his regular attacks on the Reich. An immigrant to France, Wetterlé notified the government about issues in Alsace-Lorraine and was elected to the Chamber of Deputies, serving from 1919 to 1924.
65 ADBR, 286 D 343, Ministerial Order, 2 November 1918.
66 Boswell, "From Liberation to Purge Trials."
67 Ungerer, *Tagebuch*, volume III, p. 227: "Elsässer! Jeder tote Schwob 5 Francs – also abmurxe!"
68 Pascale Hugues, "Indésirables en Alsace," *Dernières Nouvelles d'Alsace*, 11 November 2009.
69 SHAT, 16 N 1450, CP Mulhouse, report of 19–26 January 1919.
70 Brasme, *Moselle 1918*, p. 137.
71 Boswell, "From Liberation to Purge Trials"; Zahra, "The 'Minority Problem.'"

72 Pierri Zind, *Alsace-Lorraine, Elsass-Lothringen, une nation interdite, 1870–1940* (Copernic, 1979), p. 111.
73 SHAT, 16 N 1450, Bulletin de Quinzaine, Strasbourg, 4 February 1919. It is interesting to note that the report does not comment on this false number of 22,000 inhabitants "of pure extraction," while it suggests that in February 1919, only 12 per cent of the population of Strasbourg is native-born Alsatian-Lorrainer. For a realistic calculation, see Uberfill, *La société strasbourgeoise*, p. 217 (note 61).
74 Bundesarchiv Berlin-Lichterfelde (BArch), R 904/27.
75 SHAT, 16 N 1450, Bulletin de Quinzaine, Strasbourg, report of 16–28 February 1919.
76 Émile Hugel, *Chroniques de la Grande Guerre à Riquewihr. Témoignage d'un viticulteur alsacien* (Colmar: Reber, 2003), p. 246.
77 ADBR, 121 AL 906, letter from 23 December 1918.
78 BArch, R 904 / 27, Thüringische Landesstelle an die deutsche Waffenstillstandskommission in Berlin, 12 April 1919.
79 SHAT, 16 N 1464, CP Metz, report of 22–28 December 1918.
80 SHAT, 16 N 1464, CP Metz, report of 10 February 1919.
81 SHAT, 16 N 1467, CP Strasbourg, report of 19–26 January 1919.
82 *Journal d'Alsace-Lorraine*, 25 December 1918: "Et le ravitaillement ?"
83 Christian Baechler, *Les Alsaciens et le grand tournant de 1918* (Strasbourg: Hebdo, 2008), p. 112.
84 *Elsässer Tagblatt*, 4 December 1918; *Oberelsässische Landeszeitung*, 3 December 1918.
85 ADBR, 286 D 160, Strasbourg police department, report on public opinion, 30 June 1919.
86 SHAT, 16 N 1464, CP Metz, report of 7–14 June 1919.
87 Husser, *Un instituteur alsacien*, p. 204.
88 *Le Lorrain*, 30 June 1919.
89 ADBR, 121 AL 592, Letter to the Commissaire Générale de la République, 18 July 1919.
90 AN, AJ[30] 296, Report by Sir M. Cheetham to the Foreign Office in London, Political situation in Alsace Lorraine, September 1921.
91 *Lothringer Volkszeitung*, 25 January 1920.
92 SHAT, 16 N 1464, CP Metz, report of 15–21 December 1918.
93 Francis Grandhomme, "Retrouver la frontière du Rhin en 1918: l'entrée des poilus en Alsace et le retour à la France," in *Revue d'Alsace*, 139 (2013), pp. 237–58.
94 "The territories which were ceded to Germany in accordance with the Preliminaries of Peace signed at Versailles on February 26, 1871, and the Treaty of Frankfort of May 10, 1871, are restored to French sovereignty as from the date of the Armistice of November 11, 1918." Treaty of Versailles, Section V, Art. 51.

95 Baas, *Le Malaise alsacien*, op.cit.

96 See, for example, Zahra, "The 'Minority Problem,'" who compares the situation in post-war Alsace-Lorraine to Czechoslovakia, and Prott, *The Politics of Self-Determination*, who also analyses an analogous situation during the Greek-Turkish War between 1919 and 1922.

97 Zahra, "The 'Minority Problem,'" p. 158; see also Boswell, "From Liberation to Purge Trials," p. 161.

7 The "Right to Reparations," a Legal Concept in Post-war France

BRUNO CABANES

The duration and violence of the First World War created an unprecedented humanitarian crisis. Its scale required rethinking the criteria for and means of supporting the many victims left in its wake. Across Europe, at least ten million soldiers lost their lives, twenty million were injured, and eight million were maimed. In France, over one million men were permanently disabled (through mutilations, facial injuries, blinding, gassing, etc.). Families who took them in were often shocked by the extent of the injuries and trauma, their own inability to heal them, and the impossibility of returning to pre-war life. There were almost 600,000 war widows and close to 1,100,000 war orphans. In losing their only child, some parents lost the family's sole source of support. In invaded countries, physical and environmental destruction accompanied the demographic and social disaster.

For all victims of war, the recognition of their right to a pension, care, and a job was crucial. It was often a matter of life or death, given the harsh post-war living conditions.[1] From the perspective of the survivors of the Great War, it was also a matter of justice and dignity, with veterans and their assigns everywhere calling for "rights, not charity." But how were those rights to be defined after a conflict with so many victims, and with largely inadequate social legislation inherited from the nineteenth century? The issue was not merely recognizing the victims' suffering, although the need for recognition certainly underlay their larger expectations. It was also necessary to give their compensatory claims a legal basis, which required political will, a major legislative effort, and interventions by experts in labour and health law.[2] At the time, the concept of "victim of war" had not yet coalesced, and the notion of a "right to reparations" was still vague.[3] Amidst the discourse of policymakers, experts, and veterans' associations, the notion of "war reparations" assumed an international dimension with Germany as the ultimate debtor. According to Annex 1 of Article 232 of the Treaty of Versailles, that nation was to be responsible for pensions and compensation to "military victims of war … and to the dependents of such victims." Recognizing the sacrifice of victims of war and caring for them also risked exacerbating tensions between victors and vanquished in a subtle dialectic between restoring social order and destabilizing the post-war period.

For over four years, the rhetoric of a "just war" flooded the public space, co-opting legal terminology and culture in the service of national interests. "What was this so-called 'just war' combatants claimed to be waging?" asked legal historian Annie Deperchin. "What it meant was that the law had been diverted from its mission of peace to serve war, i.e., to legitimize violence. To use justice as an instrument of war was to move away from the very idea of justice. The more justice was invoked during the conflict, the greater its absence. We need to recognize that this war twisted both the law and … the legal experts."[4] Discussions of victims' rights meant first restoring humanist values in a legal landscape largely perverted by the war and re-centring reconstruction projects on the individual. The right to reparations was inseparable from the conceptual work of *what the law could do* emerging from war, and how *it must* learn lessons from the moral crisis that accompanied the conflict. This redefinition of law, in particular humanitarian and international law, was the work of prominent figures: André Mandelstam, René Cassin, Nicolas Politis, Georges Scelle, and many other legal scholars, who worked as part of a group of experts assembled by Albert Thomas at the International Labour Organization, the League of Nations, and institutions such as the Union Juridique Internationale and the Institut des Hautes Études Internationales.

Furthermore, discussions of the right to reparations developed in a context of changing personal and collective identities: soldiers became veterans and returned to their regions of origin without returning to their pre-war living conditions or ways of life; the injured, widows, and orphans demanded new rights, defined even before the official end of hostilities, and refugees often had to rebuild their lives from scratch. Originally from the department of Aisne, which was nearly 90 per cent devastated, historian Gabriel Hanotaux made this bitter observation: "The country is inaccessible, the roads closed, the bridges down, the routes detoured." Of his family home, "nothing but a shell remains, devastation … There is nothing left, everything was pillaged before the fire. I picked up a ceramic tile, and I said to my loved ones when I came home: here is your house." In his village, there was "complete solitude, an absolute void."[5] Defining the right to reparations thus ensured some continuity of identity against the traumatic devastation of the war and gave everyone a place, if not *their* place, in society. Its function was at once social and psychosocial.[6]

In theory, *victim of war* was a generic term, used in the title of the 1919 French law on pensions, which at the time included both servicemen and civilians.[7] But this does not mean that the notion of the right to reparations was uniform or that it remained unshaped by competing memories, strategies for recognition, a hierarchy of suffering, and gender roles.[8] Should and could civilian victims of the conflict, for example, enjoy the same right to reparations as the military victims, and former prisoners the same as veterans?[9]

Considering the question of the right to reparations from a gendered perspective, war widows were not recognized in their own right, but to the extent that they provided stability for the family unit. In France, however, around 140,000 widows had already remarried in 1923 and 262,500 were to do so in 1927–8, or 20 per cent and 37 per cent of all war widows. Most were widows without children or mothers of one young child.[10] Did they still need a pension? The question was raised regularly in public debates during the 1920s, a time when war widows, whether remarried or not, were increasingly involved in war victims' associations, and remarried widows remained excluded from the boards of directors of the Office National des Pupilles de la Nation and the Office National des Mutilés et Réformés.

Finally, the right to reparations involved a broader reflection on the type of society the survivors wished to see emerge from the war. The example of the devastated regions is enlightening: did repairing the destruction mean restoring pre-war landscapes, built environments, and living conditions (a pre-war inevitably idealized by those who had just gone through the tragedies of the conflict), or were the rebuilders to take the opportunity to transform and modernize the destroyed towns and villages? In other words, was the right to reparations just a nostalgia for the past or also a promise for the future – or even both?[11]

Regardless, the *desire for recognition* underlying claims for reparations, as psychiatrist Karl Abraham has aptly shown in his work on veterans,[12] almost always goes unfulfilled: the post-war reality falls short of the "horizon of expectation" (Reinhart Koselleck) and hopes forged during the conflict. In Northern France, for instance, refugees who returned home after the war grew increasingly impatient. In June 1919, the deputy from the Aisne, Olivier Deguise, talked about "populations left to their own devices, and, because of the difficulty they found themselves in, won over to a simmering revolt."[13] Learning of the peace conditions imposed on Germany on 1 July 1919, a French soldier wrote: "We have been too timid, too humble. As I have written, the men in black ruined the work of the men in blue. Our politicians have bungled matters. Foch the peacemaker would have had to become Foch the dictator."[14] It was against this conceptual, psychological, and emotional backdrop where collective dreams and individual affect met, that the experts charged with specifying the nature of war victims' rights set to work.

The definition of war victims' rights had two components. The experts had to first assess *a posteriori* the gravity of damage to people and their property and the possibility of healing, repair, and reconstruction. This assessment involved both a personal dimension (for example, documenting the exact conditions under which the damage was inflicted) and a collective one (coming up with criteria to compare the damage and draw up a compensation grid). For damage to property, assessing the losses fell to local commissions, presided over by Justices of the Peace of the canton and composed of ordinary citizens appointed by the Prefect rather than professional magistrates. This local justice was chosen for its efficiency and speed: most claims for reparations were considered between 1921 and 1923.[15]

At the same time, questions arose over society's responsibility for damages, on the basis of which victims would receive reparations. In France, the foundations, objectives, and ambitions of the very notion of reparation were redefined by the scale of the First World War's destruction. It raised questions on a national level (what was the responsibility and role of the French State in physical and moral reconstruction?) and on an international one: "Germany will pay" was one of the most common postwar slogans, but how much would it pay and when?[16] In addressing this point, French politicians fostered ambiguity, in much the same way as Clemenceau had avoided specifying the nature of veterans' rights in his famous speech in November 1917: "they have rights over us." Ultimately, it is impossible to understand the debate about reparations without returning to the work of Léon Bourgeois, the theorist of *solidarisme*, who, given the rise of poverty at the end of the nineteenth century, wanted to foster greater unity among citizens and redefine the social contract.[17] Aid to victims of the war followed this direction.[18] "The idea of solidarity between Frenchmen was just a philosophy before the war, a philosophy the war turned into a set of harsh and clear experimental truths," the deputy Léon Bérard said in a speech before the Chamber of Deputies in July 1917.

The State was therefore the financial and moral guarantor for reparations for victims' damages. Because whatever the many mutual assistance associations formed during the war could accomplish, in the growing and changing sphere of associations, only the State could manage in the long term, basing the aid received on thoughtful, fair criteria – hence the importance of German reparations.[19] The reconstruction of the northern and eastern departments of France is a good example. As early as 27 October 1914, a leaflet from the office of the Président du Conseil explained the government's ambition to help refugees and handle the reconstruction of towns and villages that were destroyed: in the months that followed, eight departments dedicated to regions that were invaded, liberated, and devastated were created in the relevant ministries (Interior, Agriculture, Public Works, etc.), in the context of an "invasion of statism."[20] This proliferation of administrative bodies at times resulted in inconsistent public policy.[21]

In November 1917, the Ministère du Blocus et des Régions Libérées was created. Its responsibilities were specified by decree the following month: "the reorganization of local life and approaches to housing, the aid given to victims to rebuild destroyed buildings, repair damage from the war, reconstitute the soil, and restore agriculture, commerce, and industry." Finally, the Charte des Sinistrés of 17 April 1919, based on the principle of equality and solidarity among French citizens for the costs of the war, made the idea of significant compensation from the State official: compensation for damages granted by the French State to those whose property was partially or completely destroyed in the invaded or occupied regions covered all of the losses suffered. If victims of war decided to rebuild (as was often the case) in the same commune or within fifty kilometres of the devastated area, they would receive up to six times the amount of the loss.

Aid to children offered the most striking example of the State's commitment to victims of war. Unlike other belligerent nations, France introduced pioneering legislation that created the designation of "ward of the nation" (*pupilles de la nation*).[22] The 27 July 1917 law established the principle of adoption by the nation, through a decision of a civil court, for children whose fathers were killed during the war or injured so badly as to be unable to provide for their families' needs. The wards of the nation were thus to be distinguished from "war orphans" – a group of steadily changing number since it included children whose fathers had been killed during the conflict or died as a consequence of a war injury after the official end to hostilities.

"For obvious reasons of moral appropriateness, it was simply not possible that sons of soldiers who fought in the war be in the same legal category as 'foundlings' or 'neglected children,'" said legislator Léon Bérard. The social consideration given to wards of the nation was demonstrated in the inviolable nature of the reparations due to them. "One of the preoccupations of the drafters of the law was that we not assimilate them with children on public assistance," legal scholar René Querenet specified. "With the designation *ward of the nation*, the law is not granting aid; it is conferring a right."[23] The wards' right to reparations originated in a fictive kinship that elevated them above their status as victims (unlike the war widows, for example) to make them children of the nation as a whole. This was behind the debates surrounding the creation of the status of ward of the nation: should their status end when they reached the age of majority or continue, seeing as the State had adopted them as its own children?

Whether for war widows or orphans, for those who were maimed or all those who lost their property and belongings during the war, the common principle was that of *a posteriori* reparations, symbolic, of course, for the losses suffered. Looking to the past in this way went hand in hand with an anticipation of future difficulties and risks. In the inter-war period, a new legal category was emerging: the *vulnerability* of the victims of the war. By *vulnerability*, lawmakers meant difficulties resulting from the war and various forms of disability that made victims fragile and exposed them *a priori*, this time, to additional risks, either physical (like aggravating physical difficulties) or social (a job loss). These risks, incurred by victims after the war, imposed on society the duty of assistance, care, and protection.[24] The gradual introduction of the idea of vulnerability attests to the fact that legal experts of the 1920s understood what recent historiography itself would keep repeating: one never fully escapes a conflict as destructive as the First World War.

Defining the right to reparations called for the creation of descriptive categories, which were constantly evolving during the conflict, as well as the work of experts. This use of experts – whether physicians to assess the extent of disability for those maimed, engineers to design prostheses, lawyers specializing in labour and inheritance law, geographers to draw the limits of the "red zone" (areas so devastated by fighting as to be rendered unfit for agricultural activity) – laid bare a reality that was hard to deny: humanitarian issues became so complex after the Great War that they required new social knowledge able to identify needs, set priorities, and distribute aid.

This practical knowledge was itself influenced by moral standards that, in the area of health care, for example, recognized certain injuries and disregarded others.[25] As a result, the physically injured and the psychologically injured had different statuses, both during and after the war. While the visible nature of bodily harm created awareness of the damage inflicted on the disabled, psychological injuries were tainted by suspicions of being faked or were considered dishonourable.[26] Disabilities resulting from the war were also perceived differently depending on the national context. In defeated countries, the injuries of those gravely wounded by the war offered a visible reminder of defeat: the maimed wore their defeat on their bodies. On the other hand, the "culture of victory" (a new concept created in opposition to the more familiar notion of the "culture of defeat")[27] transformed the war wounded and maimed into heroes or martyrs. In other words, the rights of victims of war were at the crossroads of various, and often competing, discourses: those of the legislator, the expert, and the victim.

The First World War created a new space for victims to speak out. The space contained the seeds of the first associations for the wounded and the maimed, which were formed in Paris beginning in 1915 and outside the capital in 1916–17. In March 1916, the young legal scholar René Cassin, seriously injured in October 1914, joined the disabled veterans' association in Aix-en-Provence. In his autobiography, he offered a poignant account of the beginning of the association movement:

> In this city in mourning, Aix, I would see war widows, our disabled comrades who were starting to be discharged – those from the battle of the Marne, and then the battle of Verdun, and my barber who had lost his left hand told me that the disabled in that area had started to speak out because, with a provisional allowance of 1.50 franc a day, they were living in poverty, as they were no longer able to exercise their profession. He, for his part, had been fortunate enough to be rehired by his boss ... I was the assistant secretary, since I didn't want to put myself forward. I wanted to help without drawing attention to myself. I was a newlywed at the time and swamped with work. We created the Aix association, and then associations in the surrounding villages ... Widows, even those who had jobs, were not used to going out, and a woman dressed in mourning who went into a café was frowned upon. They really needed courage![28]

The movement to recognize the right to reparations resulted from many decentralized initiatives by veterans, wounded, war widows – and not the state. It developed in a climate of dissatisfaction with the inadequate public policies for the victims of war and in response to the indifference of wider society. Leafing through the association's press reveals the following: created in 1916 by the Association Générale des Mutilés de la Guerre, the oldest of the veterans' associations, the *Journal des Mutilés et Réformés* condemned the widespread failure to consider the war injured. For example, it featured this undoubtedly fictional conversation between a factory boss and a wounded man who had come to ask him for work: "Clearly you are maimed, but that's not our fault. You have to understand that we need to put the interests of our business first and not get bogged down by the disabled.[29]

A 17 April 1916 law earmarked jobs for "soldiers and sailors discharged or retired after infirmities resulting from injuries suffered or diseases contracted during the present war," but its provisions were still too vague.[30] The law was then supplemented by the 1918 creation of the Office National des Mutilés et Réformés, part of the Ministère du Travail, and then by the law of 30 January 1923 on reserved jobs: concierges, boarding school monitors, postmasters, tobacco and match manufacturing jobs, forest rangers, peace officers, and even lighthouse keepers – although the risks the last profession posed to both the maimed and the safety of navigation led the Ministère des Travaux Publics to eventually introduce minimum physical fitness requirements, such as the ability to swim one hundred metres and pilot a boat.[31]

Reserved jobs did not simply address the social issue of giving veterans work. They also represented a form of symbolic reparations, which Clemenceau called for with his famous words: "they have rights over us." The goal of compensating damage inflicted during the conflict was accompanied by the further ambition of rendering veterans capable of contributing to the economic recovery of post-war France. "What are our maimed comrades and victims of war actually calling for? They simply want to take their place in society. They want to continue their efforts that began at the front. They want to restore our much afflicted France to its rightful place among nations, in other words, the leading place it held before the war," explained parliamentarian Marcel Ferraris. "They know their duties as good French citizens are not over. They realize they have to work to ensure the noble sacrifices were not in vain. They want to continue to work toward the prosperity of the country, which has emerged victorious from this terrible war."[32]

There were, however, noticeable differences between such rhetoric and veterans' own perspectives. In November 1917, a congress of all the associations of disabled veterans was held at the Grand Palais in Paris in an effort to create a national union. At the congress, Charles Valentino, a doctor of law and military physician,[33] spoke decisively to ensure the principle of reparations prevailed over that of assistance (he would become the Director of Pensions when that ministry was created in 1920):

> You are deemed to have a right when you can have it respected and asserted before the courts. But this right, you do not have ... The first question is therefore whether or not you have a right. Currently, it is not a right; it is assistance. The issue is whether the war wounded who saved the country will always be at the mercy of the generosity of the government or whether,

> on the contrary, they can stand before the nation as true creditors. When a man returns disabled and has spilled his blood, … this gives him a right, not to alms, but to reparations for the damage he suffered.[34]

The principle of reparations, which the attendees passed by a unanimous vote, ended up being written into the beginning of Article 1 of the law of 31 March 1919. This law represented considerable progress with respect to the legislation inherited from the July Monarchy. It no longer required the disabled to prove the origins of their injuries and instituted the principle of "presumption of origin," which worked to their advantage.[35] No more need to find witnesses to attest that a wound had been received in the heat of battle. This new provision also applied to war widows, provided the death could be officially recorded, an often long and painful process given the large number of soldiers missing in action. The new law also made the calculation of pensions more equitable by substituting the earlier pension categories of 1831 with a new system for estimating disability that ranged from 5 per cent to complete disability of 100 per cent – which modelled itself on the 1898 French law on workplace accidents. The absurdity of such an assessment is obvious: is losing a leg more serious than losing an arm? How does one estimate the relative damage of losing a thumb, a hand, or the right hand compared with the left? At the time, though, the seeming rationality of a system to evaluate disability by and large convinced veterans. Increases were arranged according to the number of children and dependents. Finally, the rights of war widows and orphans were officially recognized.

For the disabled veterans' associations, the issue of pensions was the priority, particularly since the amount, set by the law of 31 March 1919, was soon shown to be insufficient given the rising cost of living.[36] But how would they get the government to agree to an increase? If they wanted to introduce pensions worthy of the name, would they have to start by distinguishing between combatants and non-combatants, between those who fought in the trenches and those who were disabled before the war and held administrative positions in 1914–18? Justice or equality: this was another recurrent theme in post-war debates. For Cassin, it was unthinkable to establish a hierarchy among veterans of the Great War: all had served their country, whether by their labour or with their blood: no one could question the spirit of equality among veterans.[37] Secretary general of the Union Fédérale, then its vice-president, he headed up the largest veterans' association in France, along with Henri Pichot, a teacher from Loiret. "We had to be vigilant because some wanted to use the disabled for political purposes, even violent ones," he recalled. "We never allowed it and at the time we took the only republican position: we would obtain everything through the law, through democratic means!"[38] It was up to the state to find the necessary resources to provide them what they were owed – and they were owed it as citizen soldiers who did their duty during the war.

From this perspective, restoring order based on the relationship of citizens to the state is reminiscent of other debates that began during the war – for example, the trial of the soldier Baptiste Deschamps in the summer of 1916, accused of having assaulted a military neurologist who wanted to force him into electrotherapy treatment – a trial that received a great deal of press coverage and that can be seen as the starting point in a broader rethinking of the rights of shell-shocked soldiers within the military.[39] The issues in the debates immediately after the war are therefore important. In ardently defending the principle of reparations, veterans' associations argued that the state was not some higher authority bestowing rights upon veterans as it saw fit.[40] In reality, guaranteeing the rights of veterans was a pre-existing obligation of the state on account of the social contract tying it to its citizens through a series of reciprocal duties. Moreover, rights also arose from the harm suffered during the war, regardless of its nature: compromised health, job losses, delayed professional advancement, etc.

Enshrining the principle of reparations in law thus involved redefining the notion of a victim of war. There were even discussions of establishing complete equality among victims, which would have marked a significant departure from the law of 1831, which had offered significant benefits to officers over non-commissioned officers and enlisted men.[41] In the *Journal des Mutilés et Réformés*, the argument appeared as follows: "Officer, non-commissioned officer, or ordinary soldier; labourer, farmer, employee, or boss: one cannot dispute that all sacrifices were equal. And equal sacrifice requires equal reparations, according to the principles of true democratic justice."[42] In June 1793, the Convention had paved the way by elevating simple soldiers who were seriously injured to the rank of second lieutenants so they could receive decent pensions and be accepted as pensioners at the Hôtel National des Invalides.[43] Against the backdrop of preparations for the law of 31 March 1919, the principle was discussed and then abandoned. But people would continue to refer to the "sacred debt" the nation had contracted with its defenders – a term widely repeated by politicians after the Great War.[44]

Beginning in the mid-1920s, when the former central powers were still excluded from international organizations (for example, the International Research Council, founded in July 1919),[45] meetings of the Conférence Internationale des Associations de Mutilés de guerre et Anciens

Combattants (C.I.A.M.A.C.) internationalized and, in a way, radicalized the terms of the debate on the right to reparations.[46] This was precisely because such a right was no longer based on their participation in the civic community, the contract between the state and its citizens, or the sacrifices of veterans of a given country; it was founded in the name of a higher order that grew out of the rise of a humanitarian ideal, during and after the First World War.

Cassin, one of the prominent figures in the French veterans' movement, was one of the main architects of this form of transnationalization. As a member of the French delegation to the League of Nations since 1924, he forged the connection between that body and the Union Fédérale (UF), a strong association at the time with 70 federations and some 320,000 members, among whom he retained many contacts. It was also Cassin, along with Paul Brousmiche, the President of the UF, and Adrien Tixier, who was responsible for the war disabled along with Albert Thomas at the International Labour Organization, who helped redefine the issues of the right to reparations, not just in a national framework but in the larger international framework of the post-war period.

Brousmiche welcomed veterans from different countries (Germany, Austria, Italy, Romania, Serbia, etc.) to the first meeting of the C.I.A.M.A.C: "We are here among those who, having experienced the horrors of war, should have the strength to tell each other, face to face, truths that are elsewhere not easy to say or express, for reasons of national interest ... Peace? Do we not have a common interest in defending it together, not only in the moral interest of a better world, but even in the material interests of the disabled veterans and ex-servicemen, as it is only in the financial security restored by lasting peace that measures to safeguard or improve our existence can be planned and accomplished."[47]

This preliminary declaration sums up the dynamics of the aftermath of the Great War: the slow cultural demobilization still hampered by tensions between former enemies and the tangled invocations of national and international challenges, higher moral interests (the advent of a "better world"), and the interests of certain social groups like the war disabled and veterans. It also requires that we place the year 1919, which witnessed the emergence of the notion of the right to reparations in both French law (with the law of 31 March 1919 and the Charte des sinistrés of 17 April 1919) and the peace settlement (the famous part VIII of the Treaty of Versailles entitled "Réparations"), in the broader context of cultural demobilization and the reformulation of norms in the aftermath of war – a period that reaffirmed both the duties of states to their citizens and the transnational requirements of humanitarian aid. In other words, the right to reparations did not only recognize the debt that a state contracted with civilian victims or veterans, as Clemenceau's words of November 1917 suggested. It could not be summed up as a mere part of the diplomatic disputes between victors and vanquished (Article 232 recognized that "the resources of Germany are not adequate ... to make complete reparation for all such loss and damage," even as Article 231 affirmed the responsibility of the defeated countries for war damages).[48] The right to reparations also laid the foundations for a transnational reflection about the rights of all veterans, in particular the disabled, in both defeated and victorious countries.

The concrete results from the C.I.A.M.A.C.'s series of meetings remained modest. The resolution adopted in 1927 attests to this: "The Conference notes that in the majority of States, [veterans] have received no real compensation for the damage resulting from a long enlistment and premature aging, denounces the immorality of the principle according to which sacrifices for the nation in the form of money or work are compensated, while sacrifices in blood receive insufficient compensation, proclaims the need for veterans' associations to study how to introduce recognition of the particular debt owed to veterans." However, we need to avoid assessing the transnational movement of veterans that formed around René Cassin and his peers on the basis of gains or failures in the different countries. What counts much more is how this group of men severely disabled by the war incarnated the humanitarian moment of the immediate post-war period: a time when international organizations created by peace treaties, like the League of Nations and the International Labour Organization, seemed to offer hope for a new world order through the concerted efforts of the surviving witnesses of the Great War and a new generation of social experts. At the margins of traditional diplomacy – whose codes, rituals, intellectual tools, and very objectives were transformed by the war experience and its consequences – there developed a humanitarian diplomacy that offered an alternative form of diplomacy. In this new configuration, the right to reparations held a crucial place.

NOTES

1 Bruno Cabanes, "Les vivants et les morts. La France au sortir de la Grande Guerre," in Stéphane Audoin-Rouzeau and Christophe Prochasson, eds., *Sortir de la Grande Guerre. Le monde et l'après 1918* (Paris: Tallandier, 2018).

2 For instance, in the case of France, legal scholars such as Charles Valentino, author of an important Law Thesis on *Accidents du travail et blessures de guerre* (1917), Marcel Lehmann (*Le droit des mutilés,* 1918), and René Cassin.

3 Annette Becker, "Les victimes, entre 'innocence', oubli et mémoire," *Revue suisse d'histoire*, 57 no. 1 (2007).

4 Annie Deperchin, "La Grande Guerre: un non-sens juridique," in Stéphane Audoin-Rouzeau et al., eds., *La Grande Guerre dans tous les sens* (Paris: Odile Jacob, 2021).

5 Gabriel Hanotaux, *L'Aisne pendant la Grande Guerre* (Félix Alcan, 1919), quoted in Philippe Nivet, *Les réfugiés français dans la Grande Guerre. Les "Boches du Nord"* (Paris: Économica, 2004), pp. 485–6.

6 Claude Barrois, *Psychanalyse du guerrier* (Paris: Hachette, 1993).

7 Annette Becker, "Conclusion," in David El-Kenz and François-Xavier Nérard, eds., *Commémorer les victimes en Europe, XVIème–XXIème siècles* (Paris: Champ Vallon, 2011), pp. 328–9.

8 Annette Becker, *Oubliés de la Grande Guerre. Humanitaire et culture de guerre, 1914–1918*, (Paris: Noésis, 1998; Hachette Pluriel, 2003). For a study of the notion of "victims of war" in Germany, see Robert Weldon Whalen, *Bitter Wounds: German Victims of the Great War, 1914–1939*, (Ithaca et London: Cornell University Press, 1984).

9 Annex 1 of Article 232 of the Treaty of Versailles opens precisely on the damage to injured persons and to surviving dependents by personal injury or death of civilians caused by acts of war, including bombardments or other attacks on land, on sea, or from the air; of acts of cruelty, violence, or maltreatment in captivity; of damage caused to civilian victims; and of all acts injurious to "health, capacity to work, or to honour" in invaded and occupied territories. It is only from paragraph 4 onwards that the question of reparations to prisoners of war and military victims of war is addressed.

10 Peggy Bette, "Veuves françaises de la Première Guerre mondiale: Statuts, itinéraires et combats," PhD thesis, Université Lyon II, 2012, volume I.

11 The question arose again, in almost similar terms, at the time of the reconstruction of French cities bombed during World War II. On that topic, see in particular the work of Danièle Voldman, *La reconstruction des villes françaises de 1940 à 1954. Histoire d'une politique* (Paris: L'Harmattan, 1997).

12 Karl Abraham, "Contribution à la psychanalyse des névroses de guerre," in *Sur les névroses de guerre* (Paris: Payot, 2010).

13 *Journal officiel, débats de la Chambre des députés*, 1919, p. 2877, quoted in Philippe Nivet, "Le retour des réfugiés ou la violence des ruines," in *Reconstructions en Picardie après 1918* (Paris: Éditions de la Réunion des Musées Nationaux, 2000), p. 33.

14 Bruno Cabanes, "Die französischen Soldaten und der 'Verlust des Sieges,'" in Gerd Krumeich, ed., *Versailles 1919. Ziele, Wirkung, Wahrnehmung*, (Essen: Klartext Verlag, 2001), pp. 269–79.

15 Bénédicte Grailles et Patrice Marcilloux, "Les dommages de guerre," in Philippe Nivet et al., eds., *Archives de la Grande Guerre. Des sources pour l'histoire* (Archives de France / Presses Universitaires de Rennes, 2014), pp. 409–15.

16 There is a rich bibliography on the question of reparations. For an introduction, see Bruno Cabanes, "Clemenceau vu par Keynes: une réévaluation," in Sylvie Brodziak, ed., *Georges Clemenceau et la Grande Guerre* (La Crèche: Geste Éditions, 2010), pp. 203–15.

17 Several recent studies have focused on Léon Bourgeois, shedding new light on how important his influence was on politicians of the Third Republic. See especially Marie-Claude Blais, *La solidarité. Histoire d'une idée* (Paris: Gallimard, 2007) and Serge Paugal, ed., *Repenser la solidarité. L'apport des sciences sociales* (Paris: PUF, 2007). On Bourgeois's role in post-war international milieus, see Marie-Adelaide Zeyer, *Léon Bourgeois, père spirituel de la Société des Nations. Solidarité internationale et service de la France (1899–1909)*, thèse de l'École des Chartes, 2006.

18 The first mention of the concept of "reparation" for war victims appears in a law of 26 December 1914. It concerns "those who were victims in their property" at the time of the German invasion and presents the state as insurer of last resort, in the event that private insurance is lacking.

19 On the question of humanitarianism during and after World War I, see Annette Becker, *Oubliés de la Grande Guerre*, and Bruno Cabanes, *The Great War and the Origins of Humanitarianism, 1918–1924* (Cambridge: Cambridge University Press, 2014).

20 Pierre Renouvin, *Les formes du gouvernement de guerre* (Paris and New Haven, CT: Presses universitaires de France and Yale University Press, 1925).

21 Danièle Voldman, "Reconstituer les pays aplatis," in *Reconstructions en Picardie après 1918* (Paris : Éditions de la Réunion des Musées Nationaux, 2000).

22 Olivier Faron, *Les enfants du deuil. Orphelins et pupilles de la Nation de la Première guerre mondiale (1914–1941)* (Paris: La Découverte, 2001).

23 René Querenet, *Conférence faite au Comité d'entente des œuvres venant en aide aux veuves et aux orphelins de la guerre* (Paris, 1918).

24 Brian Turner, *Vulnerability and Human Rights* (University Park, PA: The Pennsylvania State University Press, 2006).

25 Didier Fassin and Richard Rechtman, *L'Empire du traumatisme* (Paris: Flammarion, 2007), transl. *The Empire of Trauma: An Enquiry into the Condition of Victimhood* (Princeton and Oxford: Princeton University Press, 2009).

26 George L. Mosse, "Shell-shock as a Social Disease," *Journal of Contemporary History*, 35, no. 1 (January 2000), pp. 101–8.

27 Wolfgang Schivelbush, *The Culture of Defeat: On National Trauma, Mourning and Recovery* (London: Granta, 2003); John Horne, "Defeat and Memory in Modern History," in Jenny Macleod, ed., *Defeat and Memory: Cultural Histories of Military Defeat in the Modern Era,* (London: Palgrave Macmillan, 2008); the notion of "culture of victory" is discussed in Julia Eichenberg and John Paul Newman, eds., *The Great War and Veterans Internationalism* (London: Palgrave Macmillan, 2013).

28 René Cassin, "Fragments autobiographiques," *La pensée et l'action* (Paris: Éditions F. Lalou, 1972), p. 197.

29 *Journal des Mutilés et Réformés,* 1 March 1917, p. 3.

30 Similar provisions applied to other war victims. In January 1915, the Minister of Finance decreed the allocation of three-quarters of vacant tobacco stores to war widows and war orphans, reviving an old practice, dating back to Napoleon I, which reserved the retail sale of tobacco to the families of deceased soldiers (decrees of 29 December 1810 and 11 January 1811).

31 Jean-Christophe Fichou, "De l'irrationalité de la loi de 1923 sur l'emploi des mutilés de guerre dans le service des Phares et Balises," *Annales de Bretagne et des Pays de l'Ouest* 121, no. 1 (2014), pp. 147–65. On health assistance and vocational rehabilitation policies, Jean-François Montès, *1915–1939. (Re)travailler ou le retour du mutilé: une histoire de l'entre-deux-guerres,* (Rapport de recherche effectué pour l'Office national des anciens combattants et victimes de guerre, 1991); Romain Pierre, "À l'origine de la réinsertion professionnelle des personnes handicapées: la prise en charge des invalides de guerre," *Revue française des affaires sociales,* no. 2 (2005), pp. 229–47; Vincent Viet, *La santé en guerre, 1914–1918. Une politique pionnière en univers incertain,* (Paris: Presses de Sciences Po, 2015); Catherine Omnès, "La réinsertion professionnelle des pensionnés de guerre en France: la loi du 26 avril 1924. Un legs de la Première Guerre mondiale?" *Revue d'histoire de la protection sociale,* no. 8 (2015), pp. 167–81.

32 Marcel Ferraris, *Chambre des députés, 30 June 1921,* quoted in Peggy Bette, "Reclasser les victimes de la Première Guerre mondiale. Le cas de la loi du 30 janvier 1923 sur les emplois réservés en France (1923–1939)," AMNIS. *Revue de civilisation contemporaine Europes/ Amériques,* 6 (2006). On the reconstruction of bodies, the return to work, and the restoration of male identities, see Julie Powell's PhD dissertation "The Labor Army of Tomorrow: Masculinity, Allied Rehabilitation, and the First World War," The Ohio State University, 2020.

33 Charles Valentino, secretary-general of the UF from 1918, became director of the Bureau of Pensions in 1920.

34 *Journal des Mutilés et Réformés,* 8 December 1917.

35 Presumption of origin was already affirmed in the law of 9 December 1916 concerning special temporary allowances for discharged soldiers (réformés no. 2).

36 The Chamber of Deputies had initially adopted an allowance scale of 2,400 francs per year for a soldier declared 100 per cent disabled, which was more or less equal to the cost of living for a year, estimated at 2,500 francs. But inflation tended to reduce veterans' purchasing power sharply at the beginning of the 1920s. See Antoine Prost, *Les anciens combattants et la société française,* (Paris: Presses de la Fondation Nationale des Sciences Politiques, 1977), vol. I, p. 55.

37 Report at the Congress of Nancy, 15–17 May 1921, pp. 126–34, quoted in Antoine Prost and Jay Winter, *René Cassin,* (Paris: Fayard, 2011), p. 55.

38 René Cassin, "Fragments autobiographiques,"p. 201.

39 Marc Roudebush, "A Patient Fights Back: Neurology in the Court of Public Opinion in France during the First World War," *Journal of Contemporary History,* 35, no. 1 (2000), pp. 29–38.

40 This theme appears again in discussions over measures for retired veterans, begun in 1930. In 1933, Cassin reaffirmed the legitimacy of these measures: "This is not generosity on the part of the State towards victims of the war and veterans, but the reparation for personal damage" (Report at the Congress of the UF in Limoges, 3–7 June 1933).

41 The law of April 1831 was based on the principle that officers discharged as a result of injury should not be forced to work: the disability pension was due to them, it was there to enable them to hold their rank, whatever the circumstances. In contrast, whether a non-commissioned officer or private received a pension was determined by the severity of the injury. If the infirmity was such that it prevented the veteran from earning a living, a pension was awarded, provided that the veteran could prove that the injury had been sustained on the battlefield. If not, the disabled veteran had to find a job upon returning to civilian life. See Antoine Prost, *Les anciens combattants et la société française,* vol. I, pp. 14–15.

42 *Journal des Mutilés et Réformés,* 1 June 1917.

43 Isser Woloch, "A Sacred Debt: Veterans and the State in Revolutionary and Napoleonic France," in David Gerber, ed., *Disabled Veterans in History* (Ann Arbor: The University of Michigan Press, 2000), pp. 145–62, and his book *The French Veterans from the Revolution to the Restoration* (Chapel Hill: The University of North Carolina Press, 1979).

44 In addition to Clemenceau's speech in November 1917, in which he said of veterans, "They have rights over us," Aristide Briand recalled, in his inaugural speech as Président du Conseil in January 1921, that the disabled and the families of soldiers killed in the Great War were "the nation's first creditors." The expression was also used by Cassin in an article in *La France*

mutilée on 30 January 1921. See Antoine Prost, "Ils ont des droits sur nous," in Jean-François Muracciole and Frédéric Rousseau, eds., *Combats. Hommage à Jules Maurin historien* (Paris: Michel Houdiard Éditeur, 2010), pp. 369–80.

45 Brigitte Schroeder-Gudehus, "Pas de Locarno pour la science. La coopération scientifique internationale et la politique étrangère des États pendant l'entre-deux-guerres," *Relations internationales*, 46 (1986), pp. 173–94.

46 For a more global study of the transnationalization of aid to the war disabled, including the Permanent Inter-Allied Committee, see Gildas Brégain, "Un problème national, interallié ou international? La difficile gestion transnationale des mutilés de guerre (1917–1923)," *Comité d'histoire de la Sécurité sociale / Revue d'histoire de la protection sociale*, no. 9 (2016), pp. 110–32. See also Julie Powell's PhD dissertation, "The Labor Army of Tomorrow."

47 A / B.I.T., MU / 7 / 9 / 5, First International Conference of Disabled Soldiers and Ex-Servicemen (C.I.A.M.A.C.), Genève, 18–19 September 1925.

48 Vincent Laniol, "L'article 231 du traité de Versailles, les faits et les représentations. Retour sur un mythe," *Relations internationales*, 158, no. 2 (2014), pp. 9–25.

8 The Wilsonians: When the Traditional Order Creates Disorder (1918–1919)

CARL BOUCHARD

I became immersed in the year of turmoil between war and peace, order and disorder, through an unusual source: letters written to US President Woodrow Wilson between November 1918 and June 1919, in large part from ordinary people. I focused specifically on the letters from French men and women for at least two reasons: they sent Wilson the most letters and France was a unique state at that point – a country victorious but weary, greatly preoccupied about the imminent peace, and anxious both about its status as a major power and its ability to make its voice heard in the negotiations that would begin in January 1919. France had put everything it had into this victory, and it bore the brunt of the war more than any other country. What did its citizens think about the peace that lay before them? How did they experience this troubled period?[1]

These letters lay bare realities on which historians have been silent or have downplayed, having generally limited their interpretation of "public opinion" to the newspapers. The letters offer a way to more accurately describe the collective emotion that gripped France at the end of the Great War, a jarring blend of relief, joy, distress, hate, hope, and expectation. Contemporaries were aware that they were living in unique times that would change the course of history: people had choices, and some believed it was indeed up to the people to shape the future world order. These feelings and the sense of urgency have not been taken seriously enough by historians, who perceive them to be an isolated phenomenon, a sort of ephemeral collective illusion (how many times has the word "illusion" been used to describe both the immediate post-war period and all interwar periods?)[2] right before the great disillusion that swept through the country in the spring of 1919.

Woodrow Wilson is not the focal point of my research. Instead, my work looks at what is revealed *through him*, the way his persona was constructed, and what it says about the times. Erez Manela provided the essential insight about Wilson, that what matters was not what he said but what the world wanted to hear.[3] The same is true about the French *Wilsonmania*. For thousands of men and women who wrote him, Wilson was a benefactor, a confidant, a powerful yet generous and surprisingly accessible leader who would hear their concerns and their distress at the ravages of war, and would help them on a myriad of issues – finding a home, a job, or a lost son; getting financial support; etc. They professed a very down-to-earth Wilsonianism. Only a minority of French men and women who wrote him referred to his ideas or commented on them: they were *Wilsonians*.

This chapter will thus address Wilsonians rather than Wilson's words or deeds. Their words and their interpretation of what happened in Paris in 1919 are unique and worthy of study. Some explicit Wilsonians did not write directly to the president, such as Fernand Pila, who will be the focus of the second half of this chapter.

What did it mean to be both a Wilsonian and French in 1919? How should we interpret the dissonance between what Wilson proposed and what the majority of France expected? Just as there are Marx and Marxists, there are, unsurprisingly, Wilson and Wilsonians: the disciples are not necessarily – in fact are rarely – in lockstep with their master; they interpret and reinterpret, merging realities to give new meaning to his original words. But there are Wilsonians because, as William Mulligan points out, World War I was from its outset a war of ideas, a central one being the notion of peace. Mulligan adds that this notion of peace lends "meaning to the conflict," forming a conceptual framework for people's sometimes muddled desires for a better world, one that is more just, more prosperous, and free of the scourge of war.[4] And yet, despite all that was said about the man, despite his inconsistencies, contradictions, messianism, and hubris, Wilson was the only leader who arrived in Paris in December 1918 with a new idea, the promise of change, and a vision of the impending peace. One can question the depth of his sincerity, his refusal to offer concrete details regarding the actual structure of the new world order, just as one can legitimately question his use of his popularity for political ends;[5] but the American president nevertheless offered people who desperately needed it meaning for the war beyond mere victory.

The first letter that mentions Wilsonians by name arrived at the president's office on 7 January 1919. It was from Cesare Norsa. The registry of civil status for the city of Paris offers a few clues about him. Born in

1874, an engineer of Italian origin who worked on the telephone system, he settled in Paris after the war. His letter, written in English, provides a fitting introduction to the topic:

> Circumstances prevented me to be what I only intend and can reasonably pretend to be: an anonymous unity in the cheering and greeting and welcoming crowds you met on your triumphal way …
>
> One day may come when something more than cheers will be wanted for the sake of this faith. I feel it necessary for me to declare that, on that day, I will be personally ready to devote myself totally to it – "soul and body" as we are used to say. – I feel that nowadays millions and millions of men would take the same oath and I dream to see them grouped in a modern, open, beneficent, universal Masonry: the "Wilsonians."
>
> I have no authority to become a founder of such a League but I shall try all in my power for its realization and for my joining it as the most modest but most active and good willing member.
>
> I am, Mister president,
> Yours very faithfully devoted.[6]

From Fleeting Wilsonians to Staunch Disciples

Any historian who has so much as touched on the atmosphere in France at the end of 1918 and the beginning of 1919 has noted the popular enthusiasm for Wilson. The consummate politician, described in virtually unanimously glowing terms by the press, set foot in Paris as a liberator, a saviour. This excitement was not limited to France: Wilson was the politician of the hour virtually around the world.[7] Photos and newsreels from the times show the popular fervour that momentous 14 December 1918, the day the American president arrived in the capital.[8] In the weeks that followed, wherever the president went, a popular movement appeared in his wake, and he was greeted with the same enthusiasm whether in England or Italy.[9] Wilsonmania peaked at the end of 1918.

The broad spectrum of Wilsonians includes fleeting supporters, who were legion in France in these initial weeks. They include the hundreds of thousands of people who greeted Wilson in Brest[10] and Paris, joined by the masses who wrote to welcome him and express their gratitude to the man who enabled France to defeat its enemy. Fleeting Wilsonians were fascinated by the power attributed to the American president, seduced by his smile and the glowing portraits of him they read in the papers. The letters take the measure of Wilson's presence during the first weeks, both in the public sphere and in private circles: they show that people were talking about the president at school, in cafés, in factories, and around the table at home.[11] But the enthusiasm was conditional. Beginning in February 1919, these fleeting French Wilsonians realized that the American president was seeking less to "punish the *Boches*" than to establish a new sort of peace: Wilson had been seen as the great avenger, and people were dismayed that he had other priorities.

This initial disappointment emerges in two ways from the letters: there was a significant decline in apologetic letters to Wilson during the winter of 1919, while requests for material assistance soared, illustrating the extent of the misery and distress in France.[12] At the same time, missives more critical of the American president started to arrive, albeit in modest numbers. Of course, the letters did not include direct attacks on the president; those who took the time to write Wilson were no less grateful for the role he played in the victory, and it was appropriate to remain polite when addressing a person of such prominence. However, concerns were raised. A recurrent one was the treatment of Germany: people were worried that he would go easy on the defeated nation. One young woman, who was enamoured of the president, made the effort to write to him in English – a strategy for access used by at least one in five people writing to Wilson – to ensure he understood the desires of the French, despite her imperfect command of English.

> Monsieur,
> Your too great goodness with everybody, your splendid idea which has for noble aim to see brotherhood and friendship between all people, is in itself wonderful. We French Nation are very proud of you and of America. But in good French give me the leave to tell you that in order of your too great greatness with the Germans people you will lose perhaps the French's esteem. Because Germany must pay before all. Monsieur you will excuse me I am perhaps very impolite to write without leave. May I present to you all my admiration.[13]

Paul Liseron was less tactful in his letter of 13 March 1919, the very day Wilson returned to France after spending a month in the United States. He was polite, but he did not go easy on the president, indulging in sarcasm when he called Wilson the "Apostle of the League of Nations":

> Mr. President,
> The French are impatiently awaiting the signature of a peace treaty, reparations, restitution, and comprehensive safeguards. Rightly or wrongly, you are being accused of lending too attentive an ear to the grumbling of

> the Germans, who are suffering from nothing more than just a bit of hunger, and even at that, not across the country. Do not lose sight of this, Apostle of the League of Nations. We find there is too much talk and not enough action at the Conference.
>
> Please accept, Mr. President, my respect and devotion.

Like hundreds of Frenchmen, Liseron sent Wilson a poem, but the tone is in keeping with the rest of the letter:

> Fast and well! We grow tense and impatient
> We have had almost five months of anticipation
> If you want our praise, facts are the thing
> Otherwise, beware of what tomorrow will bring
> Wilson, take note, your star is on the decline!
> To those other than the culprits be kind
> Or history will decide that you have warped its course
> With streams of empty words and too much discourse.[14]

Nevertheless, the vast majority of letters praised the president. Among these are letters from both longstanding and newfound disciples.

Leftist Wilsonians

The French Left was more constant in its support for Wilson. At least since Wilson's January 1917 "Peace without Victory" speech, the French section of the Workers' International – the SFIO – was Wilsonian.[15] Dominique Laurent, in his study of Wilson, the newspaper *L'Humanité*, and the SFIO in 1919, maintained that Wilson's presence in France was a political opportunity the Left could not pass up.[16] The most stirring tribute to Wilson's arrival in Paris was written by Marcel Cachin on 14 December 1918 and published in *L'Humanité*. It celebrated the arrival of "the apostle of justice." Major political figures and intellectuals contributed to the edition – Anatole France, Roman Rolland, Ferdinand Buisson, Paul d'Estournelles de Constant, Jean Longuet, Charles Gide, and others – vying to outdo each other with their impassioned words. The American president's words resonated with the way those on the Left saw the future of international relations, at least the need to profoundly change the world order and put an end to the nationalism and imperialism that had brought on the war. In 1918–19, Wilson was a useful ally for a time because he also served to attack Clemenceau's policy, which Marcel Cachin was eager to do beginning on 14 December by accusing the Tiger of having done everything within his power to prohibit the "proletarian demonstrations" in support of Wilson.[17]

The far-Left veterans' association – the Association républicaine des anciens combattants (ARAC) – founded in November 1917, illustrated the enthusiasm for Wilson in civil society and among veterans. In January 1919, at the behest of one of the association's founders, Paul Vaillant-Couturier, the ARAC sent the American president a resolution announcing its support for the ideals he defended.[18] Making it a duty to "defend humanity against deadly imperialism and forcefully oppose attempts to divide and generate hate among peoples," the ARAC also affirmed its faith in reconciliation. But most importantly, it ended its resolution on a troubling note: "given the admitted failure of certain ruling mentalities, [the association] would like to express its heartfelt gratitude to President Wilson, *the only statesman who thought of sparing human lives.*"[19] One of course wonders what prompted the ARAC to make such a statement with no real basis; perhaps it was more to accuse Clemenceau than to praise Wilson, but it nonetheless raised Wilson to the level of benefactor of humanity, well above all other politicians.

However, on the Left as well, early indications of a gradual disenchantment are to be seen in the letters to Wilson. In February, it was learned that the American president would return to the United States for one month. People were worried that during his absence the tide would turn and that what remained of his influence would be forever weakened.

René Bailly of the rail workers' union – the Syndicat CGT des cheminots d'Orléans – begged him to remain in France, urging that the winds were shifting:

> I cannot express myself as a scholar; I shall write simply from the heart, and that heart is yours, because you rose above base intrigue and emerged as an apostle of justice and reason ... Because we will need your authority to create the new order.
>
> Like my comrades, I waged a campaign for four and a half years for an ideal of what is right and just; if you can ensure this ideal does not founder as it enters port, the humblest of homes will be grateful to you.
>
> My comrades and I implore you, do not leave, Mr. President, do not leave before you have assured us of lasting peace that reflects your ideals; do not leave before fulfilling the hopes that all peoples have placed in you.[20]

Two weeks later, the great Charles Richet, 1913 Nobel Prize winner in medicine and president of the *Délégation permanente des sociétés françaises de la* paix, warned Wilson: "As you leave Paris, I would like to convey my admiration and eternal gratitude. Thanks to your remarkable energy, the dream of justice- and peace-loving men has come true. But you must come back soon, as soon as possible, so that your ideal, which we share, can finally triumph, despite the opposition of uninspired and outdated theories. Come back to ensure that the benevolent peace of justice reigns."[21]

When Wilson returned, the French papers were increasingly critical of him. Soldier Louis Bouchauveau, left-wing in his leanings, meant to reassure the president in the face of what looked like a media cabal, and attached to his letter, for the president's information, a series of "articles from opposition newspapers": "Seeing in the newspapers the difficulties you face in forming the league of nations based on generalized, progressive disarmament, I would like, on my own authority, with the support of those around me, to join my voice to yours, which already has the sincere trust of the workers of the world."[22] Dominique Laurent points out that, of all the newspapers, *L'Humanité* was the daily that remained loyal to Wilsonism the longest. In the spring of 1919, however, noting that with the League of Nations established, Wilson seemed prepared to sacrifice his principles on the altar of the political realities of negotiations, its support flagged. Wilsonism was at an impasse. On the occasion of the celebration of 1 May 1919, Marcel Cachin wrote an editorial blessing the parting of the ways: "sadly, once again, the proletariat admits its bitter disillusionment … Increasingly, disappointed peoples turn their eyes toward The Internationale; they will place their hopes in it."[23] Those on the French Left who were disillusioned opted for a radical and revolutionary path, as did other fleeting Wilsonians: Egyptians, Chinese, Koreans, and the Indochinese.[24]

Hard-Line Wilsonians

With the disavowal of fleeting Wilsonians, the disappointment, and then the rupture from the Left, were there any Wilsonians left in France in February 1919? They emerged when the president came under fire. Reacting to increasingly pointed criticism, they wrote to support Wilson against all attackers. The line of argument that many people adopted was original and drew inspiration from messianism and eschatology.[25]

There were Wilsonians among World War I French soldiers. Officers such as Schlumberger,[26] Delpech, and Michaud wrote him to confide that, despite what was being said in the papers, there were millions of Frenchmen, particularly in the army, who believed in him: "We were isolated, rudderless, until the glorious days of January 1917, when we read your message to Congress. For the first time a statesman, a powerful man, spoke the compassionate words we had been eagerly awaiting for two years. The war came to seem less cruel, the mud less heavy, the blood less difficult to spill. We knew our cause had a defender. Today there are thousands and thousands of silent soldiers who have put their hopes in you, confident that you will prevent the hate shaping this new world anticipated by all men."[27] Likewise, the rabbi and veteran Jacob Choukroun wrote Wilson from Algeria in March 1919. The rabbi offered an analogy that revealed a great deal about his admiration, saying that Wilson was "like our messiah, because you are the messiah of French soldiers and the whole world."[28]

Another Wilsonian was the soldier Albert Dufal, who still believed in the president even at the end of May 1919, at a time when few French people still supported him: "How many mothers, wives, fiancées, and children (particularly in France) owe you the life of a loved one? May your name be honoured and blessed. As a humble French soldier, my experience of the Great War was much too intense not to have felt, like balm to a wound, the fundamentally benevolent work you have done. In the midst of the chaos of injustice and selfishness in which the world struggled, no man has made your truly noble gesture or had your sense of vision, justice, and benevolence."[29]

Making Wilson a messenger of God was not a new idea at the time. Since December, a number of writers had compared him to a prophet or a messiah. Célestin Bosc wrote him this note in February 1919, emphasizing the task that lay before him, but mainly supporting his desire to reach across borders and against the forces of inertia, because Bosc believed Wilson represented the interests of humanity at the Conference:

> You have in your hands a form of power unique in the annals of humanity. No man before you, be it Caesar or Napoleon, has received from God a more expansive or less contested power.
>
> You now have the obligation to God, as to man, to be worthy of this sovereignty, and to strive to push back the assaults that slander, deceit, ambition, and greed, in their many forms, make on your good faith …
>
> You must use the sovereign mandate you have from God to make peace among the peoples – not to stoke rivalries through plans for disproportionate punishment or reparations, but through sincere efforts at healing, justice, and truth.
>
> In your eyes, there must be neither German, nor English, nor French, nor Ottoman, nor Jew, nor Christian, just men born equally to love one another under the sun that shines on us all. Your name, like that of Christ, will be revered by future generations only on this condition. No one shall condemn it.[30]

A few days later, Suzanne Louis felt compelled to write him (in English) because she felt he was being unfairly attacked. He must know – because no doubt people were trying to hide it from him – that he still had disciples in France:

> I must write to you to tell you my deep esteem. You are what all men ought to be, a soul full of justice and kindness, and in this age, in which so many low acts are to be seen, you appear so great, with so pure ideas, that we are stricken with high admiration.
>
> In this moment, you are blamed by some people, because of your being too human for the humans. For that, I admire you the more. Your thoughts are too much above the crowd to be understood. Great souls are always alone. One cannot think that it is finished with the wars. Peace, instead of treating of interests and acres ought to settle Justice and Charity in the whole world for ever.[31]

In May 1919, Augustin Hamon wrote to Wilson. The relatively well-known Leftist intellectual, militant, and pioneer in social psychology was frustrated at not having been able to defend the president in an open letter he likely sent to *L'Humanité* and chose to send it to him directly, with an introduction in English. Hamon believed he was prevented from publishing because "nearly the whole of the press defends a policy that is not desired by the *menu peuple* [humble folk] of France."[32] He added: "It is not too late to appeal publicly to all nations. By letting them know the truth of how things have been going for six months, you will free yourself and you will free them. If you do not do this, the people will free themselves, but their way will be long and grievous and bloody." Hamon believed revolution was simmering. This was followed by a copy of the open letter written in French, an analysis of the moral situation of the French people, which in passing repeated a Leftist argument about the bad faith of governments:[33]

> A profound disillusionment swept over a people that happily gave its life, blood, and strength for this to be the last war! Disillusionment is not despair, but events will inevitably lead there if you do not marshal all of your strength to demand a thorough re-examination of this treaty based on fairness, on the moral foundation of: "do unto others as you would have them do unto you." Rightly or wrongly, the humble people of France have placed their hopes in you, and in you alone, because they have no trust in their leaders. They know they will brainwash them; they know or feel instinctually that leaders played on their

> sentiments to lead and to get what they wanted. They know that now they are indifferent to their interests and will and think only of satisfying their appetites. They know or feel all of this. And all of this is brewing, rumbling, bubbling up within … [People] remember your clear Messages, your radiant Fourteen Points that are impossible to misinterpret in good faith … They want you to save them from a painful, deadly path [revolution] by interposing your will based on your Messages and the Fourteen Points you have abandoned, alas, during these six months of armistice.[34]

But if, as Hamon pointed out, Wilson had abandoned his Fourteen Points, it was not by choice but rather because of the terrible battle the other two great powers, France (in particular) and Great Britain, were waging against his ideas. For hard-line Wilsonians, the American president was the victim of, rather than the person responsible for, this abdication.

Once the situation started to degenerate, Wilsonians increasingly compared Wilson the messiah to Christ. Like Christ, he offered a new gospel; like him, he was ridiculed, taunted, and mocked by the Pharisees, in this instance being the cynics and reactionary governments; like him, he sacrificed himself so a new world could be born. An 80-year-old veteran, Constantin Bridou made this very comparison in April: "you will have done more for future peace in the world than all that has been done for it since Jesus Christ, and your name, like his, shall remain eternal. Jesus of Galilee also preached justice and fraternity among men, and was the great victim of those very things."[35]

There is a similar analogy in the letter from Madame de Colombel, who wrote him the same month:

> The French are intelligent and generous; unfortunately they do not have the energy to disrupt the conservatism that is paralyzing any initiative or progress.
>
> My heart is truly filled with sadness, in thinking that you, Mr. President, will encounter great disappointments here, when you should encounter only enthusiastic support.
>
> You are a Messiah, your noble ideas are so lofty, so insightful, that they blind closed minds, who turn their heads to avoid seeing what would disrupt their selfish habits.
>
> Christ himself was misunderstood and despised by those he wanted to enlighten and save. With Him, it must be said: "Forgive them for they know not what they do. They have eyes, but cannot see; they have ears, but do not hear."[36]

One month later, Flore Delattre, "a lowly employee," compared Wilson to the "Great Maligned One of Nazareth," and told him, like Christ, "it is among the most humble that he has the most friends":

> In these troubled times, when peace and justice appear forever denied, you alone had the noble courage to share your principles with the world, which are justice for everyone and fraternity for all. And bless you for that, my dear President Wilson.
>
> As a result, you will be spared nothing, not even slander, but that is something only the just have suffered, and since the Great Maligned One of Nazareth down to present times, all those who have wanted good for humanity have been scorned by the few – and loved by the suffering multitudes. And I know that if Our Lord Jesus were to return to Earth, He would take you by the hand and say, "You are my beloved disciple."[37]

The faith of hard-line Wilsonians was unshakeable. Beginning in February 1919, their letters showed that they understood that the sort of peace they were hoping for would not materialize. They could not, and did not want to, believe that Wilson had accepted that his ideal would be sullied simply to strike an agreement among victors: Wilson was supposed to be flawless. The great disillusion of spring 1919, which affected all of France, was above all a crushing disappointment for Wilsonians.

How should the thinking of French Wilsonians be seen in light of the order–disorder dialectic? To answer this, we must turn to a dyed-in-the-wool Wilsonian, Fernand Pila.

Fernand Pila: A Quiet Wilsonian at the Quai d'Orsay

Fernand Pila has a few lines devoted to him in the history of international relations, but he remains a little-known man, despite his relatively important role in the development of French foreign economic policy in the wake of the Great War.[38] Born in 1874, the son of a prosperous Lyon silk merchant, he joined the Quai d'Orsay at the turn of the twentieth century. Pila had expertise in economic issues and an affinity for the Far East, and these two interests were reflected in his career. Appointed *consul suppléant* to Peking in 1900, then to Shanghai from 1904 to 1905, he went on to become an authority on economic issues during World War I. In 1916, he was charged with studying France's future economic system in its relations with foreign powers, in particular Germany. In August 1918, he became bureau chief for economic services in the Ministry of Foreign Affairs' department of economy and trade. More importantly for us, in 1917, he was named to the interdepartmental committee for the

League of Nations – the Comité interministériel d'études pour la Société des Nations (CIESDN) – of which his close friend Léon Bourgeois was president. As such, he was well versed in issues related to the post-war world order; he would be active mainly when discussions at the CIESDN related to economic issues.[39] After the war, he continued to rise through the ranks of diplomatic service: from 1926 to 1933, he was director of the French foreign service – Service d'oeuvres françaises à l'étranger – and then French ambassador to Japan in 1935–6, the high point of his career.

This information is relatively well known. However, history makes no mention of the fact that shortly after the war, Fernand Pila, under the pseudonym Jean Francoeur, published a two-volume work entitled *Réflexions d'un diplomate optimiste.*[40] The volumes contain a collection of letters the diplomat wrote between 1915 and 1919 to people who remained anonymous, in particular family members but also political leaders (one such letter, perhaps to Stephen Pichon, French Minister of foreign affairs from 1917 to 1920, begins with "My dear Minister"). The first volume concludes with a letter dated 15 November 1918; the second picks up at the end of the same month, ending 25 December 1919. The desire for anonymity is understandable for a diplomat, particularly since Pila took very personal positions on war and, above all, on immediate post-war policies, which contrasted fairly radically with the official French position – even with that of the CIESDN – and were extremely critical of the mindset that held sway in France in 1919. Considering this, it is somewhat surprising that nothing in the diplomatic archives suggests that Pila was interested in anything other than the economy and the Far East.

As early as 1917, Pila solemnly affirmed that he was a "Wilsonian," but then took the trouble to add that he was also a "Clemenceau supporter," a dual loyalty that is reflected in the book, the first volume of which is dedicated to the French Président du Conseil, and the second to Wilson. Aware that to some extent this was a contradiction, the diplomat took the time to explain. While he wholeheartedly embraced Wilsonian ideas, he was also grateful for the determination and power of the man who took the reins of the national resistance against Germany in 1917. To the diplomat's way of thinking, the two men complemented each other because victory was essential to the success of the post-war project Wilson advocated. This is what drove him to his bold profession of faith: "I am a Wilsonian precisely because I am French."[41]

From then on, the Wilsonian project began to occupy the diplomat's thoughts. Pila believed that the world was witness to a new type of war: it was a war of ideas[42] and principles, a war that the allies would inevitably win because they were on the right side of history. This explained his hatred of the "defeatists" in France who did not understand the value of the battle being waged. This was also why, on this "front of ideas," "it is now time for the Wilsons, rather than the Talleyrands, of the world."[43] "To establish peace as has become necessary," Pila wrote, "antiquated principles and yesterday's methods will not suffice."[44] In other words, this new kind of war must be followed by a new kind of peace, which would do away with the existing order and old diplomatic practices.

The diplomat was particularly shocked that the French did not grasp the revolution unfolding before their very eyes, paralyzed as they were by the existential battle waged since 1914: "our thinkers, leaders and diplomats seem to see none of this. They are already judging and preparing for the work of peace drawing inspiration solely from the lessons of the past, as if nothing had changed in the customs, ideas, and desires of the world."[45] As a result, France, traditionally a beacon of new ideas, gradually yielded its leadership. It no longer held the keys to peace; Wilson's America did: "In this war, it was not France that spoke great liberal and emancipating words, sovereign calls for justice and liberty, calls that unify, illuminate and command ... America took the torch and raised it."[46]

After the armistice, Pila became increasingly critical of the situation in his own country. His criticisms of French resentment and stubbornness grew frequent. Every day, he believed, the country was moving further away from Wilson and his idea of the new order. He vehemently denounced those he called the "defeatists of peace," criticized by the diplomat with the same vigour as he previously criticized the defeatists of the war.[47] Who were these new defeatists? They were people who, he believed, had no imagination or belief in the potential of the new ideas generated by the war. How could people believe that the ideas and practices of the past, which led to the disaster of 1914, were those that should guide peace in 1919? Pila took his criticism further, even indulging in the occasional insult, when he called champions of the old order "Bismarckians," adding that it made him feel indignant "when you see our people ... insisting on putting all the weight of this cherished future on the worm-eaten crutches of old theories of international politics and dated methods of diplomacy. Blinkered traditionalism and false realism, the illusion of which would quickly become fatal, because they betray the very interests, immediate and most certain, of this country."[48]

Beginning in the winter of 1919, Pila noted that Wilson became the focus of "the persistent mistrust and even incomprehension ... of most of the scholarly and leadership elite of our country who seemed to resent him for having ideas."[49] As the months went by, he grew sorrier about the state of his country and offered the ultimate criticism: "We have the force of victory and still we are calling for guarantees that a weakened loser would demand. We want to look like victors, but we are exhibiting the morality of the vanquished."[50]

But, like all Wilsonians, Pila had to face facts in the spring of 1919: the peace he so wanted would not come to pass. The world was only seduced by Wilsonian ideas but not convinced. In Pila's letters from June 1919, there was a whiff of despondency given Wilson's defeat. However, like any good apostle, he was loath to condemn his master. The president's only mistake, Pila believed, was having been right too soon.[51]

Conclusion

At the end of 1919, Pila reached the same conclusion as his fellow Wilsonians, who wrote the American president: despite the creation of the League of Nations, the 1919 order was essentially the same that had led to global disorder in 1914–18. Who could dare believe that it would not lead to further disorder? Despite the hope, despite the promise of clearly imperfect but much-needed Wilsonism, nothing had changed. So how should one look to the future and, above all, how should one understand what had just come to an end? Five months after the signature of the Versailles Treaty, in the last pages of his reflections, Pila bitterly wrote: "We need peace created by law, not just maintained precariously through policy. If this is not done, it will truly be the failure of our victory. This war will no longer have meaning and will lose its tragic utility. All that will remain will be destruction."[52]

Wilsonians in 1919 can legitimately be criticized for their idealism, or more specifically for their lack of pragmatism regarding political realities and the persistence of hate and mistrust after the war. But they were right about the devastating moral and social consequences of a war, the meaning of which still escapes understanding today.

NOTES

1 Carl Bouchard, *Cher Monsieur le Président. Quand les Français écrivaient à Woodrow Wilson (1918–1919)* (Ceyzérieu: Champ Vallon, 2015).
2 It is "the illusion of Wilsonism," Jean-Jacques Becker and Serge Berstein argue in their *Nouvelle histoire de la France contemporaine* (Paris: Seuil, 1990). Sally Marks, in a classic work entitled the *Illusion of Peace* (New York: Palgrave, 2003), used the expression to describe the whole interwar period.

3 Erez Manela, *The Wilsonian Moment: Self-Determination and the International Origins of Anticolonial Nationalism* (Oxford: Oxford University Press, 2007).
4 William Mulligan, *The Great War for Peace* (New Haven, CT: Yale University Press, 2014), pp. 3–7.
5 One of the harshest critics of the time came from the famous British economist John Maynard Keynes: Wilson "had no plan, no scheme, no constructive idea whatever for clothing with the flesh of life the commandments which he had thundered from the White House." John Maynard Keynes, *The Economic Consequences of Peace* (London: Macmillan, 1919), pp. 54–5.
6 Library of Congress, Washington, Woodrow Wilson Papers, series 5F, reel 446 (hereinafter WWP, 5F, 446), C. Norsa to Wilson, 7 January 1919. My emphasis.
7 Manela, *The Wilsonian Moment.*
8 14–18 Mission Centenaire, Arrivée du président Wilson à Paris, le 14 décembre 1918, from the Archives de la planète, http://centenaire.org/fr/video-darchive/arrivee-du-president-wilson-paris-le-14-decembre-1918-dans-les-archives-de-la-planete, Consulted 20 May 2018.
9 Daniela Rossini, *Woodrow Wilson and the American Myth in Italy: Culture, Diplomacy, and War Propaganda* (Cambridge, MA: Harvard University Press, 2008).
10 Carl Bouchard, "'Nous nous souviendrons toujours de vous': lettres de Bretagne au président Woodrow Wilson," in Sébastien Carney, ed., *1917–1919 Brest ville américaine?* (Brest: Centre de recherche bretonne et celtique, 2018), pp. 129–48.
11 Bouchard, *Cher Monsieur,* pp. 206–8.
12 Bouchard, *Cher Monsieur,* pp. 159–60.
13 WWP, 5D, 436, Thérèse Borreil to Wilson, 7 April 1919.
14 WWP, 5D, 432, Paul Liseron to Wilson, 13 March 1919.
15 Shaul Ginsburg, "Du wilsonisme au communisme: l'itinéraire du pacifiste Raymond Lefebvre en 1919," *Revue d'histoire moderne et contemporaine,* 23, no. 4 (October–December 1976), p. 583.
16 Dominique A. Laurent, "Woodrow Wilson, L'Humanité et la SFIO, décembre 1918–juin 1919," *Cahiers d'histoire. Revue d'histoire critique* [online], 114 (2011), posted 1 January 2014; consulted 4 May 2018. URL: http://journals.openedition.org/chrhc/2266.
17 L'Humanité, 14 December 1918, p. 1.
18 WWP, 5E, 444, Association républicaine des Anciens Combattants to Wilson, 5 February 1919.
19 My emphasis.
20 WWP, 5D, René Bailly to Wilson, 1 February 1919.

21 Charles Richet to Wilson, 13 February 1919. Emphasis in the original. On Richet's peace activism, see Jean-Michel Guieu, "De la 'paix armée' à la paix 'tout court,' la contribution des pacifistes français à une réforme du système international, 1871–1914," *Bulletin de l'Institut Pierre Renouvin*, 2, no. 32 (2010), pp. 81–109.

22 WWP, 5D, 433, Louis Bouchauveau to Wilson, 20 March 1919.

23 Marcel Cachin quoted in Laurent, "Woodrow Wilson," p. 20.

24 Manela, *The Wilsonian Moment.*

25 Annette Becker, "L'histoire religieuse de la guerre 1914–1918," *Revue d'histoire de l'Église de France*, 86, no. 217 (2000), pp. 539–49.

26 He is the son of Marguerite de Witt Schlumberger, an important French feminist militant. On Marguerite de Witt Schlumberger, see Mona Siegel, *Peace on our terms: the global battle for women's rights after the First World War* (New York: Columbia University Press, 2020).

27 WWP, 5D, 441, C. Schlumberger, J. Delpech and L. Michaud to Wilson, 9 February 1919.

28 WWP, 5D, 434, Jacob Choukroun to Wilson, 23 March 1919. After the war, he would become the Chief Rabbi of Medea. He was assassinated by the FLN in 1957.

29 WWP, 5D, 440, Albert Dufal to Wilson, 28 May 1919.

30 WWP, 5D, 430, Célestin Bosc to Wilson, 3 February 1919.

31 WWP, 5B, 394, Suzanne Louis to Wilson, 12 February 1919.

32 WWP, 5B, 407, Augustin Hamon to Wilson, 26 May 1919.

33 Laurent, "Woodrow Wilson," p. 16.

34 WWP, 5B, 407, Augustin Hamon to Wilson, 26 May 1919.

35 WWP, 5D, 436, Constant Bridou to Wilson, 12 April 1919.

36 WWP, 5D, 436, Mme B.O. de Colombel to Wilson, 13 April 1919.

37 WWP, 5D, 439, Flore Delattre to Wilson, 13 May 1919.

38 Peter Jackson, *Beyond the Balance of Power. France and the Politics of National Security in the Era of the First World War* (Cambridge: Cambridge University Press, 2013), in particular chapter 4; Laurence Badel, *Un milieu libéral et européen. Le grand commerce français 1925–1948* (Paris: Institut de la gestion publique et du développement économique, 1999), pp. 98–111; Georges-Henri Soutou, *L'or et le sang. Les buts de guerre économiques de la Première Guerre mondiale* (Paris: Fayard, 1990), pp. 300–2 and 552–7.

39 See chapter 7 in Jackson, *Beyond the Balance of Power*, p. 235–75.

40 Jean Francoeur (Fernand Pila), *Réflexions d'un diplomate optimiste* (Paris: Éditions Bossard, 1920).

41 Francoeur, *Réflexions*, Volume 1, p. 351.

42 Francoeur, *Réflexions*, Volume 1, pp. 190–1.

43 Francoeur, *Réflexions*, Volume 1, p. 83.

44 Francoeur, *Réflexions*, Volume 1, p. 83.

45 Francoeur, *Réflexions*, Volume 2, p. 18.
46 Francoeur, *Réflexions*, Volume 1, pp. 291 and 351–6.
47 Francoeur, *Réflexions*, Volume 2, p. 25.
48 Francoeur, *Réflexions*, Volume 2, p. 25.
49 Francoeur, *Réflexions*, Volume 2, p. 65.
50 Francoeur, *Réflexions*, Volume 2, p. 93.
51 Francoeur, *Réflexions*, Volume 2, p. 229.
52 Francoeur, *Réflexions*, Volume 2, p. 243.

Science, Gender, and Race in a Disordered Post-war World

9 "Building for Peace": American Chemist William Noyes behind Reconciliation Efforts (1919–1924)

MARIE-EVE CHAGNON

Introduction

The dark years of the war and its resolution generated hostile exchanges and resentment between scientists in warring countries. On either side of the front lines, scientists defended their country and waged a war of minds that made it difficult to find a way back to the scientific cooperation of the pre-war years.[1] The founding by scientists from Allied countries of the International Research Council (IRC), which excluded former German and Austrian colleagues, only exacerbated tensions. The Germans responded to what they considered to be an outrage with a counter-boycott, led mainly by the *Verband der deutschen Hochschulen*, an association founded in 1920 to defend the interests of German universities.[2] The disorder generated by the war, peace treaties, and the reorganization of communities of scientists who chose to reject German science would lift the veil on an illusion widely held by scientists at the time of an international scientific community immune to politics and operating above the fray. But certain scientists within the Allied camp, specifically Americans, would work once the conflict was over to bring enemy camps together, in the hopes of recreating the fraternity of scientists as imagined before the war. Reconciliation therefore was not driven by major international scientific organizations in the post-war period but by informal channels in which American and German scientists held discussions, while waiting for the conditions to reintegrate Germany.

In fact, the opposition between the two camps was not as impermeable as it seemed. Representatives of neutral countries, such as the Netherlands, Sweden, and Denmark, were the first to try to bring the parties together.[3] While recent studies have shown the involvement of neutral counties in the post-war reconciliation process, initiatives by Allied powers and partners to unite scientists and the nature of their discussions, outside of official channels, have received very little attention.[4] In fact, there was only the appearance of consensus for a boycott in the United States, where some scientists believed that the world of science should rise above the psychological wounds of the war, to reintegrate Germans in scientific organizations.[5]

While the desire to cooperate grew more urgent beginning in 1924, one of the most influential members of the scientific community, American chemist William Noyes, took concrete action early on to do just that and to find common ground that offered scientists space for discussion, which would contribute to potential cooperation. His commitment shows not only his desire to recreate a cooperative scientific community that would contribute to the advancement of science, but also his convictions about the role of scientists in bringing enemy camps closer together. As he wrote, "The chemist and other scientific men may, if they will, contribute very much toward a better understanding."[6]

This chapter will look at Noyes's initiatives in post-war Europe and the path that led him to meet with colleagues from former warring nations, where he would try to shed light on issues related to the war. True to his training as a scientist, he set out on a quest to observe and collect the facts that he believed would reveal "the truth," which he thought would be the best guarantee of reconciliation. We will focus on his political writings, including a text entitled "Building for Peace," as well as his rich correspondence with colleagues at home and abroad. While his ideas had a relatively lukewarm reception in Europe, where tensions remained high after the war, it was better in countries where distance from what was going on in Europe allowed for greater freedom in decision-making and where the war experience was less harrowing. However, American colleagues did not completely subscribe to his initiatives, their vision being more in line with the politics of their government, which refused to officially commit to political settlements in Europe. Finally, we will see that the results of his reconciliation campaign did not live up to his ideals because the traumatic experience of the war had dashed the illusion held by the scientific community of science without borders. The inability of the international scientific community to respond to the disorder created by the war and the way it ended demonstrates that science was incapable of rising above the passions aroused by the war, and this despite the objectivity of science and the need to collaborate with foreign scholars.

The American Chemist

William Noyes grew up on a small farm in Iowa. He studied chemistry at Grinnell College in Iowa, obtaining his doctorate from Johns Hopkins University in 1882 at the age of twenty-five. In the pre-war period, spending time in German universities and labs was seen as essential to enriching an education in science. Noyes spent two semesters at the University of Munich, where he worked with the great chemist Adolf von Baeyer. The months he spent in Europe made a big impression on him, allowing him to solidify friendships with researchers not only in Germany but also in France and Great Britain. In 1907, he became director of the chemistry department at the University of Illinois, where he worked for almost twenty years developing his lab. Depicted as a visionary and a scientist mindful of the in-depth work of his contemporaries, he helped the chemistry department take its place among the great university laboratories of the world. American science was thriving at the time, and discussions with European scientists were increasingly frequent.[7] Noyes received visits from many researchers during this period, such as from German chemist Wilhelm Ostwald. During his career, he was the editor of many journals, and his connections with American scientists contributed to the success of a series of monographs in chemistry.[8] His editorial work made contact with scientists around the world essential, especially German scientists who were particularly renowned and prolific at the time.[9]

At first, the outbreak of war in 1914 did not slow discussions with German colleagues. Noyes's correspondence shows that the chemist Richard Willstätter sent him a copy of "To the Civilized World," published in October 1914. In this manifesto, ninety-three German professors, artists, and writers attempted to respond to accusations against Germany following the invasion of Belgium by defending acts perpetrated by the German Army on the ground. A number of great chemists, including Richard Willstätter, Fritz Haber, Emil Fischer, and Wilhelm Ostwald, were among the signatories.[10] The exercise was so clumsily handled that it was received with indignation by the rest of the intellectual world, which interpreted it as support from German professors for their nation's goals in the war. In the United States, many scientists denounced the manifesto but would nonetheless continue to believe in the legacy of German science and the value of its research.[11] This was particularly the case for Noyes, who corresponded with a few colleagues in Germany even though he had doubts about the statements in the manifesto.[12] He wrote Willstätter in October 1914: "Whether the nations engaged in this dreadful conflict are following the rules for a so-called civilized warfare ought, perhaps to be determined by some impartial tribunal at the close of the war."[13] He then expressed a wish for a quick resolution to the war with a fair settlement for everyone.[14]

Once the United States went to war in 1917, Noyes found himself involved in the national defence program in industrial chemistry alongside the greatest American chemists. He believed that the submarine warfare being waged by Germany justified his nation entering the war.[15] Divisions could soon be seen growing within the international scientific community during this period of turmoil. A number of his colleagues in the country turned their back on their former colleagues in Germany and developed a close working relationship with scientists from Allied countries.[16] Less than a year after the armistice, the boycott of German science nonetheless led Noyes to issues related to reconciliation. He realized the extent to which war was an anachronism and represented the worst way to settle national differences.[17]

A return to normal may have seemed simple for the scientists from neutral countries, for those who joined the conflict later, for those whose territory was never invaded, but for scientists from nations at war, it was much more complicated. The four years of the war amplified animosities and nationalist tendencies in the academic world. Rather than rebuilding bridges that fell during the war, the reorganization of the scientific world helped consolidate divisions. The newly created International Research Council (IRC) denied Germany participation in international conferences, eliminated the use of German in scientific discourse, and ended the German monopoly in bibliographic publications.[18] The IRC headed up eight international unions, each representing a scientific discipline, such as the International Union of Pure and Applied Chemistry, which would adopt the restrictions of the IRC. The members of the executive committee justified these measures by accusing the Germans of having hijacked science for criminal ends and violated universal humanitarian principles. The boycott lasted twelve years, and the Germans could not take their place again without having admitted their nation's responsibility in triggering the war and having shown some form of repentance.[19]

Yet the boycott of German science was far from airtight. Scientists who regularly travelled to Germany and enjoyed lively correspondence with foreign colleagues were more likely to be immune to national sentiment. In their private discussions, many scientists were more conciliatory towards colleagues from former enemy countries, while in public statements they were largely intransigent.[20] The promotion of reconciliation first occurred outside of official scientific institutions and the government. William Noyes was eager to serve and play a role in restoring peace; the scientific reconciliation was late in coming, although it seemed obvious and necessary for the daily practice and progress of science.[21] The men of science had to take up these issues and play a role in the reconciliation process. He realized with regret the scope of the disaster caused by scientists involved in national defence on either side and took advantage of trips to Europe to talk to researchers from both camps about these questions,[22] believing that Germany could not become a peaceable member of the international community if it continued to be ostracized.[23] He had a large circle of colleagues in Germany, actively participating in international scientific organizations, and saw no advantage to the Germans being kept out of networks for scientific cooperation.[24]

Building for Peace

The reconciliation process first required the will to re-establish the facts, the search for truth, and repentance from enemy camps to overcome emotional differences.[25] It is worth noting that when he addressed the issue of the truth, Noyes seemed to confuse pure and applied scientific truth and social scientific truth. He thought if they could just put emotion aside, the facts would come out, which, like simple scientific data, could be assembled and serve as a basis for reconciliation. While Noyes believed it was essential to re-establish the truth about events surrounding the war, he was aware of the complexity of the undertaking. He wrote: "We know the psychology of war better than we did in 1914 and know what the people of a country believe is often much more important than the truth."[26] To rebuild bridges, the scientific community would need to create space for meeting and discussion and get past the resentment and mistrust generated by the war, to find a common basis from which it could work to improve conditions.[27] The American chemist would take this winding path, hoping for an eventual rapprochement between enemy camps.

In this context, the Manifesto of the Ninety-Three, through what many saw as the lies it propagated, seemed to represent a major obstacle to any intention to resume discussions with German scientists.[28] In 1918, Noyes remarked on this, while his colleagues from the American Chemical Society removed the names of Wilhelm Ostwald, Emil Fischer, and Walther Nernst from its rolls for having signed the manifesto, an action he opposed at the time.[29]

That was what also emerged from his correspondence with French chemists Charles Moureu and Charles Marie. The former said that rather than protest the violation of Belgium and the horrors committed in the north of France, the signatories of the manifesto had instead chosen to justify the German Army's conduct.[30] Before they could consider them friends and colleagues again, German scientists would have to denounce the conduct of their military leaders. The climate was so tense that Richard Willstätter wrote in his memoirs that friend and French colleague Charles Moureu would never forgive him for signing the manifesto.[31] Moureu wrote that when he saw on the manifesto the name Willstätter, a friend he had welcomed in his home before the war, it was like a dagger to the heart.[32] French scientists who responded to Noyes's request for Franco–German reconciliation would tell him virtually the same thing. Cooperating with the Germans might seem easy for Americans far from Europe, but it was simply unacceptable for the French; for this, they would have to wait for trust to be restored.[33]

Noyes was convinced that the manifesto was just a pretext for excluding German scientists. To his German colleague Fritz Haber, he wrote: "It is clear that the Manifesto is made an excuse for not renewing relations and I know from many different sources, American and English as well as French, that this is the case."[34] For Noyes, the signatories of the manifesto had simply been caught up in patriotic fervour, and it was time for them to recognize that the statements in the text were false. He invited his German colleagues to reconsider three facts in particular. The first related to the violation of Belgian neutrality that was contrary to the treaties signed by Germany; the second concerned the fire at the Leuven Library set intentionally by German soldiers; and the third related to the atrocities committed by German soldiers on Belgian territory.[35] In addition to Fritz Haber, he wrote to Wilhelm Ostwald and Richard Willstätter to test the terrain. He thought such a statement would go a long way to restoring scientific relations in the rest of the world.[36] He nevertheless was conciliatory and recognized that the Allies had their faults too. "There is great need on both sides to begin once more on a basis of honour and justice – only that can save the world from the morass into which it has fallen."[37] The manifesto should not be an obstacle to restoring international relations, but concessions should be made on both sides.

In his response, the chemist Wilhelm Ostwald defended having signed the manifesto by pointing to his right as a citizen to take a position in wartime and said that in no way should this taint his status as a scientist. He therefore politely refused to add his name to a few refutations that came.[38] As for the rest, there were many scientists who agreed to the manifesto in 1914, based on a telegram a few lines long from the text's author, Ludwig Fulda. Many of them recognized after the war that some statements were not entirely fair but never said so publicly.[39] Noyes realized with frustration, after discussions with the German scientist, that it must be humiliating to be involved in such an exercise and that most of them would rather forget the unfortunate episode. Some would confide in him during private conversations that the statements in the manifesto were false, but he realized that an official statement was a lot to ask from the defeated nation.[40] In 1925, when he got his hands on a survey conducted by Hans Wehberg with the signatories of the Manifesto of the Ninety-Three and their position on the signature, Noyes saw an opportunity to show his French colleagues that a number of signatories were troubled by the false statements in the document. They believed asserting the facts would be the best way to bring the parties together and calm tensions.

Noyes's initiatives did not receive universal approval and were sometimes criticized. In an English chemistry journal, the publication of "Building for Peace" provoked a debate that had English scientists talking for weeks. One of the respondents praised the ideas in the document but summarized the opinion of many people when he said that Dr. Noyes had a sizeable task ahead of him if he intended to promote better relations among chemists from every country.[41] This opinion was shared by many colleagues in the country. This was the case for researcher John C. Merriam, then president of the Carnegie Institute, who did not think it was a good idea to take steps too quickly towards scientists from enemy countries; he believed premature interactions would only delay the organization's progress.[42]

Noyes did not see it that way. In addition to wondering about the veracity of the statements in the Manifesto of the Ninety-Three, he investigated the issues he considered thorny that made it difficult for the scientific community to come together. He wrote to Fritz Haber: "I hope that I may be able to do just a little toward better international relations among chemists, but the politics I question must have some settlement first."[43] Noyes wondered about the issues related to the origins of the war, the use of gas at Ypres, and reparations to be paid by Germany. He may not have considered himself a specialist on these matters but wrote that he was "only an individual who has followed events since 1914 with a keen interest and a mind open to see the truth."[44] That may be why he asked for opinions from his historian and philosopher colleagues and why he consulted many scientist colleagues in the country, as well as in France and Germany. To shed light on the documents and information he was gathering about the origins of the war and to determine their authenticity, he consulted American historians Waldo Gifford Leland and Sidney Fay, both highly involved in the international academic community in the interwar period.[45] Sidney Fay supported his project and encouraged him to pursue it. He wrote: "I think you are doing a fine work in trying to bring about a better understanding between the countries in regard to war 'responsibility' and I agree with you that moderation on both sides is what we must strive after."[46] Leland was more cautious and remarked that "the search for ultimate responsibility leads one down so many different paths and oftentimes so far afield that I think it is likely to be another generation, before the historians will feel that the question is settled with a degree of reasonable certainty."[47] He doubted that relations could be improved between the former warring countries with the search for a form of compromise regarding the origins of the war alone. He thought they simply needed to let time do its work.

Noyes's efforts show that he did not believe that reconciliation would happen on its own. His meetings with colleagues in Germany and France left him with the impression that scientists were open to starting frank, sincere discussions, provided they were conducted tactfully. "This makes me think that it is not desirable to avoid the subject of controversial questions entirely when we meet with those who differ from us."[48] He believed that his discussions with scientists on either side of the Rhine and the circulation of ideas they enabled were essential. On this matter, he wrote to Waldo Leland: "That must be the basis for resuming relations – the restoration of mutual respect in spite of differences of opinion, which are sure to persist for many years to come."[49] He thought it was essential to get back to the essence of cooperation among scientists. As early as 1922, he was addressing the issue in a scientific journal. "It has long been the custom of scientific men of the world to work together in friendly rivalry, and to share their discoveries freely with each other."[50] Intellectuals had to meet, come together on the basis of shared scientific and intellectual interests, and agree to avoid political discussions.[51] He believed that only a meeting between the two camps could overcome the misperceptions on both sides.[52] He wrote to Willstätter in 1924: "The intellectual leaders of Europe should lead in ways of peace and not merely follow after the politicians and business men."[53] He found it a shame that the scientific organizations were headed up by the IRC and had to follow its policy of excluding Germans.[54] He thought inviting Germans and Austrians to International Union of Pure and Applied Chemistry activities was essential to continue the work.

On this front, he put pressure on American physicists George Ellery Hale and Robert Millikan, two scientists who, as members of the executive committee, had more influence on the IRC.[55] In his response, Millikan acknowledged that this question was becoming urgent, but he believed that official action was not advisable until issues of reparations and the political difficulties they created were favourably resolved for everyone. He continued: "Until they are, the only action which seems to me to be possible is the development of as friendly relations as possible between individual scientists in America and in both France and Germany."[56] A few months earlier, Millikan wrote to Noyes that: "It is in my mind a question of leading and not forcing."[57] The California Institute of Technology (Caltech), a newly created research centre headed up by Robert Millikan, welcomed a few well-known German scientists for short- and long-term stays in the first half of the 1920s. Far from the turmoil of

Europe, relations with the Germans could resume without overly upsetting French and Belgian sensibilities.

The issue of the boycott was sensitive within the IRC, and George Ellery Hale told Noyes of the difficulties related to the opposition of the French, including mathematician Émile Picard, who, in 1925, still had considerable influence within the organization. For Hale, Picard's commitment to the boycott was understandable given the circumstances, and he advised Noyes to avoid at all costs provoking him by criticizing French government policy.[58] Hale confided that he agreed with the idea of inviting German representatives but could not yet see how to convince Picard to consider the idea.[59] However, Noyes did note that Hale played a leading role in blocking the German boycott during inter-allied negotiations that started with French and English representatives in 1917. The strong representation of Germans in international organizations before the war made some members uncomfortable, and the boycott offered an opportunity for the United States to counterbalance German science with a rising scientific power. Representatives at these meetings, whether French, English, or American, fervently wanted to take part in reorganizing the scientific world, to occupy a leading place within international organizations in the post-war period.[60]

Furthermore, the response of American scientists to Noyes's initiatives seemed to be more broadly in line with American politics that valued informal initiatives that did not lead to the government entering into official international agreements.[61] Colleagues within the country generally encouraged the chemist's initiatives but were cautious when they became more urgent or attempted to disrupt the order established in 1919 within international scientific organizations. He was forced to wait until 1925 and beyond before a broader movement could be organized within the scientific unions that were members of the IRC, and the American sections of unions shared difficulties they were having in their work because of the German boycott.[62]

Despite Noyes's many setbacks, he remained determined and optimistic about the resolution that came out of the congress of the International Union of Pure and Applied Chemistry in Copenhagen in 1924. "For the first time the Frenchmen were willing to discuss the question quietly and it was finally agreed that the Bureau of the Union should present a resolution asking the International Research Council to modify its statutes."[63] But he found the reconciliation process to be too slow, and his tone hardened beginning in 1925. He despaired at seeing the Manifesto of the Ninety-Three still taking up so much space, accusing the French of simply acting in bad faith. He believed that scientific associations should follow the example of the League of Nations, which would soon invite the Germans to join.[64] In fact, with the Dawes Plan in 1924 and the easing of tensions, the boycott of Germany was more difficult for the IRC to justify. It was finally lifted in 1926, after a growing number of protests within the unions and, more specifically, after Germany joined the League of Nations following the Locarno Treaties. Despite this favourable climate, German academies issued conditions deemed out of proportion by members of the IRC executive, which refused them. The Germans called for apologies for the German boycott and recognition of the German language on an equal level with French and English. The renewal of informal relations with German scientists to some extent enabled the intransigence of German academies on this matter. Negotiations would continue beyond the 1930s, and it took until 1952 for the situation to find a favourable resolution.[65]

Conclusion

In the end, William Noyes never saw the rebirth of an imagined, cooperative, inclusive community of scientists he believed he had known before the war. His efforts and his commitment at the end of the war were based on this desire to get back to a science with integrity that recognized no borders and that operated above politics, a science in which work shared at scientific meetings helped advance knowledge. He wrote: "Every scientific man must build upon the work of the past and relate his work to that of his contemporaries."[66] Noyes was convinced that science's supposed immunity to politics and ideologies would help the scientific community resume pre-war relations. This illusion was undone by the First World War and the peace treaties that marked its settlement, while international scientific organizations chose to exclude former German colleagues. While the ideal that science was to be neutral and international was shared by the vast majority of scientists at the time, it could not stand up to the disorder caused by the end of the war and the peace settlement.[67]

William Noyes was indeed a product of his times; his education, which took him to German laboratories, was typical for an American scientist of the period. While the path he took to encourage post-war reconciliation differed from some of his countrymen, that did not change who the chemist was and the vision he defended during his career. His journey also shows the myriad possible responses depending on the field, the scientific practice, personal experience, and international ties. After his first study tour to Germany, Noyes never severed ties with his European colleagues. His work in publishing made him sensitive to the need of researchers to have access to literature from their foreign colleagues. The boycott of the Germans complicated dissemination and access to recent research. He believed that scientific practice and progress required the cooperation of the entire scientific community. Noyes believed reconstruction on new foundations would be possible after the war, but the wounds were too fresh, and the European scientific elite was not prepared to go down that path so soon.

In America, reconciliation among enemy camps did not seem necessary for scientific activities to resume internationally. Discussions and meetings through channels other than major scientific organizations seemed to them to be sufficient for the moment. American scientists believed they could re-establish relations with German colleagues without trying to bring enemy camps closer together. Reconciliation was just not essential to the development of American science. It was better to let the dust settle and avoid offending European sensibilities.

For Noyes, this strategy would not help prevent a future war in Europe. His commitment went beyond his desire to reconcile for the good of science; it also revealed his pacifist streak that would further develop during the latter half of the 1920s, taking up even more place after his retirement in 1926. While he pursued his research and continued to attend activities of the American Society and the National Academy of Science, he nonetheless stepped up his involvement and efforts to maintain peace. A colleague spoke about how "he spoke earnestly for peace, disarmament and good will."[68] He became a member of the American Committee for Democracy and Intellectual Freedom, and his publications, such as *Science in Place of War* and *Who Have Paid the Cost of War*, show his hope for peace and cooperation among peoples.[69] While Noyes failed in bringing enemy camps together, his efforts were no less important; they were part of a broader scientific movement to promote scientific reconciliation between the two wars and lasting peace in Europe.

NOTES

1 John Horne and Alan Kramer, *German Atrocities 1914: A History of Denial* (London: Yale University Press, 2001).

2 On the anti-boycott, Brigitte Schröder-Güdehus, *Les scientifiques et la paix. La communauté scientifique internationale au cours des années vingt* (Montréal: Presses de l'Université de Montréal, 1978), p. 240; Brigitte Schröder-Güdehus, "Internationale Wissenschaftsbeziehungen und auswärtige Kulturpolitik 1919–1933. Vom Boykott und Gegen-Boykott zu ihrer Wiederaufnahme," in Bernhard von Brocke and Rudolf Vierhaus, ed., *Forschung im Spannungsfeld von Politik und Gesellschaft. Geschichte und Struktur der Kaiser-Wilhelm-/Max Planck-Gesellschaft* (Stuttgart: Deutsche Verlag, 1990), pp. 858–85.

3 Rebecka Letteval, Geert Somsen and Sven Widmalm, *Neutrality in Twentieth-Century Europe: Intersections of Science, Culture, and Politics after the First World War* (New York and London: Routledge, 2012).

4 Brigitte Schröder has demonstrated the dissidence at the heart of the boycott movement and has shown the debates and tensions in the scientific associations during the period. Her work remains an essential reference point today. See Brigitte Schröder-Güdehus, *Les scientifiques et la paix.*

5 On cultural demobilization, see John Horne, "Introduction," *14/18, Aujourd'hui, Today, Heute* 5, special issue "Démobilisations culturelles après la Grande Guerre," (2002), pp. 43–53.

6 The Robert Millikan Papers, California Institute of Technology, Caltech, Pasadena, California, Box 11:16, William Noyes, "America First," *Journal of Industrial and Engineering Chemistry,* 14, no. 12 (December 1922), p. 2.

7 Bernhard vom Brocke, "Der deutsch-amerikanische Professorenaustausch: preußische Wissenschaftspolitik, internationale Wissenschaftsbeziehungen und die Anfänge einer deutschen Auswärtigen Kulturpolitik vor dem ersten Weltkrieg," *Zeitschrift für Kulturaustausch* 31 (1981), pp. 128–82. Kurt Düwell, "Die deutsch-amerikanischen Wissenschaftsbeziehungen im Spiegel der Kaiser-Wilhelm- und der Max-Planck-Gesellschaft," in B. vom Brocke and R. Vierhaus, ed., *Forschung im Spannungsfeld von Politik und Gesellschaft. Geschichte und Struktur der Kaiser-Wilhelm-/Max Planck-Gesellschaft* (Stuttgart: DVA, 1990), p. 751.

8 From 1902 to 1907, he was the editor of the *Journal of the American Chemical Society.* In 1907, he founded the *Chemical Abstract, ACS Scientific Monographs* (1919–41), and *Chemical Reviews* (1924–6). William Albert Noyes (1857–1941).

9 Roy MacLeod, "Der Wissenschaftliche Internationalismus in der Krise. Die Akademien der Allierten und ihre Reaktion auf den Ersten Weltkrieg," in Wolfram Fischer, Rainer Hohlfeld, and Peter Nötzoldt, eds., *Die Preußische Akademie der Wissenschaften zu Berlin, 1914–1945* (Berlin: Akademie Verlag, 2000), p. 323.

10 Jürgen and Wolfgang Ungern-Sternberg, *Der Aufruf an die Kulturwelt, das Manifest der 93 und die Anfänge der Kriegspropaganda im ersten Weltkrieg* (Stuttgart: Steiner, 1996). Marie-Eve Chagnon, "Nationalisme et internationalisme dans les sciences au XXe siècle: l'exemple des scientifiques et des humanistes français et allemands dans la communauté scientifique internationale (1890–1933)," PhD diss., Concordia University, 2012.

11 Daniel J. Kevles, "'Into Hostile Political Camps': The Reorganization of International Science in World War I," *Isis,* 62 (1971), p. 48.

12 The William A. Noyes Papers, 1870–1942, Series number 15/5/21, University of Illinois Archives, Urbana, Box 5, Noyes to Willstätter, 28 October 1914.

13 William A. Noyes Papers, Noyes to Willstätter, 28 October 1914.

14 The William A. Noyes Papers, 1870–1942, Series number 15/5/21, University of Illinois Archives, Urbana, Box 5, MP correspondence with Ostwald, Ostwald to Noyes, 18 November 1914; Noyes to Ostwald, 17 December 1914.

15 The William A. Noyes Papers, 1870–1942, Series number 15/5/21, University of Illinois Archives, Urbana, Box 5, Noyes to Ostwald, 14 May 1923.

16 The George Ellery Hale Papers, 1882–1937, Library of Congress, Washington, correspondence with Schuster; Roy MacLeod, "Secrets Among Friends, The Research Information Service and the 'Special Relationship' in Allied Scientific Information and Intelligence, 1916–1918," *Minerva*, 37, no. 3 (1999), pp. 201–33.

17 The William A. Noyes Papers, 1870–1942, Series number 15/5/21, University of Illinois Archives, Urbana, Box 5, *Building for Peace. A Chemist's summer in Europe*, New York, The Chemical Catalog Co., 1923, p. 3.

18 Brigitte Schröder-Gudehus, *Les scientifiques et la paix*; Roy MacLeod, "Der Wissenschaftliche Internationalismus in der Krise," pp. 317–50.

19 L'Institut de France et la guerre, *Revue internationale de l'enseignement*, 69 (1915), p. 7. Roswitha Reinbothe, "L'exclusion de la science allemande et de la langue allemande des congrès scientifiques internationaux après la Première Guerre mondiale," in Pascale Rabault-Feuerhahn and Wolf Feuerhahn, eds., *La Fabrique internationale, Les congrès scientifiques de 1865–1945* (Paris: CNRS, 2010), p. 196.

20 Daniel J. Kevles, "'Into Hostile Political Camps': The Reorganization of International Science in World War I," *Isis*, 62 (1971), p. 48.

21 Austin M. Patterson, "William Albert Noyes," *American Contemporaries, Industrial and Engineering Chemistry*, 16, no. 4 (1924), p. 420.

22 The William A. Noyes Papers, 1870–1942, Series number 15/5/21, University of Illinois Archives, Urbana, Box 5, *Building for Peace. A Chemist's summer in Europe*, (New York: The Chemical Catalog Co., 1923), p. 3.

23 The Robert Millikan Papers, Caltech, Pasadena, California, Box 11:16, William Noyes, "America First," *Journal of Industrial and Engineering Chemistry*, 14, no. 12 (December 1922), p. 2.

24 The William A. Noyes Papers, 1870–1942, Series number 15/5/21, University of Illinois Archives, Urbana, Box 5, *Building for Peace. A Chemist's summer in Europe*, (New York: The Chemical Catalog Co., 1923), p. 4.

25 Tristan Anne Borer, *Telling the Truths: Truth telling and Peace Building in Post-Conflict Societies* (Notre Dame, IN: University of Notre Dame Press, 2005).

26 The William A. Noyes Papers, 1870–1942, Series number 15/5/21, University of Illinois Archives, Urbana, Box 5, *Building for Peace. A Chemist's summer in Europe*, (New York: The Chemical Catalog Co., 1923), p. 14.

27 Jodi Halpern, Harvey M. Weinstein, "Rehumanizing the Other: Empathy and Reconciliation," *Human Rights Quarterly*, 26, no. 3 (August 2004), pp. 561–83.
28 Brigitte Schröder, *Les scientifiques et la paix*, pp. 91–5.
29 The William A. Noyes Papers, 1870–1942, Series number 15/5/21, University of Illinois Archives, Urbana, Box 5, Noyes to Ostwald, 14 May 1923.
30 The William A. Noyes Papers, 1870–1942, Series number 15/5/21, University of Illinois Archives, Urbana, Box 5, *Building for Peace. A Chemist's summer in Europe*, (New York: The Chemical Catalog Co., 1923), p. 9.
31 Richard Willstätter, *Aus meinem Leben, Von Arbeit, Musse und Freunden* (Weinheim: Bergstr, 1949), p. 227.
32 The William A. Noyes Papers, 1870–1942, Series number 15/5/21, University of Illinois Archives, Urbana, Box 5, Noyes to Waldo Leland, 20 July 1924.
33 The William A. Noyes Papers, 1870–1942, Series number 15/5/21, University of Illinois Archives, Urbana, Box 5, Paul Sabatier to Noyes, 26 February 1923.
34 The William A. Noyes Papers, 1870–1942, Series number 15/5/21, University of Illinois Archives, Urbana, Box 5, Noyes to Fritz Haber, 30 April 1923.
35 William A. Noyes Papers, Noyes to Richard Willstätter, 29 April 1923.
36 The William A. Noyes Papers, 1870–1942, Series number 15/5/21, University of Illinois Archives, Urbana, Box 5, Noyes to Carl Duisberg, 9 October 1923.
37 William A. Noyes Papers, Noyes to Fritz Haber, 30 April 1923, p. 2.
38 William A. Noyes Papers, Wilhelm Ostwald to Noyes, 15 February 1923.
39 Max-Planck-Gesellschaft, Berlin, Nachlass Emil Fischer, film 17, Fischer to Baeyer, 9 January 1915; Emil Fischer to Wilhelm Waldeyer 8 July 1916.
40 The William A. Noyes Papers, 1870–1942, Series number 15/5/21, University of Illinois Archives, Urbana, Box 5, *Building for Peace. A Chemist's summer in Europe* (New York: The Chemical Catalog Co., 1923), p. 22.
41 "Editorial," *Chemistry and Industry, Journal of the Society of Chemical Industry*, 43, no. 13 (28 March 1924), p. 321.
42 The Robert Millikan Papers, Caltech, Pasadena, California, Box 8:13, John C. Merriam to George Ellery Hale, 9 January 1922.
43 The William A. Noyes Papers, 1870–1942, Series number 15/5/21, University of Illinois Archives, Urbana, Box 5, Noyes to Fritz Haber, 6 August 1923.
44 The William A. Noyes Papers, 1870–1942, Series number 15/5/21, University of Illinois Archives, Urbana, Box 5, *Building for Peace. A Chemist's summer in Europe* (New York: The Chemical Catalog Co., 1923), p. 7.

45 William A. Noyes Papers, Sidney B. Fay to Noyes, 10 June 1924. The documents and information that he assembled came primarily from his colleague Carl Duisberg, with whom he corresponded abundantly in 1923.
46 The William A. Noyes Papers, 1870–1942, Series number 15/5/21, University of Illinois Archives, Urbana, Box 5, Sidney B. Fay to Noyes, 29 August 1924.
47 William A. Noyes Papers, Waldo Leland to Noyes, 29 January 1925.
48 The William A. Noyes Papers, 1870–1942, Series number 15/5/21, University of Illinois Archives, Urbana, Box 5, Noyes to Waldo Leland, 20 July 1924.
49 The William A. Noyes Papers, 1870–1942, Series number 15/5/21, University of Illinois Archives, Urbana, Box 5, Noyes to Waldo Leland, 20 July 1924.
50 The Robert Millikan Papers, Caltech, Pasadena, California, Box 11:16, William Noyes, "America First," *Journal of Industrial and Engineering Chemistry*, 14, no. 12 (December 1922), p. 3.
51 William A. Noyes, "Correspondence International Scientific Relations," *Chemistry and Industry, Journal of the Society of Chemical Industry* (8 April 1924), p. 408.
52 The Robert Millikan Papers, Caltech, Pasadena, California, International Research Council, Noyes to Hale, 19 March 1925.
53 The William A. Noyes Papers, 1870–1942, Series number 15/5/21, University of Illinois Archives, Urbana, Box 5, Noyes to Willstätter, 6 July 1924.
54 William A. Noyes Papers, Noyes to Robert Millikan, 29 May 1923.
55 Marie-Eve Chagnon, "American Scientists and the Process of Reconciliation in the International Scientific Community, 1917–1925," in Marie-Eve Chagnon and Tomas Irish, eds., *The Academic World in the era of the Great War*, (London: Palgrave Macmillan, 2018), pp. 213–31.
56 The William A. Noyes Papers, 1870–1942, Series number 15/5/21, University of Illinois Archives, Urbana, Box 5, Robert Millikan to Noyes, 23 June 1923.
57 The Robert Millikan Papers, Caltech, Pasadena, California, International Research Council, Robert Millikan to Noyes, 19 January 1923.
58 The George Ellery Hale Papers, 1882–1937, Library of Congress, Washington, pp. 42–96, G.E. Hale to Noyes, 10 March 1925.
59 The Robert Millikan Papers, Caltech, Pasadena, California, International Research Council, G.E. Hale to Noyes, 26 February 1925.
60 Marie-Eve Chagnon, "American Scientists and the Process of Reconciliation in the International Scientific Community, 1917–1925," p. 216.
61 Melvyn P. Leffler, "American Policy and European Stability, 1921–1933," *Pacific Historical Review*, 46, no. 2 (1977), p. 211.

62 Marie-Eve Chagnon, "American Scientists and the Process of Reconciliation in the International Scientific Community, 1917–1925," pp. 223–4.
63 The William A. Noyes Papers, 1870–1942, Series number 15/5/21, University of Illinois Archives, Urbana, Box 5, Noyes to Millikan, 15 July 1924.
64 The Robert Millikan Papers, Caltech, Pasadena, California, International Research Council, Noyes to Charles Marie, 11 April 1925; Charles Moureu to Noyes, 20 May 1925.
65 Rosewitha Reinbothe, "L'exclusion de la science allemande et de la langue allemande des congrès scientifiques internationaux après la Première Guerre mondiale," p. 196.
66 The William A. Noyes Papers, 1870–1942, Series number 15/5/21, University of Illinois Archives, Urbana, Box 5, *Building for Peace. A Chemist's summer in Europe* (New York: The Chemical Catalog Co., 1923), p. 23.
67 Jimena Canales, "Of Twins and Time. Scientists, Intellectual Cooperation and the League of Nations," in Rebecka Lettvall, Geert Somsen, and Sven Widmalm, eds., *Neutrality in Twentieth-Century Europe: Intersections of Science, Culture, and Politics after the First World War*, (New York: Routledge, 2012), p. 243.
68 Roger Adams, *William Albert Noyes 1857–1941, A Biographical Memoir* (Washington DC: National Academy of Science, 1952), p. 192.
69 Adams, *William Albert Noyes*, p. 192.

10 So That Our Sons Have Not Died in Vain: Calls for Peace from Pacifist and Non-pacifist Mothers after the Great War

MARIE-MICHÈLE DOUCET

The following epitaph appears on the tombstone of a French World War I soldier: "You have not fallen in vain; your children will know Peace."[1] Repeated in 1928 by Madeleine Vernet, a prominent figure in French radical pacifism, in her magazine *La Mère Éducatrice*, these words are particularly poignant: there must be meaning in the death of these beloved men; their ultimate sacrifice must not have been in vain. This wish echoes that of many mothers I came across in my research into the Great War. This sort of discourse was not exclusive to women, but it takes on particular meaning when attributed to the notion that because mothers give life they could not bear to see their sons die in battle. It was in the name of those sons, who were promised that the Great War would be "the war to end all wars," that mothers would advocate for peace after 1918. But what sort of peace would it be? While some spoke of fraternity and reconciliation with enemies, for others the desire for vengeance was too great; they believed peace demanded the annihilation of those deemed responsible for the war: Germany. On either side of the debate, women tried to find meaning in the suffering from the conflict and called for a new world order in the name of their sons who fell in combat.

This is the perspective from which I have studied calls for peace among French mothers following the Great War. Using archival documents from feminist and pacifist movements from the 1920s and 1930s as well as women's magazines, such as *La Mère Éducatrice* and *La Française*, my research analyses women's discourse in calling for peace after the First World War. Addressing a female readership, the two magazines were notable at the beginning of the 1920s both for their discussions of peace and for their readership. While the first, edited and published by Vernet, adopted an uncompromising women's pacifist discourse from its foundation in 1917 and never exceeded more than a thousand subscribers, mainly mothers and female educators who supported the pacifist movement, the second reached a much wider audience, being the weekly journal of the Conseil national des femmes françaises (CNFF),[2] and retained its militarist spirit until the mid-1920s.[3] While one should not generalize about the discourse that emerged from these sources, they do call into question the idea that all women wanted peace, an idea which had been popular since the end of the nineteenth century. But are women truly more "biologically" pacifist than men because of their gender? While the idea was popular at the time – the famous pacifist activist Romain Rolland wrote in 1919 that "you [women] could have, and should have, fought this war in the hearts of men, before it broke out"[4] – analysing the discourse of women involved in feminist and pacifist movements between the two wars reveals debates around the issue.

An analysis of these sources shows the complexity of women's discourse around calls for peace after World War I. For the past thirty years, with the emergence of women's peace studies, historians have shown that there is no such thing as a monolithic pacifist experience among women.[5] As part of this historiographical debate, this chapter will show that, far from sharing a single mindset about matters of war and peace, French women after the war adopted ideological positions that fit into "pacifist" and "defencist" postures suggested by British historian Martin Ceadel.[6] In both cases, they wanted their sons not to have died in vain, but for the former group the war was a catalyst for pacifism, while for the latter the war had created the conviction that the only true guarantee of national security was "armed peace." By focusing on the impact of the loss of a loved one on the lives of mothers, I would like to propose a new approach to thinking about issues of war and peace after the Great War.

November 1918: Celebrating Victory and Mourning Death

On 11 November 1918, the canons fell silent, ending the bloodiest conflict the world had known up to that time. A few hours earlier, the Allied nations had signed the ceasefire with Germany. After four years of sacrifice and anxiety, peace had materialized as a breath of life for all peoples involved in the conflict, particularly those who saw fighting within their own territory. But beyond the moments of elation, no one was about to forget that the war had resulted in more than 1.3 million deaths in France and that it left in its wake devastated territories and populations in mourning.

Watching the celebrations for the signing of the armistice in Paris in November 1918, what Vernet saw was an abhorrent display: "I cried at the sight of Paris on November 12," she wrote in her magazine *La Mère Éducatrice* in December 1918:

> Yes, I cried. In front of the Place de l'Opéra where the crowd shouted and danced, I whispered the anguish of my heart: The poor souls, they are dancing on the graves of the dead ... I thought of all those abandoned in the blood-soaked mud, all of that life, all of that youth, all of those men who were so beloved, who were the future and the substance of their country and who are now piled in mass graves, where hate struck them down. I thought of all of that, and while the crowd sang and shouted, I cried.[7]

These words contrast with those of a contributor to the feminist magazine *La Française* on 16 November 1918. Relating the same events as Vernet, the writer was filled with patriotism: "Glorious Arc!" she wrote about the parades through the Arc de Triomphe in the days following armistice. "Splendid shrine raised to our many glories, inscribed with the names of our heroes, feel the immortal *Marseillaise* tremble in your belly! Behold, Paris, all of Paris will pass through it to celebrate victory!"[8] There was no mention of the dead. But she referred to the throngs of grieving mothers who attended the celebrations: "Here are the mothers, strong and proud, even in mourning. Their veils are emblems of honour. They are part of their sons' sacrifice."[9] These words would undoubtedly have made Vernet break out in a cold sweat, since in her writing she took exception to glorifications of death, but at the time they reflected the patriotic discourse that had been reserved for women since the beginning of the war.

When fighting broke out in August 1914, an entire discourse developed around the sacrifice of mothers who would have to give their sons to France. But for some of these women, there was a limit to the patriotic rhetoric: mass death, and the death of their own sons, could be the road to pacifism. Was the Great War not supposed to be the war to end all wars? Linda Forcey shows that the bond between mothers and sons influenced the relationship of women to the war,[10] as the case of Mme. Eidenschenk-Patin illustrates. After losing her only son in 1915, this mother set out on a mission after discovering a letter on her son's body: "Remember the war! Remember that while I am a dutiful soldier, I am a pacifist and hope this terrible war is the last. Join forces with those who are trying to bring this dream to fruition and rid humanity of this scourge."[11] Adding to her sorrow, Mme. Eidenschenk-Patin lost her spouse to an illness contracted at the front; a veteran of the war of 1870, he had volunteered at age 65 as an interpreter and officer after his son's death. Grieving two deaths, Mme. Eidenschenk-Patin dedicated her life to peace. In 1928, she founded the Ligue internationale des mères et des éducatrices pour la paix. With over 80,000 members internationally in 1934, the league campaigned for universal disarmament and Franco–German reconciliation.[12]

For some women, such as Vernet, the connection between motherhood and pacifism was self-evident: "A mother would never support war," she wrote in April 1919; "she has been granted the sacred mission of giving life ... she cannot be an ally of the horrific death that fills the tombs and steals her sons."[13] From the same point of view, the Catholic trade unionist Marguerite Martin explained in her speech to the Fédération française de l'Ordre maçonnique mixte international in 1925: "How can women, who are naturally sensitive and good, fail to condemn the acts of brutality and savagery inherent in war? To deny this would be to deny nature itself, ever rational nature that would not give the same person the instinct of reproduction and the desire for destruction."[14] While this discourse was widespread at the time, particularly in women's circles, which made it one of the central arguments in their fight for suffrage, drawing the connection between women and peace is not actually that simple. With the emergence of gender studies, this connection has clearly been called into question,[15] but after World War I voices were already emerging that demonstrated its limitations. In 1927, Vernet added nuance to her 1919 statements. While she still believed that women were better suited than men to fighting for peace because of their maternal instincts, she maintained that "sex has nothing to do with such matters. There are women who are hawks, just as there are women who are doves. Women clearly showed during the war that patriotic passion could lead to the excess of hatred."[16] It seems that during the period between the two wars, there was a contradictory discourse on the nature of women's pacifism. While not everyone agreed that women had a biologically determined pacifism, the dominant discourse seemed to believe that women had natural qualities that predisposed them to fight for peace.

For its duration, violence, and relentless mobilization of civil society, the Great War left an indelible mark on European populations. Ideas of "never again" and "the war to end all wars" were widespread, particularly among peace activists and veterans' groups fighting militarization and warmongering.[17] "Your son was told this would be the last war. Your son was then told there would be universal peace and general disarmament,"[18] Vernet wrote in a letter to "The unknown mother of the unknown soldier," on the first anniversary of the armistice in November 1919. But Vernet was saddened by the state of the world one year after the end of the conflict and implored French mothers to break their silence: "You know they lied to you," she explained to them, "and that they lied to your son. You know he sacrificed himself in vain, that his death was in vain, that your pain is in vain. You know that your child was not killed for peace among peoples and the advent of law."[19] For Vernet, the war was a war of greedy profiteers and arms merchants who were willing to sacrifice millions of men for their own enrichment and who continued, even after the war, to take advantage of the misfortune created by the conflict. While Vernet never officially joined the French Communist Party, its theories were clearly represented in her discourse.

Of course, Vernet's ideas were far from eliciting consensus, particularly in a society that was trying to give meaning to the carnage. A few months after the publication of her letter, Vernet published a response from a reader: "Yes! Fear not: the war has done some good," Vernet wrote at the beginning of the article. "But I am not the one saying so; it was in a letter I received and feel I must mention it."[20] The reader, whose identity she protected, explained that "the war was not in vain": "You do not create upheaval among millions of men for five years, you do not spill that much blood and gold," she wrote, "without something coming out of it."[21] Pointing to Wilsonian ideals, she explained that the war allowed notions of democracy and internationalism to take hold. For Vernet, Wilsonian ideas were laudable, but they still did not justify the deaths of thousands of men.

"We, the Mothers, … Call for the General Disarmament Our Fallen Were Promised":[22] Peace through Moral and Military Disarmament

"Franco-German reconciliation, the agreement between France and Germany, assures peace in Europe,"[23] Vernet said in 1934, in her magazine *La Mère Éducatrice.* It was an opinion shared by many of her sisters advocating for peace, particularly at the beginning of the 1930s when the Conference for the Reduction and Limitation of Armaments met in Geneva, with some of the delegates showing a keen interest in the question of moral disarmament. For these women, the rapprochement between the two enemy nations required a change in mentality. In a book entitled *La Paix? Demain si les peuples la veulent* published in 1930, Léontine Roux explained: "I believe that the first disarmament, the one that hastens and lays the groundwork for material disarmament, is the disarmament of hatred."[24] Thérèse Casevitz argued similarly in an article for *La Française* in June 1932: "Material disarmament will bring lasting results only if moral disarmament comes first … Without moral disarmament, any effort will merely create a fleeting illusion."[25] These women's opinions, however, met with strong opposition on both sides of the Rhine. For many French citizens, reconciliation with the "hereditary enemy" was either dangerous or difficult, even impossible, to imagine.

The post-war period did not ease the hatred that grew during the conflict. Jean-Jacques Becker effectively points out that, for the French, World War I was first and foremost a Franco–German war and that the Germans would eventually try to exact revenge.[26] In 1918, memories of the conflict fuelled hateful statements about the German enemy: "Listen to the people of Paris," Vernet wrote in December 1918, "listen to the conversations in the streets, on tramways, and in restaurants. You will be alarmed. What horrifies me is the rise of hatred."[27] Historians who have investigated the concept of the "sortie de guerre," or the transition from war to peace,[28] have shown the complexity of the demobilization process in post-war societies, where hateful representations forged during the conflict persisted.[29] The "sortie de guerre" required military demobilization, of course, but it also required the demobilization of minds. John Horne demonstrates that while military and economic demobilizations were necessary conditions for peace, it was cultural demobilization, i.e. the pacification of minds and the gradual re-establishment of relations between the enemy nations, that would determine "the sort of peace it will be."[30] Emerging from the war did not simply mean signing the armistice and going back to peace-time activities. Supporters of reconciliation were constantly confronted with an anti-German discourse that was very much in evidence in the public space and that received support throughout the population.

For peace activists like Vernet, it was an uphill battle. If women, by virtue of being mothers, were pacifists by nature, how did one explain that French women showed so little interest in questions of peace, particularly when it came to Franco–German reconciliation? Not only did they show no interest, but in many cases, they fuelled the hate speech towards Germany. Even pacifist circles were not immune, as Vernet noted after a November 1925 meeting of the women's league for moral disarmament, the Ligue pour le désarmement moral par les femmes. She recounts how some pacifists abruptly left the room when the discussion turned to the issue of Franco–German reconciliation: "One of them said that she refused 'to hear any good about the enemy.' And that was a woman!"[31] Vernet was astonished as she summed up the events. They needed to find a solution to this indifference among some women around discussions of peace and reconciliation, particularly among those who preferred to avoid political discussions; they had to be shown that issues of war and peace directly affected them. A fascinating maternalistic argument developed tying international issues with the day-to-day lives of women, particularly when it came to Franco–German reconciliation.

On this, the example of *La Mère Éducatrice* is particularly revealing. For Vernet, the goal was to get French mothers to understand that, contrary to the popular idea that German women were "rabid warmongers,"[32] mothers from the two nations shared the same sorrow about the last war and the same hopes for the sons they were watching grow up. For Vernet, "motherhood has no motherland. The Kabyle and the Arab women who rock their children in the sun[33] are the sisters of French and German women who put them to sleep beside the fire."[34] She would not deviate from this discourse over the years. After her return from a trip to Germany in 1928, she captured the spirit of what she saw:

> My friends, I need to tell you of a lesson in peace I recently learned ... Absolutely everywhere, familiar scenes played out before me: a mother walking with her children; another young mother rocking her little one in a doorway; under a pergola in the garden, the table was set, awaiting the family; fiancés holding one another. In a verdant schoolyard, little ones frolicking under the teacher's watchful eye; near a stream, women were doing their laundry ... And when evening fell, wisps of smoke rose from the rooftops as you crossed villages; everywhere there emerged the same details of family life.[35]

Closing her account with the idea that all mothers "have the same needs, the same joys, the same feelings" and that "everyone needs bread, a home, a family, work, and affection,"[36] Vernet wanted to show French mothers that they were no different from German mothers and that they shared the same desire for peace. She saw the sense of a shared destiny and day-to-day life as the path to reconciliation between the two nations. She thought tying the daily lives of women to international concerns was a better way to interest readers in topics that were normally the purview of men.

In the middle of the decade, the signing of the Locarno Treaties (October 1925) and Germany joining the League of Nations (1926) inaugurated a certain detente in Franco–German relations and fostered a rapprochement between the two nations.[37] Additionally, the signing of the Kellogg–Briand Pact on 27 August 1928, which condemned "the use of war to settle international disputes,"[38] created hope among some French women, particularly those calling for an end to war. Just a few days after the pact was signed, Vernet wrote in *La Mère Éducatrice*:

> My friends, we have just witnessed an important day, a day that must go down in history, a day that we will solemnly remember: emissaries of great civilized nations have *outlawed war;* they have committed to no longer waging it. A new spirit must swell in our hearts, and particularly in the hearts of young people. Because it was for the young people that our fallen wanted

> the horrific war of 1914–18 to be "the war to end all wars" … For these martyrs, for the millions of dead, we need more than just empty words on tombstones; we need an act that will deliver on the promise so often etched on their tombs: "You will not have fallen in vain; your children will know Peace."[39]

Of course, the Kellogg–Briand Pact was more symbolic than practical, and peace activists were quick to point out that nowhere did it indicate any action that would be taken in the event of a violation of commitments or disarmament measures.[40] Vernet herself admitted that "the Kellogg Pact is not a guarantee of peace, because the nations that signed it are not talking about disarmament."[41] Nonetheless, the willingness of states to sign a pact that would make war a crime seemed a step in the right direction.

Of all issues that emerged from the interwar period, physical disarmament was by far the most popular topic among peace activists. At the beginning of the 1930s, they called for disarmament so that the next generation of young men would not suffer the same fate as the previous one. When the women's international petition for disarmament began circulating in 1930, at the dawn of the Conference for the Reduction and Limitation of Armaments that met in Geneva starting on 2 February 1932, more than a hundred women wrote the organizers of the petition in France to make their wish for disarmament known.[42] In a letter signed "A widow who is crying for her home forever destroyed," the sender, who did not sign her name, expressed the fears of many mothers: "The undersigned wives and mothers are outraged at the thought that billions keep being devoted to arms that will sooner or later serve to destroy their husbands or sons."[43] This idea was shared by Mme. Vacheng, who referred to herself in her letter as an "indirect victim of war," believing that disarmament was necessary so that "[her] son, born in early 1915, would not suffer the same fate as [her] husband, who was seriously mutilated in the war."[44] In 1930, these French mothers were not prepared to make the same sacrifice as those in 1914. After seeing the human and material destruction caused by modern war, they were convinced, and rightly so, that the destruction created by a new conflict would have a precedent.

Peace through the Destruction of the German Enemy

This discourse of reconciliation, peace, and disarmament, which we see in the writing of pacifist women, did not receive universal support. For other women, there was a strong desire for vengeance, and the peace their sons fought for first required the annihilation of the German enemy.

When a group of German women sent a request to Mme. Jules Siegfried, president of France's national council of women, the Conseil national des femmes françaises, to intervene with the French government to relax the terms of the armistice in November 1918, Mme. Siegfried responded categorically: "No, we will not intervene with our government to relax the terms of the armistice, which are entirely justified by the treacherous way Germany fought the war. Through those tragic years, German women, certain of victory, kept silent about the crimes of their government, their army, and their navy. Why should we step in today against terms the sole purpose of which is to prevent another massacre of our sons? … Let German women remember and understand our silence."[45] To understand Mme. Siegfried's response, one must remember that during the war, a number of French feminist associations, like those in all warring countries, had shelved their demands to perform their patriotic duty. In France, they rallied massively behind the Union sacrée, going so far as to proclaim in December 1914 that "as long as the war lasts, the wives of the enemy are also our enemy."[46] In November 1918, these women were not ready to forget or forgive their German counterparts for the horrors of the war.

In December 1918, *La Française* again attacked the silence of German women in the face of their government's actions during the war: "We must remember that the scarcity of provisions around the world was aggravated by submarine warfare, which did not meet with disapproval from German women, and the needs of the Allies and neutral countries need to be considered first."[47] At the beginning of the 1920s, when the Comité français de secours aux enfants (CFSE) launched a campaign to raise money to help German children suffering from famine, many members refused to help those they called "little Boches." Why should the French help German children, when their fathers were responsible for the suffering of French children? That was the question a teacher asked in a letter addressed to the CFSE in December 1923, at the very moment that French troops were occupying the Ruhr: "For four and a half years, French children from the north of France and Belgium endured terrible suffering under German domination. Now German children are suffering. It is a fitting reversal of fortunes; harsh and severe, I grant you, but a much-needed lesson for the Germans. That is the instinctive thought of most of our compatriots. It is cruel, it is barbaric, it is hateful, but, alas, it is human."[48] Harsh words, undoubtedly, but far from unusual. In January 1924, some members of the CFSE shared their discontent in letters addressed to its president at the time, Mme. René Dubost. "The propaganda in the Committee's newsletter to raise French money to rescue German children means that I can no longer offer moral support to this charity and requires that I tender my resignation," a letter dated 12 January 1924 reads. It went on: "I suffered for the four years I lived in Lille under the occupation of the military regime, witnessing too many acts that ran counter to the most basic humanitarian duties ... to forget and forgive a people whose leaders speak only of revenge and who persist in bad faith and hatred."[49] In a letter dated 3 January, another writer explained: "I refuse to agree to French money being directed to help feed the children of a people raised on the hatred of the French and in hopes of massacring our loved ones. I cannot, to any degree, get behind an action that risks making victims of our own children."[50] In the end, between 1919 and 1924, the CFSE managed to raise no more than 100,000 francs for German children, having raised over 1,800,000 francs for Russian children during the same period.

In his book about letters French citizens wrote to American President Woodrow Wilson, Carl Bouchard transcribed the words of Commander Gaixet, who lost his only son, age twenty, during the first weeks of the war: "We are millions of fathers, desolate, wounded, pitying the finest of the race so thoroughly wiped out by the crime of that VILE Germany, and we are counting on you, Mr. President, on your spirit of Justice, so that we do not have to write the word DUPE on the graves of our beloved children." He took his thinking even further by pointing out that only a tough peace towards Germany would avenge the death of his son and the thousands of men who fell on the battlefield: "Our beloved heroes won, but they have not yet been avenged. And they will be only once emperors, kings, princes, ministers general, bankers, financiers, teachers, and prelates who led the GROTESQUE GERMANY in 1914, have paid with their lives for the unspeakable crime they committed. Just think of the millions of poor souls who are lying on the bloody soil. Invisible, but present, they are shouting that the blood of so many heroes must not have flowed in vain."[51] In his letter, this grieving father used the same rhetoric as mothers trying to give meaning to the death of their sons. This example also shows that this discourse was not specific to women. Fathers, like mothers, shared this profound desire that their sons not die in vain, whether that meant revenge on Germany or the reconciliation of the former enemies.

However, for mothers, the use of this maternalistic discourse had particular meaning. At the time, French women were excluded from political life in the legal sense of the term: they obtained the right to vote only in 1944. As a result, motherhood was their only social identity and became, as Louise Toupin points out, the starting point for their efforts.[52] By insisting on the fact that women want peace because they are mothers, they felt they were establishing their credibility on issues normally reserved for men.

This anti-German discourse French mothers used was still very much in evidence at the beginning of the 1930s. Among the letters sent to the organizers of the women's petition for French disarmament, only 11 of the 322 were categorically opposed to any form of reduction in French troops. Despite their limited number, these letters are particularly interesting because they present another aspect of the women's discourse on disarmament and lend nuance to the argument of pacifist women, often used by Vernet, that all women, because they were mothers, would support French disarmament. On the contrary: it was precisely because they were mothers that these women opposed it. They were afraid France would be weakened and vulnerable should it disarm. For Mme. Fournier, disarmament "leads directly to war and a fresh massacre of our children":[53] she believed that only military security would guarantee French mothers that their sons would not be sent once again "[to be killed] because we have no cannons, no munitions, and particularly no heavy artillery."[54] It was the complete opposite of the argument among those seeking disarmament; they did so precisely so their sons would not suffer the same fate as the men in the First World War. Like Mme. Fournier, Mme. Delasley wrote that it was because she wanted peace that she opposed disarmament: "As a woman and a feminist, and given that war is one of the most atrocious scourges of humanity, I want peace," but "I believe disarmament is a dangerous utopia."[55] As Cécile Brunschvicg, president of the Union française pour le suffrage des femmes, pointed out in *La Française* in November 1931: "While the French are eager for peace, they worry about disarmament because they fear being a dupe and victim of their own good faith."[56] For these women, maintaining a military force was the best way to protect the safety of France and, in turn, the safety of their sons.

What those who opposed disarmament feared was primarily a Germany bent on revenge for its defeat in 1918. The women were therefore using an argument based both on the issue of security and on hatred of Germany. For Mme. B. Gellion, planning for disarmament "is to seek war, it is to lay the groundwork for it, it is to join the program for German vengeance, the first chapter of which is the immediate disarmament of France."[57] She ended her letter with blistering criticism of French pacifists: "As such, I ask that you stop sending your magazines, leaflets, and articles to me or my friends, who condemn your criminal propaganda, precisely because we want peace, and we have a heart."[58] Mme. Fournier shared that opinion and addressed her letter directly to French mothers calling for disarmament: "You want to play the role of peacemakers and preach your doctrines to German mothers who are sowing hatred and revenge among their children, brothers, and husbands."[59] Keeping the peace and maintaining security depended therefore, as Mme. Gellion wrote, "on a single factor: appearing, being, and remaining strong."[60]

Conclusion

In April 1927, nine years after the end of the fighting, Vernet made a gloomy observation about peace: "Did we not tell the martyrs who fell in the unrest that they were dying to destroy German militarism," she wrote in *La Mère Éducatrice*, "and that after their sacrifice there would be no more war? Sadly, nine years have passed … and we no longer dare say that the war of 1914 was the last."[61] While the mothers of 1918 were mourning the deaths of their sons at the front and calling for peace in their names, those of 1930 were wondering about the fate that awaited their sons in the event of a new war.

The examples presented in this chapter illustrate the complexity of mothers' discourse around calls for peace after World War I. Whether or not they were advocates of a reconciliatory peace or a tough peace with Germany, French mothers, particularly those who had lost a son at the front, would try to ascribe meaning to their son's death somehow. In the immediate post-war period, it was in the name of their sons, to whom they had promised the Great War would be the "war to end all wars," that mothers advocated for peace. But as we have seen, they did not always agree on what making peace meant. While some argued for the ideals of fraternity and reconciliation, others talked about vengeance and refused any rapprochement with the enemy, rejecting the widespread argument of women's natural pacifism. For pacifist women, moral and material disarmament became the order of the day, while for non-pacifists, an approach focused on security and national defence was required to provide protection from the German threat. Making a connection between women and peace is therefore not as simple as some commentators at the time suggested. This does not involve a dramatic shift in how the place of women was perceived between the two wars. As Susan Grayzel points out, "the cues that women received encouraged them to see their role as mothers, specifically as producers of future soldiers, as central to their identities."[62] The cases presented in this chapter support the idea that the war seemed to have reinforced rather than disrupted gender roles. This study has also demonstrated the importance of revisiting certain concepts, such as that of the "sortie de guerre,"[63] in the context of women's pacifism. Mothers who adopted a pacifist rhetoric after the war went against the general population in speaking of disarmament when the French population was almost unanimously opposed to it. Even more so, we would argue that these women did not "come out of war" at the end of the conflict because they had never really "entered" it in the first place. Unlike the majority of the French population, which overwhelmingly supported the war effort between 1914 and 1918, these pacifists seemed to escape entirely the discourse of "defense of the patrie." Rather, their post-war actions appear to be a continuation of the work undertaken before and during the conflict. As the war raged on, they laid the groundwork for the pacifist work that they actively continued after the conflict.

On a more personal scale, the study of the discourse of French women at the end of the Great War also offers a revealing avenue for analysis. In looking at the arguments of French women after the war, we see that for many of them, the question could not be limited to the international sphere. Experiencing peace daily had a direct impact on their family life: these women called for peace so that *their offspring* would not meet the same fate as their brothers during the First World War. In this sense, their concerns were less idealistic and political than those of the pacifists. Despite their efforts for awareness and education, there was a significant gap between the discourse of pacifists, based on international morality, and the more matter-of-fact discourse of "ordinary women," for whom hatred was still very much alive. In this "familial disorder" that emerged from the end of the conflict, calls for peace took on particular meaning that brought the experience of the war and peace negotiations, often perceived as high political concerns, down to a more human level.

NOTES

1 Madeleine Vernet, "La Leçon de Paix," *La Mère Éducatrice*, 11, nos. 8–9 (August–September 1928). Unfortunately, Vernet does not give any additional information on the grave in question.

2 In 1929, the CNFF had around 150,000 members. The CNFF was formed in 1901 to promote women's rights in France.

3 With the signing of the Locarno Accords in 1925 and the Geneva Disarmament Conference in 1932, the magazine *La Française* gradually adopted a pacifist-legalist discourse, or "old style pacifism." See Norman Ingram, *The Politics of Dissent: Pacifism in France, 1919–1939* (Oxford: Clarendon Press, 1991 and 2011); and Norman Ingram, "Pacifisme ancien style, ou le pacifisme de l'Association de la paix par le droit," *Matériaux pour l'histoire de notre temps*, 30, no. 30 (1993), pp. 2–5.

4 Romain Rolland, "À l'Antigone éternelle," *Les Précurseurs* (Paris, Éditions de l'*Humanité*, 1919), p. 32.

5 Frances H. Early, "New Historical Perspectives on Gendered Peace Studies," *Women's Studies Quarterly*, 23, nos. 3/4 (Fall–Winter 1995), pp. 23–31; Linda Forcey, "Women's Studies, Peace Studies, and the Difference Debate," *Women's Studies Quarterly*, 23, nos. 3/4 (Fall–Winter 1995), pp. 9–14.
6 Martin Ceadel, *Thinking about Peace and War* (Oxford: Oxford University Press, 1987), pp. 21–42.
7 Madeleine Vernet, "Noël," *La Mère Éducatrice*, 2, no. 3 (December 1918).
8 L. Armbrustery, "Le beau cortège," *La Française*, 12, no. 480 (16 November 1918).
9 Armbrustery, "Le beau cortège," *La Française* (16 November 1918).
10 Linda Forcey, *Mothers of Sons: Toward an Understanding of Responsibility* (New York: Praeger, 1987).
11 "Une femme de bien: Mme Eidenschenk-Patin," *La Française* (1938).
12 Report of the activity of the Ligue des Mères from 1 June 1933 to 30 June 1934, *Ligue internationale des mères et des éducatrices pour la paix*, 2, no. 9 (October 1934). Bibliothèque Marguerite Durand: 327 LIG Bul.
13 Madeleine Vernet, "La Masculinisation de la femme," *La Mère Éducatrice*, 2, no. 7 (April 1919).
14 Marguerite Martin, "Le rôle des femmes dans la paix," *Le droit humain, Fédération française de l'Ordre maçonnique mixte internationale* (1925), p. 5.
15 Jean Bethke Elshtain, *Women and War* (New York: Basic Books, 1987); Cynthia H. Enloe, *Does Khaki Become You? The Militarisation of Women's Lives* (Boston: South End Press, 1983).
16 Madeleine Vernet, "L'éducation sociale de la femme," *La Mère Éducatrice*, 4, no. 8 (May 1927). It is precisely around this question that Norman Ingram's paper focuses: "Gender and the Politics of Pacifism: Feminist Pacifism and the Case of the French Section of the Women's International League for Peace and Freedom," in Eva Schöck-Quinteros, Anja Schüler, Annika Wilmers, and Kerstin R. Wolff, eds., *Politische Netzwerkerinnen: Internationale Zusammenarbeit von Frauen, 1830–1960* (Berlin: Trafo Verlag, 2007), pp. 267–85.
17 Antoine Prost, *Les Anciens Combattants, 1914–1940* (Paris: Folio-Gallimard, 2014).
18 Madeleine Vernet, "À la 'Mère inconnue' du 'Soldat inconnu,'" *La Mère Éducatrice*, 4, no. 2 (November 1919).
19 Vernet, "À la 'Mère inconnue'," *La Mère Éducatrice* (November 1919).
20 Madeleine Vernet, "Les Bienfaits de la guerre," *La Mère Éducatrice*, 4, no. 5 (February 1921).
21 Vernet, "Les Bienfaits," *La Mère Éducatrice* (February 1921).
22 Vernet, "À la 'Mère inconnue'," *La Mère Éducatrice* (November 1919).
23 Madeleine Vernet, "Si nous parlions de l'Allemagne et des Allemands," *La Mère Éducatrice*, 17, nos. 11–12, (November–December 1934).

24 Léontine Roux, *La Paix? Demain si les peuples la veulent* (Nîmes: Imprimerie de La Paix par le Droit, 1930).
25 Thérèse Casevitz, "Le désarmement moral et les victimes de la guerre," *La Française*, 25, no. 1024 (4 June 1932).
26 Jean-Jacques Becker and Gerd Krumeich, *La Grande Guerre, une histoire franco-allemande* (Paris: Éditions Tallandier, 2008), p. 9.
27 Madeleine Vernet, "Noël," *La Mère Éducatrice*, 2, no. 3 (December 1918).
28 Bruno Cabanes, *La victoire endeuillée: la sortie de guerre des soldats français, 1918–1920* (Paris, Seuil, 2004); Stéphane Audoin-Rouzeau and Christophe Prochasson, *Sortir de la Grande Guerre, le monde et l'après 1918* (Tallandier, 2008).
29 Bruno Cabanes and Guillaume Piketty, "Sortir de la guerre: jalons pour une histoire en chantier," *Histoire@Politique*, no. 3 (2007/3), pp. 1–8.
30 John Horne, "Demobilizing the Mind: France and the Legacy of the Great War, 1919–1939," *French History & Civilisation*, 2 (2009), p. 102. See also John Horne, "Guerres et réconciliations européennes au 20e siècle," *Vingtième Siècle. Revue d'histoire* no.104 (2009/4), pp. 3–15.
31 Madeleine Vernet, "Protestons toujours contre la haine et l'intolérance," *La Mère Éducatrice*, 8, no. 11 (November 1925).
32 "Une belle réunion. Le Groupe d'Amis," *La Mère Éducatrice*, 9, no. 2 (February 1926).
33 This choice is indicative of the anti-colonialist discourse defended by Madeleine Vernet in *La Mère Éducatrice* at that time. See "Les enfants adoptifs de la France," *La Mére Éducatrice*, 7, nos. 9–10 (September–October 1924); "À propose de la guerre du Maroc," *La Mère Éducatrice*, 8, no. 6 (July 1925).
34 Madeleine Vernet, "Aux mères," Supplément à *La Mère Éducatrice* (February 1921).
35 Madeleine Vernet, "La leçon de paix," *La Mère Éducatrice*, 11, nos. 8–9 (August–September 1928).
36 Vernet, "La leçon de paix," *La Mère Éducatrice* (August–September 1928).
37 Jacques Bariéty, *Les relations franco-allemandes après la Première Guerre mondiale* (Paris: Éditions Pedone, 1977).
38 Article 1, Kellogg–Briand Pact. http://mjp.univ-perp.fr/traites/1928briand-kellogg.htm.
39 Vernet, "La leçon de paix," *La Mère Éducatrice* (August–September 1928).
40 Jean-Michel Guieu, *Le rameau et le glaive. Les militants français pour la Société des Nations* (Paris: Presses de la fondation nationale des sciences politiques, 2008), p. 157.
41 Madeleine Vernet's comment following André Berthet's article, "Après le Pacte Kellogg," *La Mère Éducatrice*, 11, nos. 8–9 (August–September 1928).

42 Marie-Michèle Doucet, "Prise de parole au féminin: pétition et lettres pour le désarmement chez les femmes françaises (1931–1932)," in Isabel Valente, ed., *Pela Paz! For Peace! Pour la Paix! (1849–1939)* (Bruxelles: P.I.E. Peter Lang, 2014), pp. 307–17.
43 Letter sent to *La Française* by a group of women from Chamboulive (their names are not indicated in the letter). BDIC: 4 delta res 0028. Fonds Marie-Louise Puech.
44 Letter sent to *La Française* by R. Vacheng on 22 November 1931. BDIC: 4 delta res 0028. Fonds Marie-Louise Puech.
45 "Les Françaises refusent d'intervenir en faveur des Allemands," *La Française* (30 November 1918).
46 Jane Misme cited in Françoise Thébaud, *Les femmes au temps de la guerre de 14* (Paris, Éditions de la Seine, 2004), p. 190.
47 "Les Anglaises refusent d'intervenir en faveur des Allemands," *La Française* (21 December 1918).
48 Letter from a French schoolteacher to the CFSE, 10 December 1923. BDIC, Fonds Gabrielle Duchêne, F delta res 245.
49 Dix lettres du dossier du Comité français de secours aux enfants, Comité français de secours aux enfants, 1924. BDIC. Fonds Gabrielle Duchêne, O pièce 45100.
50 Dix lettres. BDIC. Fonds Gabrielle Duchêne, O pièce 45100.
51 Letter to Woodrow Wilson, 6 February 1919, in Carl Bouchard, *Cher Monsieur le Président: quand les Français écrivaient à Woodrow Wilson: 1918–1919* (Paris: Champ Vallon, 2016), p. 225.
52 Louise Toupin, "Des 'usages' de la maternité en histoire du féminisme," *Recherches féministes*, 9, no. 2 (1996), p. 117.
53 Letter sent by Mme. Fournier to *La Française*, December 1931. BDIC. Fonds Marie-Louise Puech. F delta res 0028.
54 Letter sent by Mme. Fournier, December 1931. BDIC. Fonds Marie-Louise Puech. F delta res 0028.
55 Letter sent by Mme. Delasley to *La Française.* BDIC. Fonds Marie-Louise Puech. F delta res 0028.
56 Mme. Brunschwicg, "L'opinion publique et le désarmement," *La Française* 25e année, no. 996 (7 November 1931).
57 Letter sent by B. Gellion, 1 December 1931, to *La Française.* BDIC. Fonds Marie-Louise Puech. F delta res 0028.
58 Letter sent by B. Gellion, 1 December 1931. BDIC. Fonds Marie-Louise Puech. F delta res 0028.
59 Letter sent by Mme. Fournier to *La Française.* BDIC. Fonds Marie-Louise Puech. F delta res 0028.
60 Letter sent by B. Gellion, 1 December 1931, to *La Française.* BDIC. Fonds Marie-Louise Puech F delta res 0028.

61 Madeleine Vernet, "Autour du désarmement," *La Mère Éducatrice*, 10, no. 4 (April 1927).

62 Susan R. Grayzel, *Women's Identities at War. Gender, Motherhood, and Politics in Britain and France during the First World War* (Chapel Hill, NC: University of North Carolina Press, 1999), p. 246.

63 Bruno Cabanes and Guillaume Piketty, "Sortir de la guerre: Jalon pour une histoire en chantier," *Histoire@Politique*, no. 3 (2007).

11 "No Women of the World Hate War and Seek Peace More Than the Colored Women": Mary Church Terrell's Bid for Racial Justice and Women's Rights in 1919

MONA L. SIEGEL

The middle-aged, American woman allowed her body to fall heavily into the seat as the train departed from Dover for London. The Channel crossing had been rougher than usual; a quiet train ride would provide much needed respite. Gazing out the window, the woman mindlessly tapped a pencil against the glass, scarcely taking notice of the young man in the freshly pressed uniform who sat beside her. As the train lurched forward, the woman lost hold of her pencil, and the soldier bent to retrieve it. "Here you go, Ma'am," he said, returning the run-away implement with a full-faced grin. "Ah, a doughboy," she thought to herself, returning the smile.

After many months in the trenches, the American soldier seemed eager to speak to a proper lady. They swapped stories about their time in France, and to the woman's embarrassment, she found herself gushing like a schoolgirl, confessing her love of Paris. The soldier didn't appear to mind. He was quite taken with her voice, telling her it was "what folks who write books call 'musical.'" Noticing her bronzed complexion, the young man commented, "You might be French yourself, ma'am, if you'll pardon me for making that remark." And so the afternoon passed pleasantly, if less quietly than the woman had anticipated.

As the train rolled into the station in London and the two new friends exchanged goodbyes, a cloud of concern darkened the young doughboy's face. Good, clean lodging was hard to find in the British capital now that everyone was returning home from the war. He'd hate for his travel companion to find herself without a place to lay her head. Though the woman protested, the soldier insisted on giving her the address of an American organization that had rooms to let, where he was himself staying, before bidding her farewell.

Later that evening, the doughboy enquired at the lodging house desk to see if his friend from the train had followed his advice. The clerk looked at the soldier curiously and then let out a hearty laugh at his expense. "You boob," she jeered, "Are you blind? Couldn't you see that woman was colored?" Confused and unsure, the young soldier retreated to his room.

Sure enough, several days later, a letter arrived in a strange hand bearing the soldier's name. "I thank you so much for your effort to get me a room," the note began. "Because you were so eager to assist me, I went to the address you gave me, in spite of the fact I had many misgivings." Rooms were available, the woman wrote in the letter, but the clerk at the American lodging house had promptly turned her away. "I am a colored woman," the letter explained. "I am so accustomed to being discriminated against on account of my race in the United States I did not want to go to the headquarters of an American organization in London, although I had hoped that right after a war fought for democracy I might be treated like an American rather than a colored woman."

"Well I'll be jiggered," the doughboy exclaimed, reading the letter to the end, "That woman certainly fooled me."[1]

Titled "A Doughboy's Fatal Mistake in London," the above tale is fictional: an abridgement of a story written in 1919, or shortly thereafter, by one of the most prominent African American feminists and civil rights activists of the early twentieth century, Mary Church Terrell. A gifted speaker and essayist, and a tireless advocate for racial justice, Terrell was not much of a fiction writer. Clunky and over earnest, her "Doughboy" story never saw the light of day.[2]

While the female protagonist of the "Doughboy" story only travelled to Europe on the printed page, Mary Church Terrell did so in person in the early months of 1919. She, like a small handful of African American women who crossed the Atlantic during or after World War I, saw the Paris Peace Conference as an unparalleled opportunity to advance the two causes closest to her heart: racial justice and gender equality.[3] Neither of these concerns were particular priorities for Allied leaders as they sat down around the negotiating table to hammer out a peace settlement and define the terms of a new world order. But if the peacemakers had their eyes firmly focused on European and imperial affairs, American President Woodrow Wilson's wartime calls for a just peace rooted in democratic governance, national self-determination, and international collaboration served as a siren song to many uninvited parties who worked their way to Paris in 1919.[4]

Feminists were prominent among the disenfranchised peoples of the world who saw in the peace conference a silent invitation to air their political grievances on the global stage. In the early months of 1919 in Europe alone, female activists organized two major international meetings in the hopes of securing for women a role in shaping the peace settlement. The first of these, the Inter-Allied Women's Conference, convened from mid-February to mid-April 1919 and served as the primary lobbying body for women's rights in Paris. The second, the International Women's Congress, met in Zurich for a week in mid-May 1919. Attracting a more radical cohort of women, many of whom had risked ridicule and even imprisonment to speak out against the war between 1914 and 1918, the International Women's Congress united women across former enemy lines to champion international governance, universal disarmament, and gender equality as pillars of a new world order.[5]

It was the second of these two meetings that drew Mary Church Terrell to Europe. Terrell was one of fifteen delegates invited by the Women's Peace Party to represent American women in Zurich, an honour she shared with other prominent progressive activists, including settlement house leader Jane Addams and America's first female legislator, Jeannette Rankin. Though less of a household name than Addams or Rankin, Terrell was no stranger to activism or the public limelight. By 1919, she was "the nation's most prominent Black suffragist," a leader in the Black women's club movement, and a preeminent member of the African American community in Washington, DC.[6]

Terrell gladly accepted the invitation, but once in Europe, she found her priorities did not always mirror those of her white co-delegates. As was the case for the protagonist in "A Doughboy's Fatal Mistake," American racism followed Mary Church Terrell across the Atlantic, feeding her understandings of feminism and pacifism and shaping her political priorities as she travelled from Paris to Zurich in 1919. During these months abroad, Terrell would make common cause with Japanese peace delegates demanding the insertion of a racial equality clause in the Covenant of the League of Nations, and she would challenge white feminists to do better than the peacemakers and adopt a similar clause of their own. In short, Terrell did her level best to sow disorder in an international political milieu where most everyone – from powerful statesmen to white feminist allies – accepted the racial status quo.

Terrell was a formidable spokeswoman for both racial justice and women's equality in Europe in 1919, but waging a simultaneous battle against two entrenched forms of global oppression was no simple feat. Even as Terrell struggled to convince white feminist internationalists to confront the pernicious legacies of racism and imperialism – alienating a few would-be allies in the process – her arguments on behalf of Africans and African Americans unintentionally complicated her quest for gender equality. Terrell asserted that peace and freedom could not be understood as abstract principles, divorced from the historical realities of slavery and colonial oppression, and she used her own life history as a compelling example of the precarious nature of African American freedom. She also repeatedly emphasized the frustrating situation of Black servicemen who had fought courageously in the world war to defend democratic rights and liberties that they themselves did not enjoy. In providing an intersectional analysis of racial and gender oppression, as well as freedom and justice, Terrell made a critical, controversial, and effective intervention in international feminist thought.[7] At the same time, however, her repeated defense of Black men in uniform had the inadvertent effect of reinforcing an understanding of racial progress that cast Black leadership in militarized and masculine terms.

Mary Church Terrell waged a lonely battle against the intertwined scourges of white supremacy and patriarchy in Europe after World War I. Her isolation speaks to the limited vision of global leaders and the peace they would forge, but it also points to the shortsightedness of both white feminists and Black civil rights leaders who resisted Black women's full and equal partnership in the fight for a democratic world order in 1919 and for many decades to follow.

In Jim Crow America

Terrell began down the path that would eventually lead to Paris as a young girl. Born in Memphis, Tennessee, on 23 September 1863, Mary Eliza Church owed much to her upbringing. Both her mother and her father were born into servitude, raised by enslaved Black or biracial mothers who had been impregnated by white men. Her parents married in 1862 with the blessings of their white fathers, and Mary was born the next year. At the end of the Civil War, freed from slavery if not from the threat of racial violence, both of Mary's parents became successful entrepreneurs: her mother ran a hair salon; her father invested in Memphis businesses and real estate.[8] The couple ultimately divorced, but both were committed to providing their daughter with the best education available to a well-off African American girl in the last third of the nineteenth century. In 1884, she graduated from Oberlin College, the first co-educational institution of higher education in America as well the first to admit students without regard to race.[9]

After college graduation, Mary's father expected her to live with him in Memphis and take up the life of a proper young lady in middle-class African American society. Mary had other plans. All during college, she said, "I had dreamed of the day when I could promote the welfare of my race."[10] Such ambitions marked Mary Church as a true daughter of what African American scholar and journalist W.E.B. Du Bois termed the "Talented Tenth": the "exceptional men" of the "Negro race" distinguished by their intelligence, education, worldliness, and propensity for leadership.[11] "Racial uplift" was their credo: a service ethos that called on members of the Black elite to help fellow African Americans develop the habits of hard work, social purity, economic prudence, and sexual virtue.[12]

Between the mid-1880s and the outbreak of the First World War, Mary Church established herself as a pillar of the Black community in Washington, DC, even as she married Harvard graduate Robert Terrell and began a family of her own. In those three decades, Mary Church Terrell worked as a teacher and later as a public lecturer and a freelance writer speaking on the intertwined problems of race and sex.[13] She also served on the Washington, DC, school board, became a charter member of the National Association for the Advancement of Colored People (the NAACP), joined the (predominantly white) National American Woman Suffrage Association, and became the first president of the National Association of Colored Women, a service club that went by the motto "Lifting as We Climb." In all her paid and voluntary work, Terrell sought to promote the welfare of the African American community. When asked to speak to gatherings of white suffragists, for example, Terrell addressed the "Progress and Problems of Colored Women."[14] With other women of colour, Terrell engaged in uplift work, but she also readily entered the political fray, for example, demanding an end to the reign of terror that resulted in the lynching of over one hundred African Americans each year.[15]

When Congress voted to declare war on the side of the Allied powers in April 1917, Terrell, along with all African Americans, faced a difficult decision. Should they protest a military effort in which Black men were expected to fight and die in segregated units for a country that denied them basic civil rights? Or should they endorse a war that President Woodrow Wilson framed as a battle for global democracy and national self-determination? Most Black Americans, including Terrell, came around to supporting the Allied war effort, hoping that through their patriotism and sacrifice, African Americans would finally win the rights of full citizenship. Some, like Du Bois, also articulated a global geopolitical argument for supporting the war. In his view, World War I marked the death throes of an imperialist world order that had been built on the backs of darker skinned peoples across the globe. African Americans stood only to gain from hastening its fall.[16]

What Du Bois argued in the abstract, a close female friend of Terrell's articulated through first-hand observation. In 1904, Ida Gibbs Hunt, one of Terrell's former college roommates at Oberlin, had moved with her diplomat husband to the French colony of Madagascar. Three years later, the couple was posted to southeastern France, where they remained throughout the world war. In the midst of the conflict, Hunt wrote letters home to Terrell describing colonial soldiers' arrival in Europe from Africa and India to help secure an Allied victory. The participation of colonial subjects in the Great War, Hunt wrote, "must change things somewhat for the darker races. [The imperial powers] must recognize and recompense some of those who fought with and for them."[17]

Back at home, World War I did open economic opportunities for African Americans, helping spur the Great Migration out of the rural South and into industrial regions in the North and Midwest. For educated women like Terrell it also opened up new jobs in government service vacated by young men heading off to war. Terrell secured a position as a typist with the federal government at the War Risk Insurance Bureau. When she arrived at work, however, she noted that her department seemed to be staffed exclusively by white women. It took Terrell's distracted boss two months to notice that her complexion was somewhat darker than that of her co-workers, at which point he abruptly fired her. Assigned next to the Census Bureau with other "coloured" female clerks, she enjoyed her work until an order was issued banning African American women in her hall from using the nearest women's bathroom, which had been re-designated for white women only. Fed up with the federal government, Terrell resigned, taking a job instead teaching French to young Black men at Howard University.[18]

After the Armistice of 11 November 1918, Terrell agreed once again to sign on to the federal payroll, this time accepting a job with the War Camp Community Service, which had money to organize recreation centers for working-class girls, including in African American communities. Terrell was settling into this position when she received a letter from the American Women's Peace Party inviting her to join a delegation preparing to travel to Europe to demand women's concerns be addressed at the Paris Peace Conference.[19]

Terrell was a member of the American Women's Peace Party and was on familiar terms with the organization's president, the famous founder of Chicago's Hull House (and future Nobel Peace Prize recipient) Jane Addams. In 1915, Addams and the Women's Peace Party had gained a certain notoriety by participating in an international women's conference at The Hague, which brought women together across enemy lines to demand an end to the bloodletting in Europe. The women's extraordinary diplomatic efforts in the midst of World War I went nowhere, but female peace activists emerged convinced of the need for women's input in the post-war negotiations. At The Hague, they vowed to reconvene at

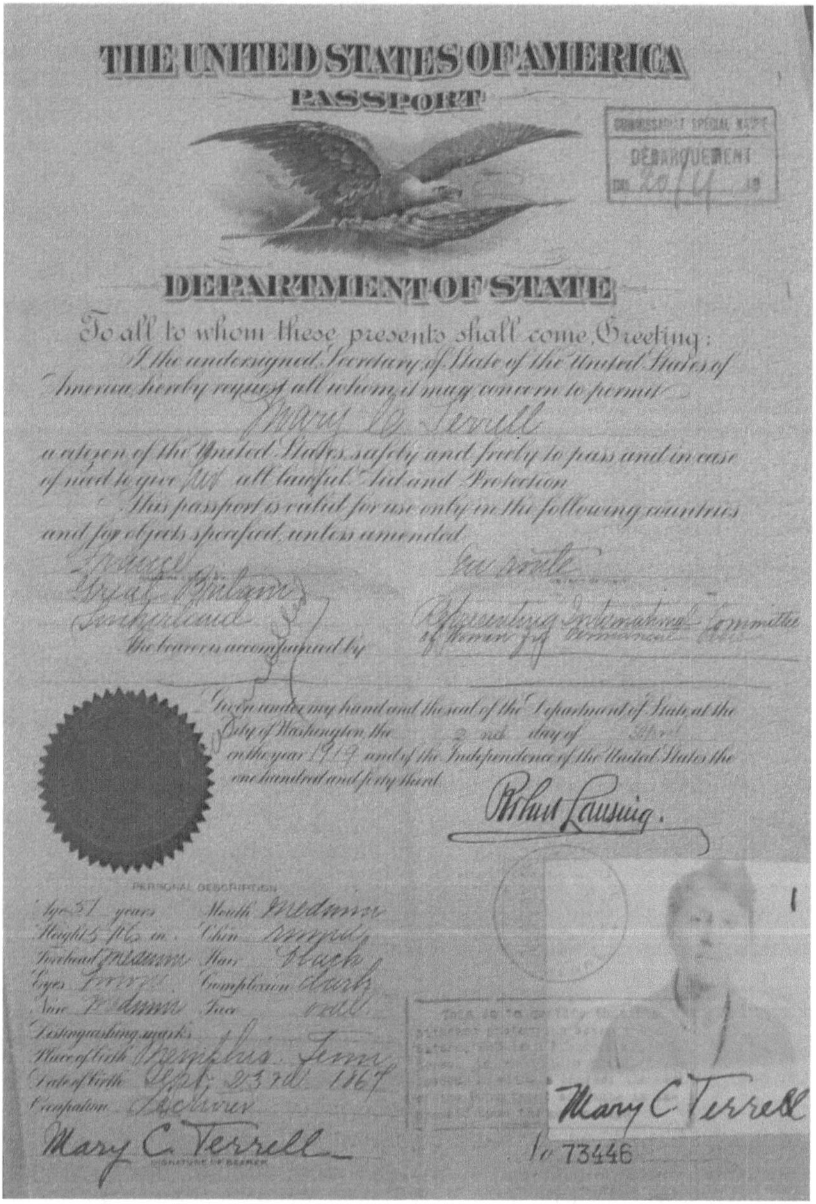

THE UNITED STATES OF AMERICA
PASSPORT

COMMISSARIAT SPÉCIAL
DÉBARQUEMENT
20/4 19

DEPARTMENT OF STATE

To all to whom these presents shall come, Greeting:
I the undersigned, Secretary of State of the United States of America, hereby request all whom it may concern to permit
Mary C. Terrell
a citizen of the United States, safely and freely to pass and in case of need to give her all lawful Aid and Protection.
This passport is valid for use only in the following countries and for objects specified, unless amended.
France / Great Britain / Switzerland — en route — Representing International Committee of Women for Permanent Peace
The bearer is accompanied by
Given under my hand and the seal of the Department of State, at the City of Washington, the 2nd day of April in the year 1919 and of the Independence of the United States the one hundred and forty third.
Robert Lansing.

PERSONAL DESCRIPTION
Age 51 years — Mouth medium
Height 5 ft. 6 in. — Chin
Forehead medium — Hair black
Eyes — Complexion dark
Nose medium — Face oval
Distinguishing marks
Place of birth Memphis Tenn
Date of birth Sept. 23rd 1867
Occupation Lecturer
Mary C. Terrell
SIGNATURE OF BEARER

Mary C. Terrell
No 73446

Mary Church Terrell, 1919 passport. Mary Church Terrell Papers, Library of Congress, Manuscript Division

the time of an eventual peace conference to make sure women had a chance to voice their concerns.

With the war over, Swiss feminists sought to fulfill this mandate by issuing a call for an International Women's Congress to meet in Zurich in May 1919. In the United States, the Women's Peace Party worked quickly to whittle its list of possible delegates down to fifteen: the number of women the American State Department reluctantly agreed to authorize to travel to Europe. Mary Church Terrell, who had not participated in the Hague Congress and who had supported the war effort, was in some respects an unlikely choice.[20] But her participation in the Zurich Congress, the members of the overwhelmingly white Women's Peace Party believed, was "terribly important for the colored people of America … for the women of America and for the cause of Permanent Peace."[21] In extending an invitation to join the American delegation, the Women's Peace Party did feel compelled to warn Terrell, "this is not an easy journey which we are inviting you to undertake under crowded conditions, in winter, to war-worn countries."[22] The intrepid activist was undeterred. African Americans, Terrell well knew, had done as much as anyone to make certain the Allies prevailed in the war to save democracy. As the sole woman of colour offered a spot on the delegation, moreover, she also felt a sense of responsibility to represent her race at the feminist congress.[23] On 9 April 1919, Terrell caught the *Noordam* in New York with Addams and the other delegates and steamed off across the Atlantic.

At the Paris Peace Conference

Terrell and her co-delegates arrived in France on Easter Sunday 1919. Their ultimate destination was Zurich, but their first stop would be in Paris, where they would have time to recuperate and to catch up on the latest diplomatic news. Setting foot on French soil, Terrell breathed a palpable sigh of relief. "How I love France and the French people!" she declared.[24] For Terrell, like for her protagonist in the Doughboy story, the indignities of daily life in Jim Crow America seemed to magically melt away in *la belle France*. "Goethe says that everybody has a fatherland and a motherland," she would later reflect. "My motherland is dear, broad-minded France, in which people with dark complexions are not discriminated against on account of their color."[25] Terrell was not blind to the fact that Black African subjects of the French empire had more reason for circumspection, but her personal experiences in Paris in 1919 largely reinforced her impression of France as a colour-blind democracy. These included a visit to the French Chamber of Deputies with Senegalese legislator and High Commissioner of Colonial Troops Blaise Diagne. There, she witnessed Black African deputies mingling with their white colleagues "just as though there were no difference in race or color at all."[26]

As Terrell soon discovered, however, even in "colour-blind France," African Americans could not escape their white compatriots' discriminatory behaviour. Upon their arrival in Paris, the other members of the WILPF delegation decided to take advantage of the time before the opening of the Zurich Congress to tour the devastated region of northern France: a major tourist draw in 1919 and an area still under military control. Convinced that an interracial party would cause a stir in a military zone where American soldiers were segregated by race, and fearful that the situation might place Terrell in an embarrassing situation, the white women in the delegation seemingly decided it would be best for all concerned to make the trip without their African American travel companion.[27] The decision was insensitive if not outright prejudicial. Terrell was hurt.

Never one to sit quietly and lick her wounds, and determined to witness the war's devastation for herself, Terrell waited for the white women to depart Paris and then went in person to the American Visitors Bureau to request permission to join a battlefield tour. The officers staffing the Bureau first delayed and then denied her request, claiming falsely that tours had been suspended. Terrell put up a loud and determined fight, going over the heads of the low-level officers staffing the Visitors Bureau and threatening to draw unwanted attention to the American military's discriminatory behaviour. Eventually, the Bureau yielded, granting her request, but even then, an African American officer was brought in to provide Terrell a personal tour, thus replicating the segregationist pattern in the military itself.[28] Terrell found the incident galling from beginning to end.

This experience explains the jarring ending Terrell gave to "A Doughboy's Fatal Mistake," in which the racial prejudices of the fictional doughboy mimicked those of the real American military officers she encountered in Paris. Everything about the character of the "doughboy" leads readers to expect him to come to the defense of his lady friend from the train as soon as her identity as a fair-skinned African American has been revealed. Instead, the soldier bemoans his own failure to perceive the woman's race and renounces the friendship. Little matter that African and African American men had risked their lives to secure a victory that was supposed to finally make the world "safe for democracy," the colour line, as far as both real and fictional white soldiers were concerned, was not to be breached.

Although the exclusion from the American women's battlefield tour stung more than she let on, Terrell put her time alone in Paris to good use, working to catch up on the swirl of discussion regarding questions of racial justice in the peace negotiations. Much had transpired prior to her arrival. In February, African American civil rights leader Du Bois and French Senegalese deputy Diagne had convened a Pan-African Congress in the French capital. Pan-African delegates, in turn, issued a series of resolutions demanding the League of Nations protect colonized peoples from exploitation and insisting that Africans and their descendants around the world "shall not be denied on account of race or color a voice in their own government, justice before the courts, and economic and social equality according to ability."[29] Terrell's college friend Ida Gibbs Hunt had been deeply engaged in planning the Pan-African Congress. Another African American acquaintance of Terrell's named Addie Waites Hunton managed to secure a spot on the program, speaking "of the importance of women in the world's reconstruction and regeneration of today, and of the necessity of seeking their cooperation and counsel."[30]

The Pan-African Congress, for all its importance to Africans at home and in the diaspora, was never given serious consideration by the peacemakers. The same cannot be said, however, of the second major effort to inject the question of racial justice into the peace negotiations: the Japanese peace delegation's proposal to insert a "racial equality clause" – prohibiting member nations from discriminating on the basis of race – in the Covenant of the League of Nations. In early January 1919, prominent African American leaders had conferred with the Japanese delegates in New York as they were in transit to Europe, encouraging them to put forward such a resolution and to make a bold stand for global racial equality at the peace conference.[31] To Black Americans, the Japanese proposal carried weighty political significance. In Paris, however, it stood little chance before the League of Nations Commission, chaired by President Woodrow Wilson, a Southerner who had allowed for the expansion of racial segregation in the federal government during his presidency.[32] Just days before Terrell's arrival in Paris, Wilson announced that the Commission was dismissing the Japanese proposal despite strong support in its favour from other peace delegates. The cause of racial equality was thus dealt a fatal blow.

Although she had reluctantly supported the American war effort, Terrell had always been sceptical of Wilson's high-minded calls for global democracy, which he belied daily by upholding the discriminatory laws and customs that permeated America's troubled Republic. Still, the news was infuriating and prompted Terrell to seek an appointment with Japanese plenipotentiary Baron Makino Nobuaki to hear firsthand what had transpired. The meeting was arranged, and together the diplomatic son of a once-great samurai family and the feminist daughter of once-enslaved parents discussed "the attitude of the proud, white races toward the dark." Makino was reserved, Terrell tells us, "a diplomat to his fingertips." Terrell was more "outspoken." "It was a great relief to my pent-up feelings," she says, "to tell him personally how shocked and sorry I was that racial equality ... had been denied Japan."[33] The meeting turned Terrell into a firm critic of the League of Nations and the entire peace process: a sentiment that would soon be echoed by anticolonial and Black nationalists disillusioned by the racism that limited global leaders' vision of a liberal, internationalist world order. The peacemakers' failure to address the legacies of racism and imperialism in the peace settlement radicalized countless men and women of colour around the globe and pointed them towards alternative ideologies in pursuit of equality and liberation.[34]

For her part, Terrell emerged from the conversation with Makino confirmed in the belief that racial justice would only become a global priority with insistent pressure applied outside the halls of power. As she packed her trunk to catch the train to Switzerland, she was already thinking about what she might do to forward the cause.

At the International Women's Congress in Zurich

The International Women's Congress, which met in Zurich from 12 to 17 May 1919, was an historic event. Although the end of the war had released international energies of all sorts, virtually all the other conferences and meetings of that year involved the Allied powers or neutral parties. In Zurich, women from the Central Powers were able to meet with women from Entente nations face to face. Together with women from neutral states, they would craft a common agenda for a just and sustainable peace. The Congress rippled with expectation and delivered its share of drama. "Attending this Congress," Terrell would later write, "was as interesting, as illuminating and as gratifying an experience as it falls to the lot of the average woman to enjoy."[35]

If the Zurich Congress was unusual due to the spectrum of the participant nations, it was less remarkable in terms of the diversity of the delegates. Looking around on opening day, Terrell could not help but notice that it was only "women from all over the white world" who were present. Given the absence of women from China, India, or Japan, let alone Africa, Terrell ultimately saw it as her responsibility to represent "the women of all the non-white countries in the world."[36] By 1919, Terrell had already built a long record of enlightening white audiences about Black Americans' travails and achievements. At the Zurich Congress, she would again be called upon to serve as an ambassador for her race, this time on a global scale.

American delegation to the 1919 Zurich Congress. Terrell is standing in the center back (seventh from the right) in a dark coat and white collar. WILPF Papers, Box 1, Folder 2, Rare and Distinctive Collections, University of Colorado Boulder Libraries

Terrell spoke twice before the Zurich Congress, both times to insist upon the centrality of racial equality to women's broader goals of peace and freedom. The first opportunity arose midway through the week, when Jane Addams asked Terrell if she would be willing to address the assembled body in a plenary session the following night. Despite the short notice, Terrell accepted eagerly. Knowing that much good will could be gained from delivering her message in the language of the host city, Terrell immediately began drafting her speech in German (a language she had mastered while living abroad for several years prior to her marriage). "Wednesday night," she says, "I did nothing but read and reread that speech until dawn."[37]

Still hard at work on Thursday morning, Terrell was obliged to set her speech aside for several hours when she was informed that a resolution she had proposed for consideration by the Congress had been placed on the agenda. Terrell first conceived the idea of asking the Congress to address the issue of racial justice a month earlier en route to Europe. "After all the other delegates on the *Noordam* had presented all the resolutions which they cared to offer," Terrell would recall, "I offered one protesting against the discriminations, humiliations and injustices perpetrated, not only upon the colored people of the United States, but upon the dark races all over the world."[38] The other American delegates equivocated, endorsing Terrell's idea in principle but seeking to alter her wording (in what manner Terrell does not tell us) right up to the last minute.[39] In the end, however, Terrell's original text was presented for the women's consideration. The resolution read: "We believe no human being should be deprived of an education, prevented from earning a living, debarred from any legitimate pursuit in which he wishes to engage or be subjected to humiliation of various kinds on account of race, color, or creed."[40]

In stark contrast to the Japanese racial equality clause, rejected in Paris, Terrell's race resolution evoked little controversy and was passed by a unanimous vote. It, in turn, became a founding principle of the Women's International League for Peace and Freedom (WILPF), the renamed, permanent organization that emerged out of the 1919 Zurich Congress. In the interwar decades, the WILPF would become the primary voice of radical feminist dissent in global policy circles.[41] "It was a proud and gratifying moment in my life when I read that resolution in person in Zürich, Switzerland," Terrell would later recount. "The only delegate who represented the dark races of the world had a chance to speak in their behalf."[42]

Later that same night, Terrell delivered her plenary address to a packed house "in a magnificent old cathedral in which women had never been allowed to speak before." From a raised pulpit looking down at the arrayed female delegates, curious Zurich residents, and international journalists, Terrell drew a deep breath and in her practiced German opened by drawing the crowd's attention to her race: "I am the only woman at this congress," she stated, "who has a drop of colored blood in her veins." Terrell commanded the Congress to recognize that the principles it claimed to profess – peace and freedom – could not be understood in the absence of a consideration of race. Offering herself up as an example, Terrell told the gathered crowd that were it not for the American Civil War, she would most likely not be in Zurich speaking to them as a free woman but instead would be "forced to live out the miserable existence of a slave."[43] Terrell's rhetorical approach was smart and deliberate. By identifying immediately as a Black woman, subject to all the risks inherent in living in non-white skin, Terrell forced her white listeners to confront their own racial preconceptions. And by simultaneously identifying as Black and embodying the ideals of civilized womanhood – refined manners, eloquent speaking, fashionable clothing – she also disrupted their understanding of racialized gender identity, both in America and around the world.[44]

The primary theme of the congress was peace, and Terrell assured her audience that despite the importance of the American Civil War to the history of her people, "No women of the world hate war and seek peace more than the colored women, whether they are in America, Africa, or some island nation." But peace, she said, could not be measured simply by the absence of conflict. "A lasting peace is an impossibility as long as the colored races are subject to injustice." This statement represented the essence of Terrell's message that evening. She warned pacifists in the audience not to put much hope in the League of Nations now that the peacemakers had rejected Japan's racial equality clause. Africa, she said, "which has been plundered so relentlessly," was no more likely to benefit from a white man's peace than were the Black victims of lynching back in the United States. A new world order demanded a new racial order as well, something the global statesmen in Paris had flatly refused to deliver. Terrell brought her speech to a close with an emotional appeal to women's sensibility and motherhood, imploring "white women of all countries" to "help the children of my race, as well as all the races who do not have white skin."[45]

Ending on a maternalist note was an astute diplomatic move. Having spent her lecture underlining the gulf of experience separating light-skinned and dark-skinned peoples, this appeal to motherhood served to remind her audience of the ties of sentiment that bound women together. Such appeals did not work on everyone. American delegate and future

WILPF secretary Emily Greene Balch, in particular, later chastised Terrell for injecting "too much militarism" into her speech.[46] But for Terrell, emphasizing the Civil War's role in ending American slavery or praising Black soldiers' wartime service did nothing to detract from the Zurich delegates' firm demand that nations renounce violence as a means of solving international disputes. Freedom and human dignity: these were virtues she emphasized through her examples. Both, she thought, were integral, not antithetical, to the establishment of peaceful world order.

Most of the Zurich delegates must have agreed, or at least they were caught up in the idealism of the moment, for they answered Terrell's speech with a long round of applause. "For once in my life I was satisfied with my effort," Terrell would later confess.[47] To the best of her ability, she had stepped onto the white women's stage and defended the basic principle that peace and freedom, sovereignty and democracy, were empty words until they extended to all people regardless of the colour of their skin.

The Zurich Congress did not so much close an era as open a new one: the beginning of women's formal engagement with international governing institutions and the adoption of women's rights as a global rallying cry. Jane Addams, who agreed to continue as president of the WILPF, left immediately for Paris to place the women's resolutions directly in the hands of the peacemakers. These included a denunciation of the draft terms of the Versailles Treaty as a victor's peace and the text of a "Woman's Charter" – calling for equal rights for men and women in the family, the economy, and in political life – which they wanted inserted in the final peace settlement.[48] Unsuccessful in altering the peace terms in 1919, the WILPF would go on to become an effective lobbying group at the League of Nations in the interwar decades. Far more than the other principal international women's organizations of the era, the WILPF spoke out against the injustices and instabilities of an imperial world order.[49] That said, it would take many decades for the WILPF, as an organization, to prioritize anticolonialism and racial equality in its campaigns for global peace and security.

In the United States, too, white WILPF members proved more open to interracial cooperation and organizing than most American feminist groups of the interwar era.[50] Terrell's commitment to the WILPF continued for many years, including several on the executive committee of the American section in the early 1920s. Other prominent African American women, including Addie Waites Hunton and Nannie Helen Burroughs, also joined the WILPF, in part due to her prodding. Even in this radical women's organization, however, Black feminists felt they had to temper their tone to gain acceptance in predominantly white feminist spaces.[51]

Terrell stuck with it because she was committed to the League's feminist, internationalist, and pacifist principles and because she firmly believed social change would only come through a united effort by whites and Blacks to challenge all forms of oppression. Nevertheless, her repeated insistence that white feminists address the racial violence and oppression that plagued Black women's lives was not always well received and may help explain why, in 1923, American WILPF members opted not to reelect her to the national executive board.[52] In response to the conflicting priorities that hindered interracial collaboration even in radical feminist circles, Terrell and other Black feminist internationalists founded their own organizations, including the International Council of Women of the Darker Races and the National Council of Negro Women, devoted to combatting the dual scourges of racism and sexism at home and around the world.

Black Men's Honour, Feminists' Frustration

Mary Church Terrell continued to pursue racial justice throughout her long life. Well into her eighties, she remained at the forefront of civil rights struggles in the United States: standing up for Black female victims of white male violence and protesting DC restaurants that refused to serve Black customers. Her leadership in initiating pickets and lawsuits challenging segregation led directly to the Supreme Court's 1953 ruling in *District of Columbia v. John R. Thompson Co. Inc.*, which desegregated public establishments in America's capital city a year before the landmark *Brown v. Board of Education* decision of 1954.[53] Terrell's engagement on behalf of the African American community knew no bounds; yet, despite her prominence as a speaker, writer, and organizer in the United States, and despite her ability and willingness to champion the rights of people of colour on the international stage – including in Paris and Zurich in 1919 – Terrell seldom was accorded the recognition she felt she deserved by male leaders of the early civil rights movement.

Like other African American women, Terrell suffered the effects of gender as well as racial discrimination. "I belong to the only group in this country which has two such huge obstacles to surmount," she would later write. "Colored men have only one – that of race."[54] Even among male allies in the struggle for racial justice, Terrell had to fight for respect and power. This was true in the NAACP, where Du Bois was eager for her endorsement and funding but less keen to give her a visible role in the organization. "I don't care how they dislike me, how nasty, mean and small they are," Terrell huffed to her husband, "they shall not stand between me and the principles I believe with all my heart."[55] Terrell's sense of marginalization in a movement that depended so heavily on her labors was shared by other Black feminist activists. Ida Gibbs Hunt, whose ideas, contacts, and organizational prowess breathed life into the 1919 Pan-African Congress, would issue similar complaints about Du Bois in the 1920s.[56] At the end of the Second World War, Mary McLeod Bethune, the head of the National Council of Negro Women, found herself similarly sidelined by Black male leaders at the United Nations Conference on International Organization.[57] Even as they struggled to convince white feminists to recognize the interconnections between racism and sexism, Terrell and other Black feminists repeatedly found their own ambitions and concerns stymied by the sexism and patriarchal assumptions of their male allies.

Ironically, in her energetic pursuit of racial justice in 1919 and after, Terrell may unintentionally have helped facilitate the marginalization of Black women like herself in the early civil rights movement. The root of the problem lay in the status of the soldier – and in this case, the Black soldier – as a cultural icon in an era defined by the traumas of war. The African American community took tremendous pride in the heroism and sacrifice of the Black men who had so admirably fought for their country in Europe, even in the face of outright hostility on the part of the nation they served. The hero's welcome accorded to the all-Black 369th Regiment out of New York – the famous Harlem Hellfighters – encapsulated the spirit of this moment. But white America's praise of Black soldiers was shallow and short-lived, and it was followed immediately by months of horrific racial violence directed, in many cases, at Black veterans perceived as a threat to white male power.[58]

Celebrating African American soldiers was a deliberate strategy on the part of Black intellectuals to counter such racial violence. It was a means of highlighting Black men's courage, responsibility, and leadership: in other words, of reclaiming their manhood in a racist society that demeaned, infantilized, and, in the most extreme cases, murdered them. African American women who had a pulpit to stand on had every reason to add to the chorus. Terrell did just that in her 1919 Zurich address, where she heaped praise on the African American soldiers of the Great War who "with astonishing sacrifice and enthusiasm" crossed the ocean in defence of democracy, despite any assurance that "the sad circumstances under which they and their loved ones lived would ever be improved."[59] Terrell also pointed out the "great number" of colonial soldiers who fought and died in the defence of civilization.[60]

Less than a year after the Zurich Congress, Terrell felt compelled yet again to defend Black men in uniform in response to what became known as the "Black Horror on the Rhine" campaign. The controversy was set off in 1920, when German women's groups began denouncing French African soldiers stationed in the occupied Rhineland for allegedly raping German girls and women. Convinced by the propaganda, and distraught at the thought of innocent German girls being thrown in harm's way, several national sections of the WILPF began circulating a petition calling for the immediate removal of all colonial soldiers from Europe. Terrell was mortified by white feminists' knee-jerk response to the unsubstantiated charges. Writing to Jane Addams, Terrell said, "I can not sign the petition asking for the removal of the black troops because I believe it is a direct appeal to race prejudice." Insisting she would resign her position on the WILPF executive board rather than sign, Terrell explained, "Because the women of my race have suffered so terribly and so long from assaults committed with impunity by men of all races," she felt real sympathy for any victims of "brutal treatment."[61] But she also insisted that she saw no evidence that non-white troops stationed in Germany were any more poorly behaved than others (and no such evidence has surfaced since).[62]

In the end, Addams sided with Terrell, the American section refused to sign the petition, and the scandal eventually blew over. Ultimately, Terrell's defense of Black soldiers led white WILPF members to reconsider their position, and Terrell could take satisfaction in having won a moral victory. In taking up the cause of Black soldiers, both from the French colonies and from the United States, however, Terrell inadvertently helped solidify a particular vision of manhood in the African American community that had begun to be used as a rhetorical bulwark against female empowerment. In particular, the New Negro movement of the 1920s – flowing out of Harlem as well as expatriate magnet cities like Paris – celebrated Black martial manhood in poetry and prose and transformed the Black officer into an icon of racial progress. The end result, historians agree, was a "highly masculinist black political culture" that lasted for decades and that was inhospitable to female leadership.[63] Such ambivalence endured, in some cases, into the later civil rights era of the 1960s, with its powerful focus on Dr. Martin Luther King Jr. and other charismatic male movement leaders.[64]

Elevating and reinforcing male hegemony was hardly the goal that Mary Church Terrell had in mind when she sailed to Europe with a group of American feminists in 1919. But the pernicious undercurrent of American racial prejudice followed Terrell across the Atlantic, much as it did for her protagonist in "A Doughboy's Fatal Mistake." Throughout her life, Terrell took it as her charge to confront white supremacy in all its guises. For Terrell, the problems of racial and gender inequality were intertwined in her daily lived experience, so much so that she could not imagine confronting one without addressing the other. "However much the white women of the country need suffrage," she would write, "colored women need it more."[65] African American women needed political – as well as social and economic – power to be able to protect their families and communities from a society that oppressed them on the basis of race *and* to be able to champion their rights in a patriarchal culture that marginalized them as women.

In 1919, Mary Church Terrell travelled to Europe hoping to convince white feminists to open their eyes to the limitations of freedom and democracy in segregated America and to demand global leaders recognize racial oppression as an impediment to lasting peace. Once in Zurich, having found herself nearly alone in a sea of white faces, Terrell extended her analysis to demand racial justice for Africans and people of colour across the colonized world. Racism, she warned, like patriarchy, threatened the new liberal internationalist order upon which Allied leaders were staking their hard-won peace. Her polished oratory impressed and influenced the radical feminists of the early WILPF, but as a lone voice speaking for women of colour in Zurich in 1919, Terrell was limited in how far she could shape the priorities of white feminists. Among the Allied statesmen and diplomats in Paris, with the exception of the Japanese, Terrell's concerns about racism and imperialism passed unnoticed and went unaddressed. Finally, for all her diplomatic savvy, Terrell's rhetorical strategies elevated a particular martial image of Black manhood that was already emerging as an obstacle to Black women's empowerment in the fledgling civil rights movement back at home. Despite Terrell's best efforts in Europe in 1919, but also in a small way because of them, patriarchy would extend its roots deeply into post-war American society, much as it would in Geneva and around the world.[66]

NOTES

My heartfelt thanks to the National Endowment for the Humanities and to the College of Arts and Letters and the Research, Scholarship, and Creative Activities subcommittee at California State University, Sacramento for generously funding this research. This essay draws on topics discussed at greater length in Chapter 2 of my book *Peace on Our Terms: The Global Battle for Women's Rights after the First World War* (New York: Columbia University Press, 2020). Following evolving journalistic and scholarly practice, the word Black is capitalized in this essay when describing a shared racial or ethnic identity.

1 Mary Church Terrell, "A Doughboy's Fatal Mistake," undated manuscript [1919], Mary Church Terrell Papers, Library of Congress (Henceforth MTC/LOC), Reel 23.

2 Alison M. Parker interprets the place of this story in Terrell's international writing and work in "What was the Relationship between Mary Church Terrell's International Experience and Her Work Against Racism in the United States?" Documents selected and interpreted by Alison M. Parker, *Women and Social Movements in the United States, 1600–2000*, Scholars Edition, Kathryn Kish Sklar and Thomas Dublin, eds.

3 For more on African American women pursuing a dual gender rights and racial equality agenda in Europe in 1919, see Adele Logan Alexander, *Parallel Worlds: The Remarkable Gibbs-Hunts and the Enduring (in)Significance of Melanin* (Charlottesville: University of Virginia Press, 2010); Brandy Thomas Wells, "1919: The National Association of Colored Women, Mary B. Talbert, & France," paper before the Annual Meeting of the American Historical Association, Chicago, IL, 6 January 2019; and Addie W. Hunton and Kathryn M. Johnson, *Two Colored Women with the American Expeditionary Forces*, intro. Adele Logan Alexander (New York: G.K. Hall, 1997).

4 On colonial nationalists' activism at and around the peace conference, see Erez Manela, *The Wilsonian Moment: Self-Determination and the International Origins of Colonial Nationalism* (Oxford: Oxford University Press, 2007).

5 In 1919, women also sought to intervene in diplomatic debates over democracy, national self-determination, and women's rights by participating in public protests in many parts of Asia and the Middle East, and they organized to champion workers' and women's economic rights at the first meeting of the International Labour Organization in Washington, DC. For the full scope of women's activism after World War I, see Siegel, *Peace on Our Terms.*

6 Martha S. Jones, *Vanguard: How Black Women Broke Barriers, Won the Vote, and Insisted on Equality for All* (New York: Basic Books, 2020), p. 152.

7 Brittany Cooper describes Terrell as one of the first African American female leaders to deliberately and effectively focus on the intersectional challenges of racial and sexual discrimination. See Brittany Cooper, *Beyond Respectability: The Intellectual Thought of Race Women* (Urbana: University of Illinois Press, 2017), pp. 64–5. On intersectional analysis, see Kimberlé Crenshaw, "Demarginalizing the Intersection of Race and Sex: A Black Feminist Critique of Antidiscrimination Doctrine, Feminist Theory, and Antiracist Politics," *University of Chicago Legal Forum*, vol. 1989, no. 1, article 8, http://chicagounbound.uchicago.edu/uclf/vol1989/iss1/8.

8 On Terrell's parents' background, see Alison M Parker, *Unceasing Militant: The Life of Mary Church Terrell* (Chapel Hill: University of North Carolina Press, 2020), pp. 5–23.

9 Terrell, *A Colored Woman*, pp. 49–80 and 93, and Beverly Washington Jones, *Quest for Equality: The Life and Writings of Mary Eliza Church Terrell, 1863–1954* (New York: Carlson Publishing, 1990), pp. 3–16. Oberlin

began admitting Black students to its baccalaureate programs in 1835 and women in 1837. Franklin College briefly admitted women in the late 1780s, then abandoned the policy for 182 years. See Oberlin College, "Oberlin History," https://www.oberlin.edu/about-oberlin/oberlin-history, and Franklin & Marshall College, "Mission and History," https://www.fandm.edu/about/mission-and-history, both accessed 26 January 2021.

10 Terrell, *A Colored Woman*, p. 93.

11 W.E.B. Du Bois, "The Talented Tenth (1903)," in *Du Bois: Writings* (New York: The Library of America, 1986), pp. 842–61.

12 Kevin K. Gaines, *Uplifting the Race: Black Leadership, Politics, and Culture in the Twentieth Century* (Chapel Hill: The University of North Carolina Press, 1996).

13 Jones, *Vanguard*, p. 156.

14 Terrell, *A Colored Woman*, p. 190.

15 On lynching statistics, see Gaines, *Uplifting the Race*, p. 25. On Terrell's anti-lynching work, see Jones, *Vanguard*, p. 156.

16 Du Bois made this argument most forcefully in the essay "The African Roots of the War," published in the *Atlantic Monthly* in May 1915. See David Levering Lewis, *W.E.B. Du Bois: Biography of a Race, 1858–1919* (New York: Henry Holt, 1993), pp. 503–5.

17 Ida Gibbs Hunt to Mary Church Terrell, 20 April 1915, MCT/LOC, Reel 4.

18 Terrell, *A Colored Woman*, pp. 291–300.

19 Alice Post to Mary Church Terrell, 10 December 1918, MCT/LOS, Reel 4.

20 Harriet Hyman Alonso, *Peace as a Women's Issue: A History of the U.S. Movement for World Peace and Women's Rights* (Syracuse: Syracuse University Press, 1993), pp. 63–9.

21 Unsigned letter to Jane Addams, 3 April 1919, MCT/LOC, Reel 4.

22 Alice Post to Mary Church Terrell, 10 December 1918, MCT/LOS, Reel 4.

23 Throughout her life, Terrell frequently found herself the sole woman of colour in white feminist spaces and continually sought opportunities for interracial cooperation, even in the face of overt racism. See Parker, *Unceasing Militant*, p. 125.

24 Terrell, *A Colored Woman*, p. 249.

25 Terrell, *A Colored Woman*, pp. 249 and 379.

26 Terrell, *A Colored Woman*, p. 379.

27 This is the likely explanation that Terrell gives for her exclusion in *A Colored Woman*, p. 384.

28 Terrell, *A Colored Woman*, pp. 385–7.

29 W.E.B. Du Bois, "The Pan African Congress," *The Crisis* (April 1919), p. 274.

30 On Ida Gibbs Hunt's role in planning the 1919 Pan-African Congress, see Alexander, *Parallel Worlds*, pp. 182–3. On Hunton's speech, see Du Bois, "The Pan African Congress," p. 273.

31 Reginald Kearney, "Japan: Ally in the Struggle against Racism, 1919–1927," *Contributions in Black Studies* 12, no. 14 (1994), available at https://scholarworks.umass.edu/cibs/vol12/iss1/14/. Thanks to Laurence Badel for bringing this essay to my attention.

32 Jennifer Keene, "Wilson and Race Relations," in Ross A. Kennedy, ed., *A Companion to Woodrow Wilson* (Chichester: Wiley-Blackwell, 2013), pp. 133–51.

33 Terrell, *A Colored Woman*. On the Japanese racial equality clause, see Margaret MacMillan, *Paris 1919: Six Months That Changed the World* (New York: Random House, 2002), pp. 316–21 and Manela, *The Wilsonian Moment*, pp. 181–2. It is not clear from Terrell's memoir if she met with Makino before or after the Zurich Congress, but the timing of other aspects of her visit suggests before.

34 Manela, *The Wilsonian Moment*, p. 212; Keisha N. Blain, *Set the World on Fire: Black Nationalist Women and the Global Struggle for Freedom* (Philadelphia: University of Pennsylvania Press, 2018).

35 Terrell, *A Colored Woman*, p. 371.

36 Terrell, *A Colored Woman*, pp. 371–2. Two other African American women, YMCA workers Addie Waites Hunton and Mary B. Talbert, also attended the Zurich Congress, as observers. Brandy Thomas Wells, "1919: The National Association of Colored Women, Mary B. Talbert, & France," paper before the Annual Meeting of the American Historical Association, Chicago, IL, 6 January 2019.

37 Terrell, *A Colored Woman*, p. 373. This was the second major address that Terrell delivered in German, having done the same in 1904 at a conference of the International Council of Women in Berlin. There are strong parallels between the two speeches.

38 Terrell, *A Colored Woman*, p. 373.

39 Terrell, *A Colored Woman*, p. 373.

40 "Resolution A VII. – Race Equality," *Report of the International Congress of Women, Zurich, 12 to 17 May 1919* (Geneva: Women's International League for Peace and Freedom, 1919), p. 110.

41 On the WILPF's radicalism, Leila J. Rupp, *Worlds of Women: The Making of an International Women's Movement* (Princeton, NJ: Princeton University Press, 1997), p. 33.

42 Terrell, *A Colored Woman*, p. 374.

43 "Mary Church Terrell (U.S.A.)," *Report of the International Congress of Women, Zurich, 12 to 17 May 1919* (Geneva: Women's International League for Peace and Freedom, 1919), pp. 212–17.

44 "On the rhetorical strategies Terrell employed at the 1904 International Conference of Women in Berlin, many of which she repeated here, see Cooper, *Beyond Respectability*, pp. 72–5.

45 "Mary Church Terrell (U.S.A.)," *Report of the International Congress of Women*, pp. 212–17.

46 On the exchange of words between Balch and Terrell, Terrell to Emily Balch, 1 February 1929, Mary Church Terrell Papers, Moorland-Spingarn Research Center, Howard University, Box 1, Folder 22.

47 "Mary Church Terrell (U.S.A.)," *Report of the International Congress of Women*, p. 217; Terrell, *A Colored Woman*, p. 376. The phrase "a colored woman in a white world" is from the title of her memoir.

48 "Congrès international de femmes, Zurich, 12–17 Mai 1919, Résolutions présentées à la conférence des puissances à Paris," Archives diplomatiques de France, André Tardieu Papers, 166PAAP/462.

49 On the WILPF's interwar anti-imperialism, see Mona L. Siegel, "The Dangers of Feminism in Colonial Indochina," *French Historical Studies* 38, no. 4 (October 2015), pp. 661–89; Mona L. Siegel, "Feminism, Pacifism and Political Violence in Europe and China in the Era of the World Wars," *Gender & History* 28, no. 3 (November 2016), pp. 641–59. On the French WILPF section, which was particularly radical on issues regarding imperialism, see Norman Ingram, *The Politics of Dissent: Pacifism in France, 1919–1939* (Oxford: Clarendon Press, 1991). On the WILPF's interracial investigation of the American occupation of Haiti, see Melinda Plastas, *A Band of Noble Women: Racial Politics in the Women's Peace Movement* (Syracuse: Syracuse University Press, 2011), pp. 114–19.

50 On interracial organizing in the American WILPF, see Michelle Rief, "Thinking Locally, Acting Globally: The International Agenda of African American Clubwomen, 1880–1940," *The Journal of African American History* 89, no. 3 (summer 2004), pp. 203–22; Joyce Blackwell, *No Peace without Freedom: Race and the Women's International League for Peace and Freedom, 1915–1975* (Carbondale: Southern Illinois University Press, 2004); and Plastas, *A Band of Noble Women*.

51 Plastas, *A Band of Noble Women*, p. 150.

52 Parker, *Unceasing Militant*, pp. 155–6.

53 Parker, *Unceasing Militant*, pp. 271–82.

54 Terrell, *A Colored Woman*, p. 29.

55 Cited in Joan Quigley, *Just Another Southern Town: Mary Church Terrell and the Struggle for Racial Justice in the Nation's Capital* (Oxford: Oxford University Press, 2016), p. 72.

56 Siegel, *Peace on Our Terms*, p. 86.

57 Jones, *Vanguard*, p. 221.

58 On African American soldiers in World War I, see Bill Harris, *The Hellfighters of Harlem: African-American Soldiers Who Fought for the Right to Fight for Their Country* (New York: Carroll & Graf Publishers, 2002). On the race riots of 1919, see Gaines, *Uplifting the Race*, p. 216; David F. Krugler, *1919, the Year*

of Racial Violence: How African Americans Fought Back (Cambridge: Cambridge University Press, 2015); and Michael Schaeffer, "Lost Riot," *Washington City Paper*, 3 April 1998, http://www.washingtoncitypaper.com/news/article/13015176/lost-riot.

59 "Mary Church Terrell (U.S.A.)," *Report of the International Congress of Women*, p. 214.

60 "Mary Church Terrell (U.S.A.)," *Report of the International Congress of Women*, p. 213.

61 Mary Church Terrell to Jane Addams, 18 March 1921, MCT/LOC Reel 5.

62 On the "Black Horror" campaign, see Sally Marks. "Black Watch on the Rhine: A Study in Propaganda, Prejudice and Prurience," *European Studies Review* 13 (1983), pp. 297–333; Erika A. Kuhlman, *Reconstructing Patriarchy after the Great War: Women, Gender, and Postwar Reconciliation between Nations* (New York: Palgrave Macmillan, 2008), pp. 42–67.

63 Plastas, *A Band of Noble Women*, p. 36. On martial manhood and Black male predominance in the New Negro movement, see Mark Whalan, *The Great War and the Culture of the New Negro* (Gainesville: University Press of Florida, 2008), pp. 6, 17, and 110–15.

64 Barbara Ransby, *Ella Baker & the Black Freedom Movement: A Radical Democratic Vision* (Chapel Hill: University of North Carolina Press, 2003), p. 176.

65 Terrell, *A Colored Woman*, p. 349.

66 For a more developed analysis of the peacemakers' response to the global sweep of demands for women's rights in 1919, see Siegel, *Peace on Our Terms*.

Contributors

Andrew Barros is an associate professor in the History Department at the Université du Québec à Montréal. His most recent publication, co-edited with Martin Thomas, is *The Civilianization of War: The Changing Civil-Military Divide, 1914–2014* (Cambridge University Press, 2018).

Carl Bouchard is Professor of Modern History and International Relations at the Université de Montréal. His research focuses on the history of peace movements and peace ideas. His latest book, *Cher Monsieur le Président. Quand les Français écrivaient à Woodrow Wilson (1918–1919)* (Champ Vallon, 2015), examined thousands of letters sent by French citizens to American President Woodrow Wilson in the aftermath of the First World War. His new project focuses on pacifism in the province of Quebec since the Boer War and more largely on how "small nations" engage in the promotion of peace.

Bruno Cabanes is Professor and the Donald G. & Mary A. Dunn Chair in Modern Military History at the Ohio State University. He is the author of several books on the First World War and its aftermath, including *La Victoire endeuillée. La sortie de guerre des soldats français, 1918–1920* (Seuil, 2004); *Août 14. La France entre en guerre* (Gallimard, 2014) (translated as: *August 1914: France, the Great War and a Month that Changed the World Forever* (Yale University Press, 2016); and *The Great War and the Origins of Humanitarianism, 1918–1924* (Cambridge University Press, 2014). He has co-edited *Une Histoire de la Guerre, du XIXe siècle à nos jours* (Seuil, 2018). He serves on the steering committee of the research centre of the Historial de la Grande Guerre and on the editorial board of *20&21. Revue d'histoire.*

Marie-Eve Chagnon is the winner of numerous prizes and fellowships, including the Society for French Historical Studies' Natalie Zemon

Davis Prize. She was a postdoctoral fellow at the Centre canadien d'études allemandes et européennes, Université de Montréal, Canada, between 2012 and 2014. Amongst other publications, she is the editor (with Tomas Irish) of *The Academic World in the Era of the Great War* (Palgrave Macmillan, 2018). Her current research looks at the role played by the American scientific community in the reconciliation process between the wars.

Sebastian Döderlein is a lecturer in German at the Université du Québec à Montréal, where he teaches German language, history, and culture. He holds the Staatsexamen from the University of Cologne and a PhD from Concordia University. His thesis, entitled "Un pivot de l'histoire? – La société alsacienne-lorraine et les sorties ambiguës de la Première Guerre mondiale (1918–1919)," examined the different ways the population of Alsace-Lorraine experienced the end of the Great War. He has been the recipient of many prizes and fellowships, including the Natalie Zemon Davis Prize from the Society for French Historical Studies.

Marie-Michèle Doucet is an assistant professor in the Department of History at the Royal Military College of Canada. She teaches European social history, the history of international relations in the first half of the twentieth century, as well as specialized classes in the history of genocide and women's history. Her main field of research is European peace movements after the First World War, largely through the lens of feminist pacifism.

Talbot Imlay is a professor in the Department of History at the Université Laval in Quebec City, Canada. His most recent book is *The Practice of Socialist Internationalism: European Socialists and International Politics, 1914–1960* (Oxford University Press, 2018). He is currently working on a book on Clarence Streit and his campaign for a federation of the North Atlantic democracies during the twentieth century.

Norman Ingram is Professor of Modern French History at Concordia University in Montreal. He is the author of *The Politics of Dissent: Pacifism in France, 1919–1939* (Clarendon Press, 1991 and 2011) and *The War Guilt Problem and the Ligue des droits de l'homme, 1914–1944* (Oxford University Press, 2019). He has held Visiting Fellowships at Magdalen College, Oxford; the Institute for Advanced Studies in the Humanities at the University of Edinburgh; and the University of St Andrews. He has served as co-president of the Society for French Historical Studies in the United States and is a Fellow of the Royal Historical Society in the United Kingdom.

Peter Jackson holds the Chair in Global Security at the University of Glasgow and is Director of the Scottish Council on Global Affairs. He has been Professeur invité at the Université de Paris (Panthéon-Sorbonne) and the Institut d'Études Politiques in Paris. Among his many publications are most notably *France and the Nazi Menace: Intelligence and Policy Making, 1933–1939* (Oxford University Press, 2000); *Beyond the Balance of Power: France and the Politics of National Security in the Era of the First World War* (Cambridge University Press, 2014); and, most recently, *Le Renseignement et relations internationales de 1789 à nos jours* (Editions Nouveau monde, 2021) [forthcoming with Bloomsbury as *The Rise of Modern Intelligence, 1789–2020*]. He is a fellow of the Royal Society of Edinburgh and of the Royal Historical Society.

William Mulligan is a professor in the School of History at University College Dublin. He has written widely about international history in the early twentieth century, including *The Great War for Peace* (Yale University Press, 2014) and *The Origins of the First World War* (second edition, Cambridge University Press, 2017).

Mona L. Siegel is a professor of history at California State University, Sacramento, and a specialist in the histories of feminism, pacifism, and internationalism in the twentieth century. Her first book, *The Moral Disarmament of France: Education, Pacifism, and Patriotism, 1914–1940* (Cambridge University Press, 2004), was awarded the 2006 History of Education Society Outstanding Book Award. Her second book, *Peace on Our Terms: The Global Battle for Women's Rights After the First World War* (Columbia University Press, 2020), has been selected for honourable mention by the Barbara "Penny" Kanner Award Committee of the Western Association of Women Historians.

Index

Page numbers in *italics* refer to figures.

www.ingramcontent.com/pod-product-compliance
Lightning Source LLC
LaVergne TN
LVHW041114090826
844660LV00062B/902/J